# The Durhams of Fairfield:
## An African American Genealogy

## By Robert L. Uzzel, Ph.D.

EAKIN PRESS ⋈ Fort Worth, Texas
**www.EakinPress.com**

*Photo Courtesy of Marc Durham*

## Table of Contents

*"Thou shalt not remove thy neighbor's landmark,
which they of old time have set in thine inheritance,
which thou shall inherit in the land
that the Lord thy God giveth thee to possess it."*
Deuteronomy 19:14

## *Prologue*

The Durhams of Fairfield are truly a great African American family. In this book, the name "Fairfield" has two meanings. The first is Fairfield County, South Carolina, whose county seat is Winnsboro. Evidence indicates that Gobi, the patriarch of the Durham family, along with his wife and five older sons, were slaves in this county and that this was the site of Gobi's brutal murder. The second meaning of "Fairfield" is Fairfield, Texas, the county seat of Freestone County, the county where Isaac Durham was born and where his five brothers had settled by 1870. They appear to have come with their masters to DeSoto Parish, Louisiana and joined their mother and brother in Texas shortly after Emancipation.

The six Durham brothers—Belton, Allen, Minor, Christopher, Anderson, and Isaac—lived east of Fairfield in the Butler community of Freestone County. Each of these brothers has descendants living today in Butler, where "Durham" is one of the most common surnames. Some, like their ancestors, continue to till the soil. Others are involved in many different occupations and professions. Durhams and related families with roots in the Butler community now can be found throughout the United States, where they contribute to their communities, their states, their nation, and the world.

The Durhams of Fairfield are truly a remarkable family with a great and noble legacy! If the reading of this book will inspire Durhams and others to have a greater appreciation for this legacy, then these humble efforts will be well rewarded.

You cannot really know who you are unless you know where you came from!

### *Dedication*

This book is dedicated to the memory of the African Gobi, Allen Durham, Rance Durham, Willie Anderson Durham, and Gladys Durham Henry, from whom my mother-in-law, my wife, my children, my grandchildren, and my great grandchild are descended. May the Durham Legacy ever be preserved!

# Acknowledgements

The Durhams of Fairfield are truly a great family—a family with a very interesting history. I have been on trail of the Durham family for over 35 years. How did I become so interested in this family? I married into it. On 19 February 1977, I married Debra Bass of Fairfield, Texas. Debra is the daughter of Aldessa Henry Bass, the granddaughter of Gladys Durham Henry, the great-granddaughter of Willie Anderson Durham, the great-great granddaughter of Rance Durham, the great-great-great granddaughter of Allen Durham, and the great-great-great-great granddaughter of the African Gobi.

Many people with connections to the Durham family and/or roots in the Butler community of Freestone County, Texas have provided invaluable help. Many of them, sadly, did not live to see the completion of this project. Such included Luke Durham; Archie Durham; Mitcheola Durham; Julious Durham; Isaiah Durham; Hobart Durham, Jr.; Alonzo Durham; Hubert Durham; Dorris "Jim" Durham; Thelma Lee Durham Roquemore; Therman Rogene Durham; Mary O. Edwards; Clara Durham Peters; Gladys Durham Henry; Katie Mae Durham Tatum; Mary Nelson Durham; Johnnie Johnson, Jr.; Ruby Jo Durham; Leophia Carden; Houston Slaughter; Rev. W. E. Henry; Charles Simmons; and Rosa Lee Quarles.

Those who are, happily, still in the land of the living and either provided an interview or completed a questionnaire include my mother-in-law Aldessa Henry Bass; Juanita Henry Durham; Maurine Durham Jones; Bobbie Jean Durham; Eddie Marie Durham; Clara Durham McIlvene; LaRue Durham Hooks; George Douglas Durham; Isaac Newton Durham; Richard Eugene Durham, Sr.; Richard Eugene Durham, Jr.; Allie Faye Durham Moore; Bascom Gerald Durham; James Ronnie Durham; Daydrian Durham; Keith Isaac Durham; Michael Cornell Durham; Cecliea Rena Durham Woods; Norah Burns Durham; Amy Durham; Raquila Durham; James Durham; Walter Durham, Jr.; Beauford Durham; Gale Lynn Durham; Harold Glenn Durham; Shirley Givens Durham; Texanita Durham Bluitt; Ernestine Durham Williams; Ike Durham; Eddie Lee Durham; Teaner Annie Durham

Johnson; Jimmy R. Durham; Linda Kay ("Katie") Durham Collins; Diana Faye Durham Massey; Laura Woodard; Mary Durham Rabb; Maurice Durham; Hellen Durham-Jones; Clara Durham Page; Gennelle Durham Moseley; Josephine Daniels; Alice Jarmon; and Dorsey Strawther.

I am grateful to my wife's five siblings—Kenneth LaClaire "Buck" Bass; Celia Marketta Bass Strickland; Cilkay Vanessa Bass Jessie; Teresa Maria Bass Haynes; and LaCharles Michael Bass, along with their children--who have been very helpful in providing information about their immediate families.

Charles Bass (my brother-in-law since 1977) and Kenneth Prox (my son-in-law since 1995) played very important roles in making this book possible. In August 2003, Charles drove Kenneth and me to DeSoto Parish, Louisiana, where we conducted research and took pictures at various cemeteries and at the Mansfield State Historical Park. In August 2012, Kenneth drove not only me but also his daughters Kendra and Kayla to Fairfield County, South Carolina for a trip that was years in the making. Kenneth well expressed our mutual feelings about the Palmetto State when he said "We did not meet one mean person. Everyone we met was nice and really tried to help us." Research at the local library and museum resulted in much valuable information. Visits to various places in the county were enjoyable. After taking pictures at White Oak Baptist Church, we were heading down the road and I asked Kenneth to turn around because we failed to photograph the church cornerstone. This resulted in an encounter with a young man on a rider mower named Julius Durham, Jr., who directed us to aunt and uncle down the road--Boykin Durham and his sister Katherine Durham Pope. Thus, two very good interviews were conducted. My grandson Richard Walker took pictures at both Lone Star Cemetery and Pine Top Cemetery in the Butler community of Freestone County, Texas. Lone Star and Pine Top are the final resting places of many members of the Durham family. Thank you so much, Charles, Kenneth, and Richard.

Much information on the Durham slaveholders and their previous residence in Fairfield County, South Carolina and DeSoto Parish, Louisiana was obtained with the help of the following individuals to whom I am very grateful: Pelham Lyles, Sarah McMaster, Tom Harrison, and Johnny Harrison of Winnsboro, South Carolina; Raymond Powell of Mansfield, Louisiana; the late J. Murray Durham of Bossier City, Louisiana; the late Colonel James Michael Durham of Farnham, Virginia; the late Major Robert Scott Durham of Fort Worth, Texas; Thomas Wittington Durham of Shreveport, Louisiana; and the late Lieutenant Colonel Donald Smith Durham of Shawnee, Kansas. My first contacts by mail and telephone with the latter individual occurred in 1983, when Don was living in Manassas, Virginia and employed at the Pentagon. I thought of him on 11 September 2001 when I heard about the terrorist attacks on the headquarters of the U. S. military. I was greatly relieved to learn that he had retired from the Army and, when I reached him by telephone, I said "Thank God you are no longer at the Pentagon." I appreciate the help provided by Andi Grindle, librarian at the Grand Lodge of the State of Louisiana, F.&A.M., with my research on General Richard Strother Taylor, Confederate commander at the Battle of Mansfield. I also am grateful to Mildred Burkhalter, mayor of Rentiesville, Oklahoma, for providing information on the life of Dr. Abner Durham, my wife's great-great uncle. The late Dallas attorney William E. Walton was quite helpful in supplying information on his great uncle, the legendary Dallas attorney William J. Durham. Although he may not have been related to the Durhams of Fairfield, the latter individual played an important role in the Civil Rights Era. I am also grateful to another unrelated individual, Major General Archer L. Durham (U. S. Air Force Retired) for taking the time to answer my letter of inquiry.

I extend special thanks to Odis Rich of Germantown, Maryland, who has conducted extensive research on the Titus family. Willie Anderson Durham married Ellen Titus and they had twelve children. This very special couple—my wife's great-grandparents—now have numerous descendants. Odis' research and my research obviously overlap. The same is true of Paula Woodard Andrews of Arlington, Texas, who has done research on several African American families of the Butler community, including the Durhams. I am grateful to them for sharing their findings with me.

I am also grateful to Dr. Emilia Gay Griffith Means, co-author of *Images of America: DeSoto Parish* for permission to use information from her book, her interest in my research, and her enthusiasm for history and genealogy. There is a special bond that unites writers.

I have been a Civil War buff since childhood and believe that it is more than coincidental that this book is being published during the Civil War Sesquicentennial. I am very thankful that I was able to attend the commemoration of the 150th Anniversary of the Battle of Mansfield, Louisiana on 26 April 2014. Walter Donald Kennedy, co-author of *The South was Right!*, gave me permission to reprint the picture of DeSoto Parish's celebrated black Confederate soldier Levy Carnine that was drawn by the late Shreveport artist Jim Whittington. It is possible that Carnine knew some DeSoto Parish Durhams, white and black. In recent years there has been considerable research on African American participation in the Civil War. While most of the focus has been on blacks who wore the Union blue, there is evidence that some black men also wore the Confederate gray. Thank you, Donnie for granting this permission. My use of this picture, however, does not indicate agreement with all of the ideas expressed in *The South was Right!* We should all be able to agree to disagree and still remain friends.

My Facebook friend Marc Durham of Salisbury, Maryland gave me permission to use the needlepoint design "Durham Renowned the World Around" from a sewing circle in North Carolina. I appreciate this permission and also Marc's enthusiastic support for this project.

I am also grateful to many individuals and institutions for help in my research. Adrianne Pierce of the Texas/Dallas History and Archives Division of the Dallas Public Library was very helpful in locating a picture of Lawyer William J. Durham of Dallas. The staff members of the Genealogy Department of the Dallas Public Library, the Waco-McLennan County Library, the Texas Collection of Baylor University, the Ennis Public Library, the Freestone County Courthouse, the Freestone County Genealogical Society, *Fairfield Recorder*, the Mansfield Female College Museum, the DeSoto Parish Courthouse, the Fairfield County Library, the Fairfield County Museum, and *Herald Independent* of Winnsboro, South Carolina have been quite helpful during my visits over the years. I am very grateful to Kevin Boozer of the latter publication for the two articles he wrote about me during my 2012 visit to Fairfield County.

Also helpful have been the staff members of various libraries to which I have written for information. I am grateful to these and to many unnamed individuals too numerous to mention who helped in so many ways, if only by providing an encouraging word.

I extend love and thanks to my wife Debra, our four children—Ericha, Eric, JoAnna, and Rob, our seven grandchildren—Richard, Dominique, Alicia, Kendra, Daveon, Kayla, and Kayleigh—and our one great grandchild, Chaz. They are truly the apple of our eye. Finally, I concur with the words of the Apostle Paul in Ephesians 1:3: "Blessed be the God and Father of our Lord Jesus Christ, Who hath blessed us with all spiritual blessings in heavenly places in Christ." At the end of our lives, may we all, like Debra's great-great grandfather Rance Durham, merit the following epitaph: "He died as he lived, a Christian."

# Chapter I
## *The Historical and Geographical Background to the Durham Story*
### Fairfield County, South Carolina

Evidence indicates that the ancestors of the Durham family of Freestone County, Texas (whose county seat is Fairfield) were slaves in Fairfield County, South Carolina.

The first colony of what became South Carolina was established along the Ashley River in 1671. By an act ratified in 1769, the province of South Carolina was divided into seven judicial districts. This system of governmental organization continued after the province was admitted to the union as the eighth state in 1788. The judicial districts—then numbering thirty—did not become counties until the adoption of the South Carolina Constitution of 1868.[1] Thus, to speak of counties in South Carolina prior to 1868 is to employ an anachronism. The writer, however, has chosen to do so because this term is more familiar to readers.

The town of Winnsboro, which was settled around 1755 and incorporated in 1832, is the county seat.[2] Fairfield County was settled both by Scotch-Irish immigrants from the Upcountry and English and French Huguenot planters from the Lowcountry. Situated between the Broad River on the west and the Wateree River (now Lake Wateree) on the east, the area was hunting ground for several Indian tribes.[3] The first settler was Thomas Nightingale in 1740. Mount Zion Institute in Winnsboro, established in 1777, was the first school in the South Carolina Upcountry. This place of learning continued to operate until 1991.[4] During the years following the Civil War, the faculty included Rev. William PorcherDuBose, Fairfield County native who became a prominent Episcopal priest and theologian.[5]

A number of other schools operated in Winnsboro, including the Jefferson-Monticello Academy, whose trustees and founders sent a petition to the General Assembly of South Carolina on 2 November 1802. Petitioners included Charnel and Joshua Durham.[6] Furman Academy and Theological Institute (now Furman University) was established in Edgefield County,

1

South Carolina in 1826; moved to Fairfield County in 1836; and finally settled in Greenville in 1851.[7]

During the American Revolution, General Charles Cornwallis made his headquarters in Winnsboro between October 1780 and January 1781. The house where he stayed during the occupation is still standing. There is a legend that, when Cornwallis looked out over the horizon, he said "What fair fields these are."[8]   Not everyone, however, accepts such claims. The county was formed in 1785 as a part of Camden District. The credit for naming the county has been given to Judge Henry Pendleton, who may have got the idea from Col. John Pearson or Capt. James Kincaid.[9]

The Fairfield County Courthouse was designed by South Carolina architect Robert Mills and completed in 1823. Across from this building is the Town Clock which was added to a narrow building modeled after Independence Hall in Philadelphia. Residents boast that the clock is the longest continuously running clock in the United States. The county has numerous churches, some of which are over 200 years old. Such include the celebrated Old Brick Church, which was built in 1788 and served as the site of the organization of the Synod for the Carolinas for the Associate Reformed Presbyterian Church in 1803.[10]   Ministers of the Gospel representing various denominations have had great influence throughout the history of Fairfield County. An important study indicated:

> *In 1942 for whites there were in Fairfield County 13 Methodist Churches, 14 Baptists with a membership of 1643, eight Presbyterian Churches with a membership of about 875, four Associate Reform Presbyterian with a membership of about 285, two Episcopal Churches, one Lutheran with one other preaching point, one Church of the Nazarene, one Pentecostal Holiness, and one Mormon Church. With a white population of 9,300 in 1826 against 8,000 in 1942, there were many more churches and apparently a considerably larger membership in 1942.*
>
> *According to the best available information in 1942 there were Negro churches in Fairfield as follows: 39 Baptist Churches, 20 Methodist, seven Presbyterian, one Episcopal, one House of Prayer, and one Holiness Church, a total of 69. So far as known there were no separate churches for Negroes before the Confederate War, the Negroes being members of the same churches with the white people.[11]*

During the Civil War, Fairfield County furnished about 2000 men to the Confederate armies, including General John Bratton. Pvt. W. S. and Pvt. F. M. Durham served in the Fairfield Fencibles, while Pvt. William Durham and Sgt. W. S. Durham served in Hampton's Legion.[12]  Toward the end of the war, the county was invaded by Union troops under the command of General William Tecumseh Sherman.  With Mount Zion Institute being used as a military hospital, classes were moved to the Baptist Church and other buildings.  A note penciled on the wall of the Old Brick Church expresses a Union soldier's regret at the church's floor boards being taken up to build a river crossing.[13]  Union solders marched via White Oak to Wateree Church and destroyed the railroad between Winnsboro and White Oak.[14]

Ridgeway, the second largest town in Fairfield County, was originally known as "New Town."  The name was changed when the owners of Charlotte and South Carolina Railway decided not to build the railroad on the Camden route but to use the ridge way."[15]  During the years after the Civil War, young people enjoyed dancing at the local hotel in the large-ceilinged dining room with its huge open fireplace.  By 1942, Ridgeway had five churches—one black and four white—and also had Masonic and Knights of Pythias lodges.[16]

During the mid-1700s, early settlers brought cotton to the county and it remained the main crop until soil depletion and the boll weevil brought devastation.[17]

Agriculture has always played a prominent role in Fairfield County.  In 1850, Fairfield farmers included Osmond Woodward, John Durham, and Robert Durham.  In 1860, such included O. Woodward, R. C. Woodward, and M. D. Durham.[18]  It is interesting to note that:

> *Fairfield County in company with the whole State of South Carolina had no industrial development before the Confederate War.  One may say with a degree of assurance that Fairfield, preeminently a slave-holding county above all the counties north of the coast counties, was dominated by the large planter class, who did not encourage industrialism.*
>
> *The numerous small water courses of the county were well dotted with flour and grist mills.  In 1841, in "The Southern Agriculturist" of Charleston, is found a communication from "Humanity" urging that every plantation have a grist mill to grind corn for the whole plantation, including the slaves, instead of requiring the slaves to grind their own meal and grits after working hours.  It says that mills made by McCreight and Son of Winnsboro would grind enough in a day for the whole plantation.[19]*

The Winnsboro Cotton Mill, owned by the U. S. Rubber Company, had a plant, including a mill village, valued at over $4,000,000.  The mill had 52,316 spindles and 16 looms.  It made automobile tire cord.  As late as

1942, employees worked three shifts a day and consumed about 200 bales of cotton a day, twice the national average.[20] This mill was the setting for the popular labor song "Winnsboro Cotton Mill Blues," which was written by an unnamed mill hand in Winnsboro during the 1920s. The tune was borrowed from another popular song of the day—"Alcoholic Blues." It has been sung by Huddie Ledbetter, Pete Seeger, and other artists and was reworked by composer/pianist Frederic Rzewski.[21] This mill is now owned by Performance Fibers Group.[22]

Fairfield County is known for its "pines, ponds, and pastures" and as a place for people to enjoy living in a serene country atmosphere. Residents are quite proud of their heritage, which includes over 100 historical buildings, churches, and homes. The county's monuments and memories speak of the unique traditions and culture of the Upcountry.[23]

Today, Fairfield County's African American population has been estimated to be 70% of the total population. Apparently, this black predominance is nothing new. In 1800, there were 2,224 slaves in Fairfield County. In 1820, there were 7,748 slaves and 48 free blacks. According to an important study by a Fairfield County native:

> In contrast with neighboring counties Fairfield shows remarkable differences in Negro population. In 1840 the Negro population of Fairfield was 12, 5788, of Chester, 7,858, of Kershaw, 8293, of Richland, 11,071 and of Newberry, 10,142. In 1880, of Fairfield, 20,880; of Chester, 16,517; of Kershaw, 13, 642; of Richland, 19,388; and of Newberry, 18,261. Each of the other counties named had a larger white population than Fairfield.
>
> In 1860, just before the Confederate War, Fairfield had 15,504 Negroes, Chester, 10,838; Kershaw, 7,841; Richland, 11,005; Newberry, 13,695. Since the Confederate War, Fairfield has been the one "black" county in the Piedmont.[24]

In 1860, Fairfield County's slave population was 59%.[25] 1860 was the year of the last antebellum census. That year, there were 6,373 whites, 204 free blacks, and 15, 534 slaves in Fairfield County. In 1870, the white population was 5,787 and the black population was 14,101.[26] In several subsequent census reports, the black population of Fairfield ranked third among South Carolina counties. For example, in 1920, the black population of Beaufort was 78.4%, Allendale, 77.6%, and Fairfield, 76.1%.[27] No doubt most of Fairfield's black residents were former slaves and many continued to work in agriculture. However, in 1920, only 12% of Fairfield farm owners were black.[28] Many, no doubt, were tenant farmers and sharecroppers. Some probably had the surname of "Durham." In 1960, the white population of Fairfield County was 8,394, while the black population was 12,318.[29]

## DeSoto Parish, Louisiana

As previously stated, evidence indicates that the ancestors of the Durham family of Freestone County, Texas were slaves in Fairfield County, South Carolina and later moved with their masters to DeSoto Parish, Louisiana.

An interesting pictorial history presents the following assessment of important events related to DeSoto Parish:

> *DeSoto Parish rests in Northwest Louisiana as a stopping point along the wagon roads of American westward expansion. Immigrants poured into the region from such eastern states as Georgia and South Carolina. Oftentimes spurred by letters from family and friends that celebrated the fertile soil and salubrious climate of northern Louisiana, South Carolina slaveholders transplanted their way of life to northern DeSoto Parish. Such settlers might have thought of themselves as pioneers pouring into new and unchartered territory, but the land on which they would build farms, towns, and communities already had a long, rich history. . . .*
>
> *Recognizing the rapid growth of the region between Natchitoches and the Sabine River, the State of Louisiana carved out DeSoto Parish from portions of Natchitoches and Caddo Parishes through Act 88 of the 16th Legislature of Louisiana in 1843. The name was in honor of Marcel DeSoto, who brought the first settlers to the area that became DeSoto Parish. Anglo-American settlers from crowded eastern states moved westward into northern Louisiana as the cotton regime began to unfold. The parish seat was named for English Lord Chief Justice Mansfield.*
>
> *The beginning of the great cotton kingdom of the 1840s lasted to the early 20th century and defined life in DeSoto Parish for this era of development. Anglo-American settlers eager for land on which to earn a better way of life came westward to establish their own farms. They left places like Society Hill, South Carolina, to come to DeSoto Parish and build houses that were architecturally identical to what they had left behind. . . .*
>
> *As in other areas across the South, the Civil War was a pivotal event for DeSoto Parish. The war affected every single individual in the parish. Enslaved men and women whose forced labor made possible the explosive growth of the cotton economy found liberation in the war's outcome. Thousands of young men from the parish enlisted, fought, and perished in the war.[30]*

From the early 1850s until 1930, DeSoto Parish was the home of Mansfield Female College, which was reportedly the oldest female college west of the Mississippi River.  The earliest record known of a girls' school in Mansfield is a tuition statement, dated 1852, from the Mansfield Seminary Company.  This was also the year that Rev. Henry Coleman Thweatt, a Doctor of Divinity and a minister in the Louisiana Conference of the Methodist Episcopal Church, South, became the school's first president.  In 1854, construction of the three-story, $33,000 main building was begun.  In January 1855, the Board of Trustees initiated formal transfer of the school to the Louisiana Conference.  Two months later, it was legally incorporated as Mansfield Female College.  That same year, the Louisiana legislature appropriated $5000 to assist the building program.  At the beginning of its first official academic year (1855-56), the school was organized into three departments—Primary, Academic (Secondary), and Collegiate.  On 24 June 1856--the Feast Day of Saint John the Baptist—the cornerstone of the main building was laid.[31] A former student recalled this impressive ceremony:

> *These were to be gala days, and we could think and talk of nothing else, except what we would wear.  No doubt the anticipation afforded more pleasure than the realization.  But just here in the midst of our happiness, was the first real trouble my little heart had ever known, and oh what mountains we make of molehills in our childhood! Masonry was in its zenith in Mansfield, but, unfortunately, my father did not belong to that fraternity. The daughter of the Master of the Lodge said, in the presence of my companions: "Sallie Moss, you can't wear a white dress and blue sash, nor join the procession on St. John's Day, because your father is not a Mason. . . ."*
>
> *The president, faculty and pupils assembled in the Academy, and to my great joy, we were without distinction commanded to fall in line, in pairs, ready for the procession.  A number of Masons, with their aprons and other insignia, soon made their appearances, followed by a large crowd.  After parading all around the campus to our hearts' content that warm June day . . . the Masons stopped at the northeast corner, and with the customary ceremonies, the cornerstone was laid.  We anti-mason girls were very much amused with the "So mote it be" responses, but had no idea what it meant.  But we managed to see every article that was deposited under that stone—the wine, corn and oil, newspapers, kid gloves, coins of different denominations, etc.  There they have reposed for nearly half-a-century, and there may they remain until time shall be no more.  Many of us saw the first cornerstone laid that day.[32]*

One week later, the school held its first commencement exercises.[33]

Like other institutions, Mansfield Female College was affected by the Civil War. Despite declining enrollment, the school continued to operate, with classes graduating in 1862 and 1863. The students did their part to support the Confederate cause, raising $95 to aid sick and wounded Louisiana soldiers. The school did not reopen in the fall of 1863. The college buildings, as well as many other structures in the parish, were pressed into Confederate service as a hospital before, during, and after the battles of Mansfield and Pleasant Hill in April 1864.[34]

The school reopened in the fall of 1865. It had developed into one of Louisiana's most prosperous colleges by 1880. The campus consisted of nine acres during the 1928-29 school year. Buildings included Thweatt Hall, Sheppard Annex, Bobbitt Dining Hall, and Epworth Auditorium, as well as tennis courts and a large swimming pool.[35] A victim of the Great Depression, the school closed in 1930, when it was merged with Centenary College in Shreveport.[36] In view of the segregation of the time, no African American students attended this institution. There were African American employees, perhaps some with the surname of "Durham."

The school's property was purchased by the Riemer Calhoun Family. In 2002, this family's heirs donated the building and grounds to the State of Louisiana for use as a museum. Through much work of the Friends of the Mansfield Female College Museum and former State Representative Beverly Bruce, the historic facility was added to the Secretary of State's Museums Program during the 2003 legislative session. Today, the Mansfield Female College Museum — housed in one of the original buildings— is one of 17 museums operated by the state.[37]

Some of the Durham slaves were, no doubt, still in DeSoto Parish at the time of the Battle of Mansfield, which occurred on 8 April 1864. At that time, Union General Nathaniel P. Banks[38] and a large Federal army was moving up the Red River toward Shreveport. On 8 April, the Confederate army commanded by General Richard Strother Taylor[39] fought against Banks' troops at Mansfield in the largest battle west of the Mississippi. After a two-hour cavalry fight near Wilson's Farm, Taylor decided to defend a site about four miles south of Mansfield, which today marks the location of an important state historic site. Since Banks did not expect the Confederates to fight until he reached Shreveport, Taylor was able to deal with the much larger Union army of equal terms. The Union troops formed a line of battle along a rail fence and a ridge known as Honeycutt Hill. On order from Taylor, General Alfred Mouton's Division charged the rail fence. Mouton was killed while leading the attack but General C. J. Polignac led the Rebels in an attack, overwhelming the Union line. Although 2,000 Union troops formed another line of battle, they were routed by Taylor's forces, who took many prisoners and seized guns, small arms, and wagons, abandoned by the fleeing soldiers. Thus, the Union advance up the Red River was halted and the land invasion of Texas was delayed. Among the most important weapons captured by the victorious Rebels was the Val Verde Cannon, a model 1861 Ordnance Rifle made of wrought iron, weighing 816 pounds, which was manufactured by Phoenix Iron Company of Phoenixville, Pennsylvania and put into Union service on 25 October 1862. The Val Verde Battery played an important part in the Confederate victory at Mansfield.[40] Approximately 1,000 Confederate soldiers were killed or wounded in this battle, along with approximately 2,400 casualties on the Union side. In private homes and on the campus of Mansfield Female College, the wounded and dying on both sides were given care.[41]

Somehow, a legend developed that General Taylor was alerted of the approach of General Banks by John Franklin Durham, II, a member of the Durham family from Fairfield County who was quoted as saying:

> *A slave came flying down the road, crying "The Yankees is comin' dis way!" I jumped on my little gray pony as soon as I knew the direction of Banks' army and started in the direction of General Dick Taylor's motley army. When I whispered in the little mare's ear the urgency for speed, she literally flew-straight to the Confederate forces. I had the privilege of speaking directly to General Taylor, who commended my swiftness and accuracy of directions. He said, "Go home, son, get your women folk to safety, bury your treasures—but don't worry, we will beat Banks since you have given us time! And he patted me on the shoulder!*
>
> *Back we flew, the little gray mare and I, home as swiftly as we had come. Our ladies were sent to the furtherest neighbors, the silver buried, livestock taken to another location, and we didn't worry—we just waited. Dick Taylor did win a decisive victory, the last of the Civil War. Thus, Mansfield and Shreveport were both saved.*[42]

Descendants of John Franklin Durham, II, deny this story, insisting that he was only five years old at the time of the Battle of Mansfield.[43]

On the following day, the Confederate Army pursued retreating Union soldiers south and fought the Battle of Pleasant Hill in neighboring Sabine Parish, where the two sides suffered another 2,2000 casualties. At Pleasant Hill, a store and a Methodist church were used as hospitals and the Union dead were buried in mass trenches behind Peace-Payne College. Following the disasters at Mansfield and Pleasant Hill, General Banks halted his offensive and abandoned plans to invade Texas.[44] According to the aforementioned history of DeSoto Parish:

> *For over five generations, the families of the men who fought and died at Mansfield and Pleasant Hill never forgot these two engagements. The United Daughters of the Confederacy organized a chapter named for the Prince de Polignac, a French aristocrat who served as an officer at the Battle of Mansfield and played a pivotal role in the establishment of a state park at the site of the engagement. DeSoto Parish Episcopalians renamed their church Christ Memorial in memory of both Union and Confederate dead.*[45]

Many DeSoto Parish men served in the Pelican Rifles, which was designated Company D of the 2nd Louisiana on 11 May 1981 and saw much combat during the next four years. This company included a black man named Levy Carnine, who started out as a body servant and cook but eventually bore arms for the Confederacy. Canine died on 9 April 1924—sixty years and one day after the Battle of Mansfield.[46] It is possible that he knew some DeSoto Parish Durhams, white and black. Apparently, he was well respected in DeSoto Parish, as indicated by the following:

> *Of the 151 enlistments in the Pelican Rifles, only 32 returned home at war's end. Those 32 remained in touch for the duration of their lives and met regularly in Mansfield. Levy Carnine, thought not an enlistment in the company, was always considered an honored member and was for the rest of his life a part of that organization—its 233rd member. When he died, Levy Carnine was buried with full military honors at the expense of the surviving members of the Pelican Rifles. He rests among the soldiers in the Confederate section of the Mansfield Cemetery beneath a small Confederate-type flat-topped gravestone, which read "L. S. Carnine, CSA." As long as any member of the Pelican Rifles lived, his grave was always decorated with flowers and sometimes miniature Confederate flags, just like all the other Confederate graves. On February 18, 2001, he was honored once more as some 35 persons attended a memorial service for him. His newly repaired and restored gravestone bore a small Confederate battle flag as in decades past, and the strains of Dixie and Amazing Grace were played on the bagpipes, just for Levy. Among the dignitaries were the Commander in Chief of the Sons of Confederate Veterans—successor organization to the original United Confederate Veterans—as well as officers of regional SCV*

*camps (as SCV chapters are called), members of the leadership of the DeSoto Parish black community, and others. Confederate colors were presented and a musket volley was fired to salute Levy Carnine. It was a fitting tribute to a soldier—for indeed he was that—who risked his life for his friends, his country, and his fellow men.*[47]

After the surrender of General Robert E. Lee at Appomatox Courthouse, Virginia on 9 April 1865—exatly one year after the Battle of Pleasant Hill--Freestone County soldiers under the command of Captain T. D. Nettles who had fought at Mansfield carried the Val Verde Cannon back to Texas and disbanded at Fairfield. For many years, the cannon was fired during meetings of the United Confederate Veterans at the Moody Reunion Grounds in Fairfield. Later, the cannon was mounted on a concrete pedestal and placed on the lawn of the Freestone County Courthouse. In 1964, the Freestone County Historical Survey Committee had the cannon remounted. In April of that year, it was carried to Mansfield, Louisiana and fired during the centennial celebration of the Battle of Mansfield.[48] The Fairfield High School Band participated in this celebration and was designated as the official band for the state of Texas at this event. Freestone County residents played a prominent role on this occasion, as they had on the battlefield one hundred years earlier.[49]

On 8 August 1997, the cannon was restored to its present condition from funds raised by the Johnson-Sayers-Nettles Camp #1012 of the Sons of Confederate Veterans.[50] While the cannon can no longer be fired, it was again taken to Louisiana and placed on display at the 150th Anniversary of the Battle of Mansfield that was held 24-27 April 2014. More than 700 re-enactors from various states converged on the Mansfield State Historic Site. The Saturday morning events included the commemoration program of the Crescent Regiment in Mouton's Trail area and a special presentation near the park museum by Louisiana Lt. Gov. Jay Dardenne regarding the acquisition of acreage that was part of the original land where the battle was fought by the Civil War Trust, a nonprofit organization dedicated to the preservation of endangered Civil War battlefields. Tom Gilmore, real estate director for the Trust, announced that 282 acres to the northeast of the museum at the state-owned site are under contract. Remarks were made by Mansfield Mayor Curtis W. McCoy and by Carolyn Calhoun Huckaby, Reimer Calhoun, Jr., and Thomas Allen Calhoun. The 1848 ancestral home of the latter three, which served as a field hospital during the war, will be incorporated into the battle site. On Saturday afternoon, there was a re-enactment of the battle. The writer traveled to Mansfield on Saturday 26 April and attended the special presentation and the re-enactment. He met many people from Texas, Louisiana, and other states with whom he shares a passion for history. His Masonic brother Earlie Hewitt, Worshipful Master of Stars of Prince Hall Lodge #241, met him at the battlefield and, afterward, they had dinner at Black Smoke BBQ on State Highway 175 across from his lodge hall and not far from the Mansfield State Historic Site.[51]

The Durhams—like all other slaves in the South—were freed as a result of the Civil War. It is interesting that they relocated from DeSoto Parish, Louisiana—the site of an important Civil War battle in which the Val Verde Cannon was used--to Freestone County, Texas, where the same Civil War weapon found its permanent home.

Interstate Highway 84 runs directly from Mansfield, Louisiana to Fairfield, Texas. More than likely, the Freestone County men who had fought at Mansfield traveled this route home after the war. More than likely, the newly freed Durhams—Belton, Allen, Minor, Christopher, and Anderson—traveled this route when they joined their younger brother Isaac in their new home in the Butler community.

## Freestone County, Texas

Freestone County is located in east central Texas in the center of a group of counties once called the Trinity Star. It is bounded on the east by Anderson County, on the south by Leon County, on the west by Limestone County, and on the north by Navarro and Henderson counties. Early settlers included the Caddo Indians. By the 1830s, the Caddoan tribe called the Keechis had a small settlement near what is now Butler while some Caddoan Tawakonis lived around Tehuacana Creek.[52]

By the 1840s, the white population of the northeastern part of Limestone County had grown significantly. In 1850, the Texas legislature carved Freestone County out of Limestone County. By the following year, the county has been organized and the town of Mound Prairie was selected as the county seat. Soon the name of Mound Prairie was changed to Fairfield. Some early towns included Cotton Gin, Avant Prairie, Butler, and Bonner Community.[53]

There were 290 slaves in Freestone County at the time of the 1851 organization. The number had grown to 2,167 by 1855.[54] According to the 1860 census, the county's total population was then 6,881, including 3,613 slaves. That year's agricultural census found 417 farms, encompassing 282,803 acres, in Freestone County. While more than half of these farms were smaller than 100 acres, a few large plantations had developed.

Two local landowners owned more than 100 slaves each, and four owned between 70 and 100 slaves. Fifty-seven slaveholders owned at least 20 slaves. Corn was the most important agricultural product. However, cotton was also an important staple. Over 6,900 bales of cotton were ginned in 1860. Local farmers also produced 5,200 pounds of tobacco. Other important crops included wheat, oats, and sweet potatoes. At this time, local ranchers were raising almost 19,300 cattle and 7,700 sheep.[55] The late Professor P. D. Browne, a Fairfield native and expert on Freestone County history[56] wrote concerning slavery in the county:

> *Many old settlers declare that the slaveholders who emigrated to the county brought their slaves with them, and seldom was the occasion that a planter went beyond the borders of the county to buy more slaves after he had located. The slave families were very prolific. Early and frequent marriages, large families, and a constant, large immigration caused the slave population to keep pace with the white and finally surpass it, as shown by the United States Census for 1860.*

> *Slaves were seldom sold or traded even in the county, little actual profits were made from their labor, and few planters found themselves sufficiently remunerated to be encouraged to purchase more Negroes. The natural increase of the slave families on the plantation, together with accepting a few occasionally for debts, was sufficient to meet the needs and satisfy the wants of the planter class. . . .*

> *As has already been indicated the increase in numbers of slaves was prodigious. In less than ten years their number increased from less than three hundred to more than three thousand. The number was nearly fifty per cent greater than in Leon County, twice as many as in Navarro, more than three times as many as in Limestone, and practically equal to the number in Anderson. Some three hundred and seven slaveholders held from one to more than one hundred slaves each. Of those who held five or less there were one hundred and forty, fifteen others owned more than forty each, while two of them owned more than one hundred each. Freestone's great wealth for 1860 was rendered for taxes at $1,921,459 or practically two-thirds of the total property valuation in the county. But the highest valuation of the Negroes was not reached until 1864, after some two thousand or more Negroes had been brought into the county in 1863, when an attempt was made to save slave property from the liberating Union Army in Arkansas and Louisiana. In 1864, five thousand six hundred and thirteen*

*Negroes were valued at $4,153,500.*[57]

Many Freestone County plantations were large, including seven that were larger than five hundred acres. It is interesting to note that only two plantations of this size operated in Anderson County, the wealthier county to the east. Reportedly, most of the masters treated their slaves fairly well. However, slavery is always a bitter pill to swallow. In May 1855, a slave of Hillary Manning, near West Point Landing, drowned himself, apparently to escape punishment by an overseer. In July 1861, Dr. A. G. Grayson's overseer was killed by a rebellious slave. Masters R. Oliver, Robert A. Gordon, Reuben Manning, and William Carter placed advertisements in The Texas State Gazette, offering $50 for the return of runaway slaves. There were no free blacks in Freestone County during this time.[58]

By the 1860s, a number of cultural institutions existed in Freestone County. A combination school and Masonic lodge was built in Fairfield in 1853 and at least two colleges were established before or during the Civil War, including Fairfield Female Academy (chartered in 1860) and Woodland College for Boys (established in 1863). By 1860, there were 13 churches (mostly Baptist and Methodist) operating in various parts of the county.[59] Ministry was not limited to the county's white population. Reportedly:

> All the laurels for church work among the slaves go to the Methodist. Some time previous to 1858 they organized the Trinity African Mission on the Fairfield circuit and placed a white missionary in charge. By 1860 they had as many as seventy-six members in full connection and thirty-six on probation. At the annual church conference for that year it was stated that the mission work among the colored was the crowning glory of Southern Methodism. Though their policy was often denounced, they steadily adhered to the scriptural position of preaching to poor and rich alike. "We will preach the gospel to the slaves, and their salvation shall be our rich reward" was the spirit in which the denomination pursued its work. . . .[60]

At the Secession Convention in Austin in 1861, Freestone County, represented by John Gregg and W. M. Peck, voted to leave the Union. After the convention, county residents voted 585 to 3 in favor of secession. Many Freestone County men fought and some died for the "Lost Cause."[61] The war had the following impact on the local economy:

> Freestone County's main cash crop, like that of much of the South, was cotton. The big problem was an inability to eat cotton, and food was a necessity for the Confederacy. . . .

*Corn was always a big crop in the county and during wartime this was fortunate. They were indeed fortunate to have Washington Steward's grist mill within the county. At Steward's Mill, corn was ground into meal to make the cornbread common on every table. Whole wheat could also be ground into flour there. The destruction of this mill by raiders during the war's latter days was an unfortunate event for the entire area. . . .*

*For Freestone County, the war was the end of an era, and a way of life was gone. Maintaining its agricultural dependence, the county would slowly decline for almost a century. However, it would be a sleeping giant with her strength in her land and her people. Freestone County would find new sources of energy in a new age and rise once again to the forefront of Texas.[62]*

In 1865, the end of the Civil War brought freedom to slaves in Freestone County and throughout the South. While some former slaves worked as sharecroppers for their former masters, others left the plantations, some departing from the South completely.[63]

Prof. Browne insisted that Texas did not suffer as severely during the Reconstruction years (1865-77) as other states of the old Confederacy and Freestone County less than many other places in Texas.[64] In September 1865, E. A. McCracken was appointed chief justice of the county court. At this time, a guard of six men was appointed to watch the town of Fairfield and vicinity to protect persons and property from damage. These six men were William Cotton, J. J. DeBoarde, Lewis Watson, J. H. McIlveen, John Karner, and J. C. Yarbre.[65] Texas was officially readmitted to the Union on 30 March 1870. Military rule in Texas ended on 16 April 1870. State authority returned to civil officers but carpetbaggers and state police played a prominent role in Texas politics until 1873. Radical Republican Governor Edmund J. Davis declared martial law in Freestone and Limestone counties on 9 October 1971, following a racially-related homicide in Groesbeck. One month later, martial law was lifted.[66]

By 1870, the area production of corn and cotton was considerably lower than in 1860. However, the coming of two railroads—the Houston and Texas Central to the west and the International-Great Northern to the south of the county brought considerable economic opportunity. The number of farms nearly doubled between 1870 and 1880 and, by 1900, the number of "improved" acres of farmland nearly tripled.[67]

During this time, the agricultural economy was marked by a significant rise in both cotton and corn production. In 1906, the Trinity and Brazos

Valley Railway was built across the county and partially solved the problem of getting crops to market. By 1920, almost 100,000 acres were devoted to cotton, while more than 50,600 were planted in cereal crops, primarily corn. At this time, the Freestone County population had arisen to 23,264.[68]

Local agriculture declined considerably during the early 1920s, as 777 farms were lost. During this time of Prohibition, one of the most lucrative enterprises was bootlegging, centered around Young's Mill. Illegal whiskey, known as Freestone County Bourbon Deluxe, was transported out of the county. Reportedly, a number of local families "became wealthy, directly or indirectly," from the liquor trade.[69]

The economic slump worsened during the Great Depression of the 1930s. Partly due to newly imposed federal crop restrictions, cropland harvested in the county dropped considerably. Hundreds of farmers left. Due partly to farm consolidations, the population declined between 1940 and 1970. With the advent of new businesses in the 1970s and 1980s, however, the population began to increase. While farming and livestock remained important, the biggest gains were in the mining industry, which employed over 500 workers in 1988. A new electric generating plant outside Fairfield caused public utilities to more than double their workforce from 1980 to 1986. Service and retail industries experienced considerable growth. By 1990, the county's population had increased to 20,946.[70]

Between the 1860s and the present, the Durham family has been quite visible in the Butler community and other parts of the county, making many positive contributions to historic developments.

## The Butler Community of Freestone County

Members of the Durham family who had been in slavery in Fairfield County, South Carolina and DeSoto Parish, Louisiana settled after the Civil War in the Butler community in the eastern part of Freestone County, Texas, between Fairfield and Palestine. Census records indicate that they were firmly established there by 1870. Today, although they are now scattered throughout the country, many still call Butler home.

It appears that, from Reconstruction to the present day, Butler has been a predominately black community. It has not always been so. First settled in the 1830s, Butler once had fifteen stores, a Masonic hall, a post office, a male and female academy, cotton gins, a blacksmith shop, two churches, and a school. The major source of revenue was the cotton plantations that surrounded it. The community was named for Butler County, Alabama, home of the earliest settters. Some of these settlers were named Gill, Bonner,

McDaniel, Mayes, Franklin, Wood, Mobley, Dunan, O'Neal, Creel, Looney, Edwards, Logan, Cornwell, Gorman, Murdock, Peevy, Stevens, Perry, Colly, Evans, Claypool, Prayther, Bateman, Tyus, Manning, Ray, Cobb, Hall, and Walker.[71]

Community Union Church was a nondenominational body originally located at Hickory Grove, about a mile east of Bonner Springs on the Old Palestine Road. It was later moved closer to the metropolis of Butler and became the center for most of the activity of the community. Slaves went to church with their masters and the names of slaves were recorded on the church roll. After Emancipation, a separate black congregation was built by Raymond O'Neal.[72]

Butler Baptist Church played a major role in the history of Butler. From 1864 to 1866, this church's pastor was George Washington Baines, the great-grandfather of President Lyndon Baines Johnson.[73]

Butler was known for many social activities, including great parties and dances, known as "in-fairs." Hosted by various plantation owners, these gala events were attended by people from many miles away. Reportedly:

> *The slim-waisted, bright eyed young ladies, complete with hoop skirts and velvet slipper, flirted and danced and strolled in the gardens with their beaus, who were clad in their white linen suits and silk top hats. Many a lass has "tipped a light fantastic" or "put her little foot" till dawn of the music of the fiddle and the bow (all properly chaperoned, of course.)[74]*

During the Civil War, there were two soldiers' homes in Butler. One was operated by Hillary Manning, a plantation owner; and the other by William McDonald. These homes furnished meals and lodging to soldiers traveling to and from the army and were reimbursed by the Freestone County Commissioners' Court in Confederate money.[75]

While Butler usually had a resident physician, much health care took the form of folk medicine, as thus described:

> *Sassafras tea, made by boiling the root of the tree, was used as a general tonic to "thin the blood."*

> *The leaves of the Madeiravine were mashed to a pulp and applied to boils.*

> *Catnip tea was given to the babies to make them sleep well, and when they started to cut teeth, the two front feet of a mole were hung around the baby's neck "to help the teeth scratch through."*

> *If a person had rheumatism, he would have to steal an irish potato from the grocery store and carry it with him at all times.[76]*

In 1872, when the International and Great Northern Railroad wanted the right of way to come through Butler, the company could not reach an agreement with landowners. As a result, they went through Oakwood and Palestine instead. By 1880, when the railway was finished, many Butler residents had moved to the major rail centers. As the steamboats along the Trinity River gave way to the railroads, the plantations disappeared. In 1971, Butler schools were closed and Butler students began attending schools in the Fairfield Independent School District.[77]

The old plantations were divided into smaller farms, operated mainly by former slaves, some as owners and some as sharecroppers. Many of these farmers had been in bondage to white Durhams in South Carolina and Louisiana. Thus, after obtaining their freedom, they adopted the surname of "Durham."

### *Fairfield Sesquicentennial Celebration*

On Saturday 27 October 2001, the Fairfield Sesquicentennial Celebration was held. That morning, the last order of Confederate General Joseph Burton Johnson was honored as he was reburied in the Fairfield City Cemetery. The Sons of Confederate Veterans, the Masons, and the National Grange of the Patrons of Husbandry were involved in this ceremony. The writer and his grandson, Dominique Bass-Parker, were in attendance. That afternoon, they participated in the Sesquicentennial Parade. That night, they attended a Freestone County History Pageant at Fairfield High School. This pageant included the following ten scenes: Indian family, frontier family, the reliance steamboat, Old South scene, Confederate soldiers, cabin scene, auctioneer scene, oil field scene, and Prohibition scene. Rose Nemons, an African American woman from Teague, told how Freestone County blacks, many of whom remained loyal to the South, nevertheless longed for their freedom. She then described the achievements of local African Americans, including Blind Lemon Jefferson, the famous blues recording artist from Wortham. Rev. K. M. Williams, the "Texas Country Blues Preacher," sang the following Blind Lemon songs: "Black Snake Moan," "'Lectric Chair Blues," "See That My Grave Is Kept Clean," "Prison Cell Blues," and "Blues Came to Texas." Prior to his performance, Rev. Williams invited the writer on stage to promote his Blind Lemon biography.[78]

Good Hope Baptist Church in Fairfield County, SC.

Author at Good Hope Baptist Church and Cemetery in Fairfield County, South Carolina.

Gravesite of Julius Durham in the Good Hope Cemetery in Fairfield County, SC.

Author and son-law Kenneth Prox at White Oak Cemetery in Fairfield County, SC.

Author at the gravesite of Willie Mae and Elie M. Durham in the White Oak Cemetery in Fairfield County, SC.

Author in front of the Fairfield County Library in Winnsboro, SC.

White Oak Baptist Church and Cemetery in Fairfield County SC.

Author in front of the Fairfield County Museum in Winnsboro, SC.

Author with Katherine Durham Pope

Boykin Durham

Ruff Store at Ridgeway, SC

Author, Granddaughters Kendra and Kayla Prox, and Son-in-Law Kenneth Prox at Harrison Store near Lake Wateree.

Durham Mercantile at Blackstock, SC

Bob Uzzel at a Durham grave in Desoto Parish, Louisiana.

Gravesite of Reverend Ezra John Durham in Kingston Cemetery near Mansfield, La.

The site of Keachi College near Mansfield, La.

Mansfield Female College in Mansfield, La.

Star Light Lodge in Mansfield, La.

Saint James AME Church in Mansfield, La.

Levi Carnine was African American Confederate soldier from Mansfield, La.

People gathering at the 150th anniversary of the Battle of Mansfield.

Richard Strother Taylor,
Confederate General
at Mansfield

Nathaniel Prentice Banks,
Union General
at Mansfield

Author with a cannon at the Mansfield
State Historic Site.

The Val Verde Cannon in Fairfield, Texas.

Calvin Nicholson with the Val Verde Cannon at the reeanctment of the Battle of
Mansfield.

Confederate forces at the reenactment of the Battle of Mansfield, near Mansfield, La.

Union forces at the reenactment of the Battle of Mansfield.

Author at the Fairfied Memorial Hospital in Fairfield, Tx.

Author in front of the Fairfield Memorial Hospital in Winnsboro, SC.

Union (formerly Pine Top) Methodist Church at Butler in Freestone County, Tx.

Pine Top Cemetery at Butler in Freestone County, Tx.

Lone Star Baptist Church at Butler in Free-stone County, Tx.

Lone Star Cemetery at Butler in Freestone County, Tx.

## Chapter II
## *The Durham Slaveholders and Their Descendants*

Evidence indicates that the Durham family that settled in Freestone County, Texas are descendants of the slaves owned by the family of Robert Winfield Durham, who moved from Fairfield County, South Carolina to DeSoto Parish, Louisiana after his death.

It appears that the first Durham to settle in Fairfield County was Capt. Charnel Durham, who was born at Northern Neck, Virginia on 2 July 1753, the son of John Durham. He married Nancy Echols on 2 January 1777. They had three other children—John, Robert Winfield, and Lucretia. They settled in Fairfield County, near the source of Dutchman's Creek, where he cultivated the soil until called to bear arms in the American Revolution. He enlisted on 1 July 1774 and served three years under Thomas Woodward, Richard Winn, and Frank Boykin in Col. William Thompson's South Carolina Rangers. During the spring of 1780, he was captured by Tories and imprisoned at Charleston, South Carolina. Thirteen months later, he escaped. An American soldier named Hightower also escaped. Apparently, they had developed such a bond during their time in captivity that they agreed to name one of their descendants for each other so they would know they got away safely. Years later, Capt. Durham learned of a man named Durham Hightower living in Georgia. Since he had no more children after the war, the family agreed that a grandson would be named Charnel Hightower Durham. In 1781, he served for three months under Col. William Bratton and three months under Col. John Pearson.[1] His last years have been, thus, described:

> *Capt. Durham ... after a toilsome journey of some weeks, concealing him by day and traveling by night, reached home and rejoined his command, where he continued actively to serve his country until her independence was assured and peace proclaimed. Then returning to his farm he there spent his remaining days amid the quietude of his rural home and the endearments of the domestic circle, dying only after he had transcended man's allotted time of three score and ten years. His wife survived him two years. Their remains were interred within the garden adjoining the family mansion.[2]*

Capt. Durham died in Fairfield County on 13 April 1836. The old family burial ground is near Ridgeway.[3] The following indicates the importance of the Durham and Woodward families:

> *A few miles distant the Woodwards and Durhams lie interred in the Woodward burial ground just below Winnsboro. Seeming to stand as sentinel is the famous anvil rock easily seen to the right from the car window as you go south after leaving Winnsboro.*
>
> *The first of the Durhams to arrive in this country came in the ship Confidence arriving at Old Point or Jamestown in 1721. Some of them settled in Folkstone County, Virginia. . . . Capt. Durham and his wife were both Virginians. Capt. Durham had three children. John Durham married Cynthia Woodward, granddaughter of Thomas Woodward, known in history as the Regulator. Robert Winfield married a daughter of Judge Abner Ross. . . . Lucretia married John Ford, son of Nathaniel Ford, who came from Caroline County, Virginia.[4]*

Robert Winfield Durham was born on 10 September 1784 in Fairfield County, South Carolina, the son of Charnel and Nancy Winfield Echols Durham.[5]   On 9 April 1816, he married Molsie Eliza Ross.[6]   They lived on the Durham Cotton Plantation in Fairfield County until his death. To this marriage, the following children were born: Osman Lawrence (23 April 1817-1908), Charnel Hightower (27 December 1818-16 December 1882), Mary Elizabeth (26 July 1821-4 October 1857), Joel Ross (21 February 1823-8 October 1855), Abner Ross (21 July 1825-12 June 1847), Robert James Durham (29 September 1829-19 April 1847), William Thomas Sumpter (11 July 1832-May 1863), John Franklin (17 December 1829-15 November 1918), Mary Elizabeth Whitaker (21 June 1834-22 January 1917), Emma Harriet (6 October 1836-?), Ross Durham (22 May 1841; died in infancy), and Robert Winfield. Both Abner Ross and Robert James Durham were killed in the Mexican War. Their father died on 13 February 1852. He is buried in the family graveyard on the Durham Cotton Plantation.[7]

Molsey Eliza Ross Durham, the widow of Robert Winfield Durham, arrived with two of her sons in DeSoto Parish, Louisiana in 1858. The family brought their slaves with them.[8]   In a list of slaveholders who paid taxes on nine or more slaves in 1861, she is listed as the owner of twenty-six slaves.[9] She died on 17 February 1873 and is buried in the Old Hazelwood Cemetery in Grand Cane.[10]

Capt. Osman Lawrence Durham, the oldest son of Robert Winfield and

Osman Lawrence Durham

Molsie Eliza Durham, was born in Fairfield County on 23 April 1817.[11] He emigrated to Lowndes County, Alabama in 1839. He had children born there as late as 1847. However, he was firmly established in DeSoto Parish by the time of the 1850 Census. From his earliest boyhood, he was familiar with farming. Upon his removal to Louisiana, he purchased some land which was in very poor condition. He immediately began making improvements and eventually acquired at least 1,000 acres, of which 350 acres were cleared and devoted to such crops as cotton and corn. He also became quite adept at the raising of livestock. Throughout the area, he developed a reputation as a thrifty and prosperous farmer.[12]

In 1862, Capt. Durham enlisted in the Confederate Army, becoming commander of the Dixie Rebels of the Twenty-seventh Louisiana Regiment. Later, he was transferred to the quartermaster's department, collecting food and horses for his regiment. He continued to serve the Confederacy in this capacity until he was mustered out at Shreveport in 1865.[13]

In 1839, Capt. Durham married Martha Jane Haywood in Lowndes County, Alabama. To this union, five children were born: Osmond Ross, Robert H., Melissa C., Mark E., and Emma V. Martha Jane Durham died in 1880. He married Mary Thomas ("Tommie") Scott in DeSoto Parish on 15 November 1893.[14]

Capt. Durham was a very active Baptist, serving as chair of the District Baptist Association, composed of DeSoto and Caddo parishes. He served for a number of years as president of the local school board and was one of the founders of Keatchie College.[15]

On 1 September 1860, Capt. Durham sold to Francis L. Carroll of Natchitoches Parish, Louisiana, "one certain Negro man named Adam, aged about 30 years, of griff complexion." This document was signed by O. L. Durham and F. L Carroll.[16] In a list of slaveholders who paid taxes on nine or more slaves in 1861, he is listed as the owner of twenty-three slaves.[17] On 23

January 1866, he was appointed as administrator of "Tobe Shannon, Alic Shannon, Lewis Shannon, Edmund Starke, Julia Young, all minors, all black children, minors until they reach of age of 21 years for boys, 18 years for girls, under apprenticeship."[18]

Capt. Durham died on 5 April 1908. He is buried in Old Hazlewood Cemetery.[19]

Tommie Scott Durham—the second wife of Capt. O. L. Durham—was born in Kingston, Louisiana on 18 October 1860, the daughter of Thomas F. and Sarah Moss DuBose Scott. She taught school in DeSoto Parish for many years. She spent her last years living with a sister in Shreveport. She died on 28 May 1936 and is buried in Evergreen Cemetery near Frierson, Louisiana.[20]

Charnel Hightower Durham, M.D., was born on 27 December 1818 in Fairfield County, South Carolina. He later settled in DeSoto Parish, Louisiana, bringing his slaves with him.[21] On 10 February 1859, he sold to B. F. Jenkins a nineteen-year-old slave named Cane.[22] In a list of slaveholders who paid taxes on nine or more slaves in 1861, he is listed as the owner of ten slaves.[23] Dr. Durham practiced medicine in Louisiana for many years. He died on 16 December 1882. He is buried in Mansfield Cemetery. His wife, Lizzie E. Smith Durham was born in South Carolina on 1 January 1833 and died on 18 July 1861. She is buried in Hazelwood Cemetery.[24]

Lt. John Franklin Durham was born in 1829 in South Carolina. His wife, Elizabeth Jemima Ashford Durham, was born there in 1833. He was the sixth child of Robert Winfield and Molzey Eliza Ross Durham. She was the youngest child of William Ashford and Martha Matilda Robertson. They married in South Carolina on 17 February 1854. They had settled in DeSoto Parish, Louisiana by 1859. They brought their slaves with them.[25] In a list of slaveholders who paid taxes on nine or more slaves in 1861, he is listed as the owner of ten slaves.[26] He was a farmer and she was a house-keeper. Their children were Ruth Anna (15 September 1854-1909?), Martha Matilda—nicknamed "Tay" (9 December 1855-March 1934), Emma Melissa (30 August 1857-15 November 1933), John Franklin II (1 April 1859-1942), William David—nicknamed "Willie" (13 March 1861-?), Joel Ashford—nicknamed "Tedie" ((21 November 1864-12 May 1932), Thomas Ashford (19 May 1867-31 August 1903), Mary Belle (21 May 1869-29 June 1929), Fannie Lee Durham (5 June 1871-2 February 1947), Cornelia E.—nick-named "Nellie" (1873-23 October 1957).[27]

On 3 May 1862, in Mansfield, Louisiana, John Franklin Durham enlisted in the Confederate Army as a Second Lieutenant, Company D, 11th Bn La Inf. He was present on rolls from May to October 1862. He was granted a furlough on 20 August 1862. This furlough was extended and he was placed on sick leave in January 1863. He resigned his commission on 8 March 1863 and placed on 30-day furlough in April 1863. Apparently, his military career was quite brief. He died in 1918.[28]

Osman L., Charnal Hightower, and John Franklin Durham had other siblings. A sister, Martha Durham, settled in DeSoto Parish and never married. Two brothers died in the Mexican War. Joel Ross Durham died in 1855 in South Carolina. William Durham served in the Confederate Army and was killed at the Battle of Malvern Hill, Virginia in 1862. Mary Eliza Whitaker Durham married James Monroe Nelson in South Carolina and came to DeSoto Parish with the Nelson family. She died in Beaumont, Texas. The youngest child, Emma Durham, married William Ball and settled in DeSoto Parish.[29]

John Franklin Durham, II, was born on 1 April 1859 in DeSoto Parish. He married Leonora Scott on 10 January 1883. The following children were born to this union: Edna Leonora, Mitchell Judson, John Earl, Mary Belle, James Murray, Sarah Thomas, Viola Vivian, Gladys, Frank Leon, Marguerite, Lillie Frank, and Ashford.[30]

Mitchell Judson Durham, the son of John Franklin and Leonora Scott Durham, was born on 12 September 1884 in DeSoto Parish. For many years, he was overseer for a plantation at Curtis, Louisiana. He married Carrie Mai Smith, the daughter of James Aticus and Mary Eliza Wynn Smith of Arkansas.[31] The following children were born to this union: Judson Burney, Frank Lee, James Franklin, and Alan Curtis. Mitchell Judson and Carrie were members of the First United Methodist Church of Bossier City, Louisiana. She died on 17 December 1970. He died on 6 November 1973.[32]

Judson Burney Durham was born on 15 November 1910 in Kingston, Louisiana. He settled in Shreveport, where he worked as an accountant for John David Crow Drilling Company and served as an elder at Broadmoor Presbyterian Church. He married Edith Eloise Whittington (born 30 March 1910) on 8 August 1933.[33] Judson died on 28 March 1993. Eloise died on 28 December 2001. They are buried in Forest Park East Cemetery in Shreveport.[34]

Four sons were born to the union of Judson Burney and Eloise Whittington Durham. The first, Col. James Michael Durham, was born in Shreveport on 27 May 1937. A 1954 graduate of Byrd High School in Shreveport, he attended Rensselaer Polytechnic Institute, where he was a member of Pi Kappa Alpha fraternity; and graduated from Centenary College in 1959. Upon graduation, he was commissioned a Second Lieutenant in the U.S. Army's Ordnance Corps and advanced through the rank of Colonel during his twenty-seven-year Army career.    He married Constance Manuela Alvarez on 4 June 1960.[35]   He earned Master's degrees from New Mexico State University, the University of Southern California, and Michigan State University and was a graduate of the U.S. Army War College and the U.S. Army Command and General Staff College.   He was a veteran of the Vietnam War, where he earned the Bronze Star and various campaign awards. His other awards included the Legion of Merit (two awards), Meritorious Service Medal (two awards), Joint Service Commendation Medal, and Army Commendation Medal.   His Army assignments in included commanding the 703rd Maintenance Battalion, the 3rd Materiel Maintenance Command, and the Mainz Army Depot.   He was also Product Manager for the Heavy Equipment Transport and, in his final assignment, Program Manager, Tactical Vehicles. As PM(TV), he was responsible for the engineering, production, fielding, logistics, and support of over fifty separate systems. These systems ranged from light tactical vehicles such as the High Mobility Multipurpose Wheeled Vehicle (HMMWV or Humvee) to the Family of Medium Trucks to the Army's largest vehicles such as the Heavy Expanded Mobility Tactical Truck (HEMTT). During his tenure he oversaw the initial fielding of the Humvee which replaced the World War II vintage Army Jeep.   After retiring from the Army he held various positions within the defense industry including Director, Tank Automotive Programs for Cypress International, Vice President of Government Business for Cummins Engine Co, Inc., President, Cummins Military Systems, Inc., and Vice President of Marketing and Business Development for Lear Siegler Services, Inc. In 1995 he established JD Interests, Inc., an aerospace and defense systems marketing and business development consultant services firm.   He settled in Farnham, in the Northern Neck of Virginia, not far from where his ancestors once lived. Active in his local community, he served on the boards of the Richmond and Westmoreland Counties Chapter of Habitat for Humanity, the Northern Neck Chapter of the Association for the Preservation of Virginia Antiquities, the Potomac Chapter of the Military Officers Association of America, and the Historical Society of the Northern Neck of Virginia.

Col. Durham died on 23 January 2004.  He was interred with full military honors at Arlington National Cemetery on February 20, 2004. He was survived by his wife; daughter Jennifer Esperanza; sons and daughters-in-law Dr. James M. Durham, Jr. and Kathy Durham, Christopher Durham and Kari Durham, Commander David Durham of the United States Navy and Lisa Durham, and Matthew and Karin Durham; and eight grandchildren, Caitlin Durham, Emily Esperanza, Ryan Durham, Rebecca Durham, Anna Durham, Gabriel Kessler, Owen Durham, Zoe Durham, and Tess Durham.[36]

The second son of Judson Burney and Eloise Whittington Durham, Maj. Robert Scott Durham, was born on 5 December 1938 and married Carole Kopcsak on 7 June 1969. After his service in the U. S. Army, he moved to Houston, Texas, where he worked in banking and later taught mathematics at a high school. After retirement, he moved to Fort Worth, where he died on Sunday 24 February 2013, after a courageous 21-month battle with renal cancer. A memorial service was held on Sunday 10 March at Saint Stephen Presbyterian Church in Fort Worth. He was survived by his wife, Carole Kopcsak Durham; their daughter, Kathryn McGlinchey and her husband, Parnell; and grandchildren.[37]

The third son of Judson Burney and Eloise Whittington Durham, Thomas Whittington Durham, was born on 5 February 1946 and has remained in Shreveport, where he has worked for many years in the office supply business.[38] In 1983, the author sent him a letter regarding the family history and he forwarded to his brother Donald Smith Durham, who was then living in Manassas, Virginia. This resulted in a telephone call from Don and a major breakthrough in the author's research.

The fourth son of Judson Burney and Eloise Whittington Durham was Lt. Col. Donald Smith Durham, who was born on 15 February 1947, in Shreveport. He graduated from Byrd High School in Shreveport and received an undergraduate degree from Northwestern Louisiana and a Master of Business Administration degree from Tulane University. He entered the U. S. Army as a commissioned officer in June 1969, and served until his retirement with rank of lieutenant colonel on 31 December 1989. His military career included tours of duty in Germany; Fort Hood, Texas; Vietnam; Korea; Hampton, Virginia; and the Pentagon in Washington, DC, where he met his wife, Carol M. White Zagorsky. They were married in a military wedding at Fort Meyers, Virginia, on 5 May 1984. While employed at the Pentagon, he lived in Manassas, Virginia.[39] At the time of his retirement, he was the leader on the Force Modernization Division at the U. S. Army Command and General Staff College at Fort Leavenworth, Kansas. He received numerous awards and decorations during his Army career. After his retirement, he worked for four years as a defense contractor and then joined American Express Financial Advisors. He was known for maintaining the highest standard of honesty and integrity and expecting the same in those with whom he dealt. He died on February 16, 2006, at his home in Shawnee, Kansas, after a long and courageous battle with colon cancer. He was survived by his wife Carol; their son, Trent Zagorsky and daughter-in-law, Layla, of Lenexa, Kansas; their daughter, Shawn Zagorsky; and their grandson, Ryan White, of Denver, Colorado. A memorial services was held on Wednesday February 22, 2006 at Porter Funeral Home in Lenexa, Kansas. Final burial with full military honors was at Arlington National Cemetery.[40]

# Chapter III
## *The Durhams of Fairfield County, South Carolina*

The Durham population—white and black—of Fairfield County, South Carolina has diminished over the years. Nevertheless, there remain some Durhams in the area who are more than likely distant relatives of the Durhams who came to Freestone County, Texas via DeSoto Parish, Louisiana.

John Woodward Durham, the only child of John and Cynthia Woodward Durham, was born on 2 December 1807 and died on 21 January 1858. He is buried in Woodward Cemetery. His older son John Woodward Durham, Jr. lived from 1827 to 1871. During the Civil War, he served in the South Carolina Cavalry Battalion, Hampton Legion, Company B. His younger son William Strother Durham was born on 16 May 1835 in Fairfield County. He attended school at Shirley's Institute in Fairfield County. In June 1856, he received an A.B. degree from South Carolina College, where he was a member of the Euphradian Literary Society. For two years, he taught in a number of rural schools. At the beginning of the Civil War, he enlisted in the Fairfield Fencibles and, several months later, became a member of the Congaree Troop, which eventually became part of the Hampton Legion Cavalry and was upgraded to a regiment, becoming known as the Second South Carolina Cavalry. He served with Company H of this cavalry until the close of the war. After the war, he resumed his teaching career, serving on the faculty of Blythewood Female College, West Point Male Academy, and Sumter Graded Schools. In 1882, he retired to his Fairfield County farm, where he lived until his death on 22 November 1909. He is buried in the Sandy Level Baptist Church Cemetery in Blythewood, South Carolina.[1]

William Shedd Durham, son of Robert Winfield Durham, was born in 1832 and served as a corporal in the South Carolina Cavalry Battalion, Hampton Legion, Company D. He was killed at the Battle of Malvern Hill in Henrico County, Virginia on 1 July 1862.[2]

A review of cemetery records reveals the gravesites of a number of white Durhams. The following a buried in the cemetery of Union Memorial Presbyterian Church: Abner Robert Durham M-12 (25 November 1850-11 October 1924), son of Rebecca Shedd and Joel Ross Durham; Abner Ross Durham N-26 (6 March 1879-16 April 1944); Eva Fant Durham N-25 (4 January 1884-20 August 1961), wife of Abner Ross Durham; Foride Durham N-15 (14 July 1898-1 May 1990), daughter of W. S. and M. V. Durham; Mary E. Durham M-14 (7 February 1882010 February 1916, daughter of Mary V. and W. S. Durham; Mary V. Estes Durham M-15; 20 October 1856-7 May 1943, wife of William S. Durham; and Maude Durham N-16 (6 August 1853-7 December 1917).[3]   The following are buried in the Catholic Presbyterian Cemetery: Daisy Hill Durham (8 April 1897-6 December 1979); William S. Durham (27 May 1890-2 November 1987); Alberta Durham, (30 April 1871-27 November 1954), Cynthia Anna Durham (15 February 1868-9 March 1950); John Woodward Durham (24 August 1875-20 November 1932); Lottie Durham (born and died in 1862, three months old), daughter of A. K. and E. D. Durham; Lutie McNulty Durham (11 March 1880-1 January 1961); Margaret Daniel Durham (3 March 1813-2 June 1899), Marvin McNulty Durham (8 September 1845-5 July 1936); William McNulty Durham (no dates), infant son of William and Marvin Durham; and William S. Durham (16 May 1835-21 November 1909).[4]

For many years, a store called Durham Mercantile, owned by William S. ("Will") Durham, played a prominent role in the community of Blackstock, located on the Fairfield-Chester County Line.   In a senior thesis, John I. Sanders wrote:

*Tucked away in the pines of the South Carolina midlands is the tiny Blackstock community. In 2007 one might place it geographically by saying it is one hour north of Columbia on I-77 and one hour south of Charlotte on the same interstate. . . . For most of the 20th century there was a business and social center to the community. That center was the grand brick building erected in 1894 when the town was rapidly expanding. . . The owner was Mr. Will Durham. . . Mr. Will was coming into his prime just as Blackstock was hitting its peak. When Will took over the store in 1920 he was 30 years old and fresh home from World War I. The charm of Mr. Durham and his locally iconic general store were central pieces of the Blackstock community for decades. Even in the 1980s, after the store had closed for business, a 90-year-old Will Durham would open the store so that his neighbors could still gather there. Now, when the community members look back at their community in the years between 1920 and 1940 their stories are laced with references to Mr. Will Durham and his country store. The link is strong and fittingly so. A close look at the economic and social history of Blackstock reveals that Mr. Will Durham was the community's quiet hero for more than 20 years.*[5]

In the 1870 U. S. Census, the following Durhams (all natives of South Carolina) were listed as Winnsboro residents:

| Name | Age | Gender | Race |
| --- | --- | --- | --- |
| Angelina | 24 | Female | Black |
| Charlotte | 30 | Female | Black |
| Frances | 60 | Female | Black |
| John | 35 | Male | Black |
| Margaret | 58 | Female | White |
| Mary | 65 | Female | Black |
| Oliver | 21 | Male | Black |
| Osmond | 40 | Male | Black |
| Philip | 30 | Male | Black |
| Ransom | 35 | Male | Black |
| Robert | 2 | Male | Black |
| Sarah | 45 | Female | Black |
| William | 35 | Male | White[6] |

By 1880, the Durham population of Farfield County had experienced much growth, with black Durhams in the majority. Each of these was a native South Carolinian:

| Name | Age | Gender | Race |
| --- | --- | --- | --- |
| Adeline | 25 | Female | Black |
| Albert | 17 | Male | Black |
| Alverta | 9 | Female | White |
| Anjaline | 26 | Female | Black |
| Annie | 26 | Female | Black |
| Boseman | 7 | Male | Mulatto |
| Boykin | 2 | Male | Mulatto |
| Charity | 24 | Female | Black |
| Cynthia | 12 | Female | White |
| Ellison | 8 | Female | Black |
| Fannie | 65 | Female | Black |
| Frances | 16 | Female | Black |
| George | 12 | Male | Black |
| Hannah | 28 | Female | Black |
| Ida | 3 | Female | Mulatto |
| Ida | 2 | Female | Black |
| Jane | 10 | Female | Black |
| John | 8 | Male | Mulatto |
| John Woodward | 4 | Male | White |
| Julias | 32 | Male | Mulatto |
| Kate | 4 | Female | Black |
| Layle | 21 | Female | Mulatto |

| | | | |
|---|---|---|---|
| Levi | 29 | Male | Black |
| Lilla | 4 | Female | Mulatto |
| Lizzie | 1 | Female | Black |
| Lucy | 1 | Female | White |
| Lucy | 30 | Female | Mulatto |
| Maggie | 6 | Female | Mulatto |
| Margaret | 63 | Female | White |
| Marnin | 35 | Male | White |
| Martha | 19 | Female | Black |
| Ransom | 34 | Male | Black |
| Reuben | 8 | Male | Black |
| Rhodesta | 9 | Female | Black |
| Robert | 30 | Male | Black |
| Stilla | 5 | Female | Black |
| Thomas | 15 | Male | Black |
| William | 2 | Male | Black |
| William | 60 | Male | Black |
| William S. | 45 | Male | White |
| Willie | 6 | Male | Black[7] |

In 1900, only seven Durhams were listed in the Fairfield County Census:

| *Name* | *Age* | *Gender* | *Race* |
|---|---|---|---|
| Calvin | 30 | Male | Black |
| Joe | 18 | Male | Black |
| Joe | 40 | Male | Black |
| John | 28 | Male | Black |
| Lilla | 23 | Female | Black |
| William | 45 | Male | Black |
| Willie | 26 | Male | Black[8] |

By 1910, the Durham population of Fairfield County had, again, increased:

| *Name* | *Age* | *Gender* | *Race* |
|---|---|---|---|
| Allen | 15 | Male | Black |
| Boykin | 32 | Male | Mulatto |
| Charlie | 34 | Male | Black |
| Cluie | 11 | Male | Black |
| Henry | 12 | Male | Black |
| Hope | 35 | Male | Mulatto |
| Isaiah | 18 | Male | Black |
| Joe | 45 | Male | Mulatto |
| Julious | 60 | Male | Black |
| Liler | 31 | Male | Mulatto |
| Lizzie | 31 | Female | Black |
| Robert | 35 | Male | Black |
| Will | 35 | Male | Black |
| William | 24 | Male | Black[9] |

By the beginning of the "Roaring 20s," the Durham population of Fairfield County had, again, dropped:

| Name | Age | Gender | Race |
|------|-----|--------|------|
| Boykin | 43 | Male | Mulatto |
| Charles | 48 | Male | Black |
| Hattie MC | 35 | Female | White |
| Julious | 66 | Male | Mulatto |
| Robert | 40 | Male | Black |
| W. D. | 44 | Male | Black |
| William | 45 | Male | Black |
| William S. | 29 | Male | White[10] |

At the beginning of the Great Depression, only seven Durhams were listed in the Fairfield County Census:

| Name | Year of Birth |
|------|---------------|
| William | About 1875 |
| Boykin | About 1876 |
| Bill | About 1882 |
| Robert | About 1882 |
| Mood | About 1891 |
| Richard | About 1905 |
| Clarence | About 1918[11] |

In 1940—the last year for which census records are available—the following Durhams were listed in Fairfield County:

| Name | Spouse | Year of Birth | Other Info |
|------|--------|---------------|------------|
| Boykin | Mary | About 1875 | |
| Will | Sarah | About 1875 | |
| Sarah | Will | About 1877 | |
| Robert | Bessie | About 1882 | |
| Mary | Boykin | About 1882 | |
| Bessie | Robert | About 1882 | |
| William S. | Daisy H. | About 1891 | Blackstock |
| Mood | Bertha | About 1892 | |
| Paul | Mamie | About 1896 | Blackstock |
| Daisy H. | William S. | About 1897 | Blackstock |
| Richard | Memie | About 1903 | |
| Willie, Jr. | | About 1904 | Son of Will and Sarah |
| Mamie | Paul | About 1905 | Blackstock |
| Memie | Richard | About 1905 | |
| James | | About 1908 | Son of Will and Sarah |
| Bertha | Mood | About 1908 | |
| Willie | Clara | About 1916 | |
| Norvell | | About 1916 | |
| Will | | About 1917 | |

During the early years of the writer's research for this book, there were only two Durhams listed in the Winnsboro, South Carolina telephone directory. He wrote letters to both of them. He received the following reply from

W. C. Durham:

> *I am a white Durham from Indianapolis, Indiana. I moved to Fairfield County 20 years ago and have no relatives in the South. Please write to Mr. Bill Taylor, 211 West Liberty Street, Winnsboro, S. C. 29180. He is the head of the museum and historical society of Fairfield County and should be able to help you.*[12]

The other Durham listed in the directory was a black woman named Clara Durham. Having received no reply, I telephoned her. She told me that her maiden name was Brown and that she was married to Willie Durham, a native of Fairfield County who died 20 years earlier. She said she never met her husband's father and met his mother only once. She stated that her husband had two sisters, Francena and Lucinda, both deceased; and she did not know if he had any brothers. She knew of a few other black Durhams in the area, including Bertha Durham, who lived toward Middlesex, on the Old Camden Road. She also knew of Richard Durham, whose family was light-skinned and who lived on the "Back Water." She was unsure of any kinship with her husband. She knew nothing about the Durham slaveholders in Fairfield County.[13]

On 22 August 2012, I obtained a copy of her funeral program and those of other black Durhams at the Fairfield County Library. Thus, I learned that Clara Brown Durham was born in Fairfield County to Charlie and Georgia Ann McCullough Brown. She was a lifelong resident of Fairfield County and a member of Small's Chapel African Methodist Episcopal Zion Church in Winnsboro and of the Sons and Daughters of Zion. She died on 27 July 1993. Her funeral was held on 1 August 1993 at Small's Chapel, with the eulogy delivered by Rev. S. Lai, followed by interment in Small's Chapel Cemetery. She was survived by two sons—Willie Durham and Charlie Durham; and one daughter Georgia Ann Durham.[14]

Katherine Durham Pope, who lives on "Durham Hill" in the Lake Wateree area near the Fairfield County city of Ridgeway, was born on 27 December 1934 in Fairfield County. She is the daughter of William B. ("Willie") Durham, the granddaughter of Boykin Durham, and great granddaughter of Julius Durham. She left South Carolina at age 13 and grew up in Baltimore, Maryland. She was employed as a nursing assistant, retiring from a Baltimore hospital. She also worked at Wal-Mart. After retirement, she returned to Fairfield County. She is a member of White Oak Baptist Church. She was married to John A. Pope, who died on 1 January 1990. They had one son, John L. Pope. On 27 September 2005, a tornado landed in Fairfield County.

She was taken up by the storm, causing three fractured ribs. She thanks God that she survived. Her brother Julius Durham died in this tornado. He, along with two other brothers—Willie James Durham and Elex Durham—are buried in White Oak Baptist Cemetery.[15]

Boykin Durham, who lives next door to his sister on "Durham Hill," was born on 13 September 1948 in Fairfield County. He is the son of William B. ("Willie") Durham, the grandson of Boykin Durham, and the great-grandson of Julius Durham. He was a farmer for many years, raising over twenty acres of cotton and corn. He also was employed in construction, having jobs in many places, including the Raleigh-Durham area of North Carolina, where he put in several traffic lanes. He is now retired. He recalls his family at times talked about slavery and that his grandmother, Mary Hogan Durham, cleaned houses for white people. He is a widower with a daughter named Briana and a son named Frederick. He is a member of Good Hope Baptist Church but often visits White Oak Baptist Church. Both churches have had many Durhams on their rolls throughout their history. He was named for his grandfather and was aware of the Boykin family in nearby Boykin, South Carolina.[16]

A number of Durhams are buried in the White Oak Baptist Cemetery. Such include the following. Julius Durham, the son of Frances Durham, was born on 14 November 1851 and died on 4 March 1924. His wife, Lucy Boykin Durham, was born in 1855 and died on 1 January 1936. Robert Durham was born on 12 May 1879 and died on 15 December 1957. His wife Betsy M. Durham was born on 18 December 1881 and died on 31 January 1960. Katie Durham Tidwell, the daughter of Julius and Lucy Durham, was born on 24 July 1884 and died on 13 January 1970. Edward Durham, the son of Julius and Lucy Durham, was born in October 1888 and died on 2 March 1936.

W. M. Durham was born in 1890 and died on 13 October 1952. Mood Durham, the son of Julius and Lucy Durham, was born on 4 July 1892 and died on 20 March 1959. His wife Alberta Harrison Durham, was born on 4 January 1908 and died on 14 January 1988. Minnie Canty Durham was born on 16 February 1908 and died on 3 June 1989.[17]

William B. ("Willie") Durham, the father of the above two interviewees, was born on 18 July 1911 in Fairfield County, the son of Boykin and Mary Harrison Durham. At an early age, he joined White Oak Baptist Church. He died on 18 July 1992 at Fairfield Memorial Hospital in Winnsboro. He was preceded in death by his brothers Richard and Linder Durham and his son Elie Durham. He was survived by his wife, Sallie H. Durham; five sons—

Walter, Willie James, Boykin, Paul, and Julius Durham; and six daughters-Beulah Washington, Elouise Perry, Katherine Pope, Mary Canzator, and Sallie Canzator. His funeral was held at White Oak Baptist Church, with the eulogy delivered by Rev. Arthur A. Gayten. Interment was in White Oak Baptist Cemetery.[19]

John Durham, the son of Charles and Maggie Durham, was born on 5 May 1920 and died on 13 May 1920. He is buried in White Oak Baptist Cemetery.

Willie Mae Adams Durham was born on 12 February 1939. She was the daughter of Willie and Nannie Bell Adams of Ridgeway, South Carolina. She grew up in Ridgeway and was educated in Fairfield County. On 9 June 1957, she married Deacon Elie M. Durham. She was employed by Fairfield Manufacturing Company, Ridgeway School District, Knitwear Inc. of Great Falls, South Carolina. She was survived by her husband; two sons—James Curtis and Darrin Durham; and one daughter—Shirley D. Durham Simmons; and seven grandchildren. Her funeral was held on 29 January 2000 at White Oak Baptist Church.[20] Her husband, Elie M. Durham, was born on 22 August 1934, the son of Mood and Albertha Harrison Durham. He attended Fairfield County Schools, served in the U. S. Army, worked at Winnsboro Mills, and retired from employment as a security officer for Fairfield County Detention Center. Following Willie Mae's death, he married a woman named Dorethea, who survived him. He died on 11 October 2006. His funeral was held at White Oak Baptist Church. The eulogy was delivered by Rev. James Addison. Interment was in White Oak Baptist Cemetery.[21]

Herman "Slicks" Durham was born on 8 August 1928 in Winnsboro at the "Flats" to Richard and Minnie Durham. He grew up in White Oak Baptist Church. He later moved to Washington, D. C., where he worked as an orderly until returning to Ridgeway. He died on 11 February 2007. He was preceded death by his sister Lillie Durham Kennedy and his brothers George and Daniel Durham. He was survived by his brother Linder Durham and his sister Mamie Durham Jones. His funeral was held on 15 February 2007 at White Oak Baptist Church. The eulogy was delivered by Rev. James Adamson. Interment was in White Oak Cemetery.[22]

# Chapter IV
## *The Durhams of DeSoto Parish, Louisiana*

The U. S. Census of 1870—the first census taken after the abolition of slavery—listed the following Durhams in DeSoto Parish, Louisiana:

| Name | Age | Sex | Race | Birthplace |
|------|-----|-----|------|-----------|
| Alfred | 30 | Male | Black | South Carolina |
| Emma | 16 | Female | White | Louisiana |
| Jack | 28 | Male | Black | Alabama |
| John | 40 | Male | White | South Carolina |
| M. E. | 70 | Female | White | South Carolina |
| Rose | 9 | Female | Black | Louisiana |
| William | 30 | Male | White | Alabama[1] |

Ten years later, the white Durham population of DeSoto Parish had experienced substantial growth, accompanied by substantial decline in the black Durham population, as indicated by the following census records:

| Name | Age | Sex | Race | Birthplace |
|------|-----|-----|------|-----------|
| Bissie | 20 | Female | White | Louisiana |
| C. H. | 67 | Male | White | South Carolina |
| E. M. | 22 | Female | White | South Carolina |
| Emma | 7 | Female | White | South Carolina |
| F. C. | 6 | Female | White | Louisiana |
| Fanie | 8 | Female | White | Louisiana |
| J. F. | 21 | Male | White | Louisiana |
| J. F. | 51 | Male | White | South Carolina |
| J. T. | 48 | Female | White | South Carolina |
| Joel | 15 | Male | White | Louisiana |
| John F. | 21 | Male | White | Louisiana |
| M. M. | 23 | Female | White | South Carolina |
| N. J. | 60 | Female | White | Alabama |
| O. L. | 63 | Male | White | South Carolina |
| R. A. | 25 | Female | White | South Carolina |
| R. H. | 35 | Male | White | Louisiana |
| Rose | 20 | Female | Black | Louisiana |
| T. A. | 13 | Male | White | Louisiana |
| W. D. | 19 | Male | White | Louisiana[2] |

At the turn of the century, there were still Durhams living in DeSoto Parish, with greater racial balance than twenty years earlier:

| Name | Age | Sex | Race | Birthplace |
| --- | --- | --- | --- | --- |
| Emma | 23 | Female | Black | Louisiana |
| Henry | 35 | Male | Black | Louisiana |
| Jene | 44 | Female | White | Louisiana |
| John B. | 11 | Male | Black | Louisiana |
| John F. | 71 | Male | Black | South Carolina |
| Jos | 69 | Male | White | South Carolina |
| Owen | 83 | Male | White | South Carolina |
| Sophia | 76 | Female | White | Alabama |
| Tyra | 36 | Female | Black | Louisiana[3] |

The 1910 U. S. Census revealed that the Durham population of DeSoto Parish—both black and white-had dropped. The following Durhams are listed:

| Name | Age | Sex | Race | Birthplace |
| --- | --- | --- | --- | --- |
| Henry | 40 | Male | Black | Louisiana |
| J. F., Jr. | 51 | Male | White | Louisiana |
| Joel A. | 42 | Male | White | Louisiana |
| John L. | 80 | Male | White | Louisiana |

Henry Durham's wife Fannie was also a Louisiana native and was 35 at that time.[4]

No black Durhams were listed in DeSoto Parish in the 1920 or 1930 U. S. Census. In 1940, a black woman named Fannie Durham—a 65-year-old widow—is listed as living on Walker Road in DeSoto Parish.[5]

During the author's visit to DeSoto Parish on 11 March 2013, telephone calls to the two local black-owned funeral homes revealed no recollections of burying anyone named Durham.

## Chapter V
### *Gobi—Patriarch of the Durham Family*
#### The First Generation

I have often told members of the Durham family of Freestone County, Texas: "Alex Haley had Kunta Kinte and you have Gobi."[1] I first heard of Gobi from Mary Durham of Fort Worth, the widow of Rev. General Bev Durham. Mary reported that her husband was the great-grandson of an African named "Gobi." Another Fort Worth resident and cousin of Rev. Durham, Mary Edwards, told me that General was the son of Boykin Durham and the grandson of Belton Durham.[2]

According to Mary Edwards' brother Johnny Johnson of Butler, Gobi (also called Gubbie) is buried in South Carolina. He said that, once, there was a rain spell and they could not work. The straw boss (overseer) and Gobi went hunting for bears. In a bear cave, they uncovered some gold. The straw boss died first. Gobi had sworn never to reveal the whereabouts of the gold. Some men tied Gobi to a tree in a bottom and wrapped a rope around him. Gobi refused to reveal where the gold was hidden, even when surrounded by mosquitoes. As a result, his tongue was torn out by its roots and he was left there to die. Five of his sons—Belton, Allen, Minor, Christopher, and Anderson—were born in South Carolina. His youngest son, Isaac, was born in Texas.[3]

Apparently, after Gobi's death, his pregnant widow Mary Allen Durham (who was born in Richmond, Virginia in 1810) was brought to Freestone County, Texas. Shortly after her arrival, she gave birth to their youngest son, Isaac Durham, on 15 August 1860. She died on 10 November 1880 and is buried in Lone Star Cemetery.[4]

The meaning of his African name should be explored. It is interesting that it is similar to the Gobi Desert of Asia. His African birthplace will be difficult to find. Nevertheless, he is a very important man and was the patriarch of a great family of African Americans who left their mark in Fairfield County, South Carolina; DeSoto Parish, Louisiana; Freestone County, Texas; and many other places.

Gobi and Mary were the First Generation of Durhams who are the focus of this book. Belton, Allen, Minor, Christopher, Anderson, and Isaac are the Second Generation.

## Chapter VI
## *Belton Durham and His Descendants*
### The Second Generation

Belton Durham, the son of the African Gobi and Mary Allen Durham, was born in 1836 in Fairfield County, South Carolina. He later moved with his master to DeSoto Parish, Louisiana. His wife Amanda—better known as "Mandy"—was born on 17 March 1849 in South Carolina. Mandy was part Cherokee. Their son Edmond was born in September 1866 and their son Adam was born in 1867—both in Louisiana. They were settled in the Butler community of Freestone County, Texas by 1869, the year of their daughter Patsy's birth. Also born in Freestone County were their son Boykin (1873), their daughter Savannah (1875), their son George (1877), and their son Willis (March 1882). Some daughters of Edmond, Adam, and Boykin later lived in Breckenridge, Texas. Belton worked as a farmer and was one of the first deacons at Lone Star Baptist Church. He did a lot of fishing in the Trinity River.[1]

Belton and Mandy are listed in the 1900 Freestone County Census. At the time, two grandchildren—Ida Williams (born February 1892) and Morris Williams (born November 1895) were living with them. Mandy died on 19 May 1905 and was buried in Lone Star Cemetery. Belton married Sylvia Simmons in 1907. Sylvia was born in South Carolina in 1856. The couple, along with Sylvia's daughter Nellie, are listed in the 1910 Census. Belton died in June 1927.[2] Sylvia's son David Simmons and his wife Rebecca had a daughter named Ovena who married Walter Titus "Nit" Durham on 7 February 1935. Sylvia had a total of ten children.[3]

### The Third Generation

Boykin Durham, the son of Belton Durham, was born in Freestone County in November 1873. He married Elizabeth Coutler on 16 January 1894. The ceremony was performed by Rev. George W. Solomon, the first pastor of Lone Star Baptist Church. His wife was born in Texas in March 1875. The following children were born to this union: Silvan (April 1892), Heuzie (November 1894), Garfield (June 1895), General Beve (29 January

45

1898), and Clark (1901). Boykin is listed in the 1900 Census but not in the 1910 Census.

Savannah Durham, the daughter of Belton Durham, married Johnnie Johnson, Sr. Thirteen children were born to this union: Annie Bell; Johnnie, Jr.; Bealer; Annie Beatrice; Dusty; Paul; Georgia; Avery; L. C., Robert; Mary; and Birl.[4]

## The Fourth Generation

General Beve Durham, the son of Boykin Durham and grandson of Belton Durham, was born on 29 January 1898 in Freestone County. He married Elnora Session and to this union four children were born. This marriage was dissolved. On 4 July 1928, he married Mary Nelson in Fort Worth, Texas. No children were born to this union. In Fort Worth, he joined Magnolia Avenue Church of God in Christ. In 1961, he accepted the call to the Gospel ministry and became pastor of Boaz Mission Church of God in Christ. He served as pastor there until his death on 28 December 1966.[5] This congregation's name was later changed to Durham Memorial Church of God in Christ and was located near the Butler Housing Project.[6]

Bealer Johnson, the son of Johnnie and Savannah Durham Johnson, was born on 20 June 1898 in Freestone County. He was baptized at an early age at Lone Star Baptist Church in Butler. In 1922, he united with Henry Chapel AME Church in Oakwood. He was active as a Sunday School superintendent, steward, and trustee of Henry Chapel. He married Callie Perry and to this union seven children were born. Following her death, he married Lavana Henry and to this union one child was born. He spent his last two years in Fort Worth, where he became a member of Durham Memorial Church of God in Christ. He died on 16 September 1968. His funeral was held at New Hope Baptist Church in Oakwood on 21 September 1968. He was buried in Oakwood Cemetery.[7]

Bib Durham, the son of Silvan and Betty Shed Durham, was born on 4 January 1908 in Freestone County. He married Zellie Lee Durham and they lived for many years in the Freestone County city of Teague. He died on 1 February 1993 in the Wortham Nursing Home. His funeral was held on 7 February 1993 at Salem Missionary Baptist Church, with burial at Salem Cemetery. He was preceded in death by his son Willie R. Durham and his brother Moses Shed. He was survived by his wife, his son Charles Durham of Dallas, and seven daughters: Lorine Pate of Donie, Texas; Bennie Carrington of Mart, Texas; Louise Ogendip of Galesburg, Illinois; and Hazel Johnson, Ella Montgomery, Bettye Davis, and Fannie Price of Dallas.[8]

The last surviving child of Johnnie and Savannah Durham Johnson was Mary O. Edwards, who was a big help to this writer in compiling this history. Mary was born in Butler on 4 February 1916 and attended school there. She lived for many years in Fort Worth. She married J. T. McCutcheon and two children were born to this union. She later married Fred Edwards. Her second marriage, which resulted in no children, lasted for forty-two years. She worked for Atlanta Life Insurance Company as an agent and later as district manager. She also worked for Cedar Hill Insurance Group. She fell asleep in the arms of Jesus on Saturday 13 October 2012 at her residence. A celebration of her life was held on Friday 19 October 2012 at the Pauline Minor Memorial Chapel of Gregory W. Spencer Funeral Directors in Fort Worth. The eulogy was delivered by Rev. Raymond Oliver. Interment was in Cedar Hill Memorial Park near Kennedale, Texas.[9]

## Chapter VII
### *Allen Durham and His Descendants*
## The Second Generation

Allen Durham, the son of the African Gobi and Mary Allen Durham, was born around 1836 in Fairfield County, South Carolina. He later moved with his master to DeSoto Parish, Louisiana. He was living in Freestone County, Texas by 1870.[1]

The name of Allen's first wife was Alice Mack.[2] She was the mother of the following children: George (born in South Carolina); Tethia (born in South Carolina in 1857); Rance (born in Louisiana on 22 July 1859); Wash (born in Louisiana in 1861); Sylvia (born in Louisiana in 1864 or 1866); Taylor (born in Louisiana in 1867); and Johnnie (born in Louisiana in 1868). It is believed that she died before Allen came to Texas. He later married Hanna Wafer and to this union the following children were all born in Texas: Syrenia (September 1869); Henry (1875); William (1876); Samuel (October 1879); Richmond (1880); Luke (27 November 1888), and Leona.[3]

According to his grandson Archie Durham, Allen lived with his son Johnnie until his death, date unknown.[4] According to his son Luke Durham, he died around 1900, when Luke was 12 years old.[5]

## The Third Generation

Ransom Durham—"Granpa Rance" or "Uncle Rance," as he was commonly known—was one of the most respected members of his community, Owens Chapel, and all the other surrounding communities, for his sharp mind, his ability to get things done, and his concern for his fellowman. The son of Allen and Hannah Wafer Durham, Rance was born in slavery on 22 July 1859 in DeSoto Parish, Louisiana. He came with his family to Freestone County, Texas when he was about ten years old. He spent the rest of his life in Freestone County. He was very active in the Pine Top (now Union) Methodist Church, Pine Top (now Rising Star) Masonic Lodge, in politics, and as a devoted family man.[6]

Rance Durham and Alice McDonald were united in marriage on 2 January 1879 by Rev. G. W. Solomon.[7]  To this union were born four children: Willie Anderson, Abner, Tezia, and Georgia.[8]

Grandpa Rance's community activities made him well known enough to be selected in October 1912 as the Republican District and County Chairman.  This position kept him politically active for years afterwards, helping members of the black community become registered voters.  He was also elected as one of the only black road commissioners in the history of Freestone County.[9]

Grandpa Rance was unable to complete his formal schooling but did much to educate himself on his own.  This made him one of the most knowledgeable persons in the county.  He did all he could to help promote the education of the black youth of the community by seeking to secure books, equipment, and other supplies for the community school.[10]

Grandpa Rance bought property near Red Lake that he farmed.  He later built a cotton gin and syrup mill on his property.  He and other community residents made use of these facilities.  His farm became the regular meeting place for the surrounding communities.[11]  He bought land on a number of occasions and no one knows the extent of his holdings.  As a farmer and businessman, he was a daring entrepreneur and employed a number of people in his various enterprises.  His granddaughter recalled seeing workers clearing new ground and cutting down trees to provide wood for fences.[12]

Grandpa Rance's community spirit can be seen in his donation of part of his personal property for a community park.  The Rance Durham Park was the scene of many Juneteenth celebrations where baseball, barbecue, watermelons, and general socializing became a longtime tradition that many older members of Freestone County's African American community remember with fondness.[13]

Grandpa Rance became a kind of father figure for many people.  He gave legal and personal advice to many.  He helped members of the Pine Top community to organize a burial society.  This helped defray the costs of burial at a time when most blacks were unable to obtain insurance from mainline companies.  People of all ages, black and white alike, knew and respected him.[14]

During his last years, Grandpa Rance suffered severe headaches and eventually lost his eyesight.  While blindness forced him to curtail many of his activities, his wit, cheerfulness, sense of humor, and sharp mind was a lasting trademark which remained until his death.[15]  His great-granddaughter recalled that, even after he lost his sight, he knew his land and his community well enough that he could walk all over his land and even down the road to the grocery store without getting lost.[16]

Grandpa Rance died in Freestone County on 6 March 1950 of natural causes due to age. He was 90 years, 7 months, and 11 days old. He was buried in Pine Top Cemetery on 12 March 1950 by Updack Funeral Home in Palestine.[17] The marker on his grave contains the following inscription: "He died as he lived—a Christian." While he is gone, many of his works live on in those he helped.[18]

Grandma Alice McDonald Durham, the daughter of Anderson McDonald and Claudia Jones, was born in Texas on 20 December 1859. She died on 18 October 1957, at the age of 97. At the time, she was suffering from senility and arterial hypertension. She was buried in Pine Top Cemetery on 23 October 1957 by L. E. Roberson Funeral Home.[19]

Taylor Durham was born in May 1867 in DeSoto Parish, Louisiana.[20] His wife Fannie was born in 1869 in Texas. They were married around 1886. The following children were born to this union: Anderson (1888); Hannah (1890); Surrena (December 1891); Taylor, Jr. (1893); and Anna Bell (August 1896).[21]

Johnnie Durham, the son of Allen and Hannah Wafer Durham, was born around 1868 in DeSoto Parish, Louisiana. He came to Freestone County, Texas as a child. He lived for a number of years at West Point, near Blue Lake, on land owned by Jeff D. Reagan. At the time, his principle transportation was oxen. In 1898, he relocated to some land he purchased from Reagan which was bound on the east by the Boggy Slue, on the north by the Devil's Backbone, on the west by the Franklins, and on the south by Calvin Lewis and Henry Howard. He used an ax to clear the land until it was suitable for farming. His wife, Starrie Simmons Durham, was born around 1875. They had the following children: Travis (1903), Archie (1906), Gladys (1907), and Lorey (1910). Johnnie Durham drowned in the Trinity River on 8 July 1951.[22]

Richmond Virginia Durham, the son of Allen and Hannah Wafer Durham, was born in the Butler community of Freestone County on 7 January 1882. He lived for many years in Palestine, the county seat of neighboring Anderson County. He worked for the railroad and operated orchards in both Palestine and Wortham. He married Anna Jackson and two daughters—Evelyn L. and Arilla-- were born to this union. After Anna's death, he married a nurse named Maudie Bell, a native of Grapeland, Texas. He also had a son, Houston Slaughter, by his first cousin, Matilda Durham, the daughter of Anderson Durham.[23]   He died on 7 August 1968.   He is buried in Palestine Memorial Cemetery.[24]

Luke Durham, the son of Allen and Hannah Wafer Durham, was born in the Butler community of Freestone County on 27 November 1888.   He had a very good memory at the age of 90, remembering some of the songs his mother sang as well as what one of her favorite dresses looked like! He also remembered that, when his mother died, his father took him to Elkhart in nearby Anderson County, Texas and found someone there to take care of him.  He said he stayed there only a short time, soon returning to Butler to live with his father.  Their home was close to the area called the "Crossroads," about a mile or so from Highway 84 near what is now Gaston's Temple.   Around 1900, Allen became very ill and died.  After his father's death, Uncle Luke—as he was affectionately called--lived for awhile with his sister Sylvia and his brother Henry.[25]

In 1908, when he was 28 years old, Uncle Luke walked from Butler to Palestine, where he went to work for the Railroad Round House.  He held several other positions  in the Palestine area and also worked for awhile in the Freestone County city of Teague, ten miles west of Fairfield.[26]

In the early 1900s, Uncle Luke married Mollie Morgan, the daughter of M. Morgan and Mattie Smith.  Mollie was born in Texas on 25 December 1896.  To this union were born five children: Sylvia (1909-1918),  Classie (1913), Lela Corine (1914), Coleman (1916), and Carlton (14 April 1918-6 September 1950).[27]  Mollie died on 17 August 1947.  The cause of her death was Major Carditis Nephritis, which was diagnosed by R. E. Bing, M.D., of Oakwood.  She was buried in Lone Star Cemetery on 20 August 1947 by Leslie D. Radford of Fairfield.[28]  They farmed the land of Carl Franklin for eighteen years.  Following Molly's death, Uncle Luke worked for Caleb Evans in Freestone County and later worked for a family in the McLennan County community of Mart.[29]

Eventually, Uncle Luke returned to Butler, where his nephew Willie Anderson Durham and his great nephew Walter Titus (Nit) Durham lived across from the grocery store which was the meeting place for the residents of Lone Star, Bethel, Shiloh, Rabbit Ridge, and other communities. There he met Everleane Nayme Hayes Jones, a widow with nine children at home.  He soon began visiting her.  On 18 December 1951, they were married.  To this union was born one son, Luke Durham, Jr., on 13 October 1952.[30]

As a child, Uncle Luke joined Lone Star Baptist Church in Butler.  On 14 February 1982, he joined Trueway Church of God in Christ in Dallas.

He died on 28 March 1982. His funeral was held on 3 April 1982 at Owens Chapel Church of God in Christ in Butler, with Pastor J. I. Hemphill officiating. He was buried in Lone Star Cemetery.[31]

## The Fourth Generation

Willie Anderson "Papa Bud" Durham was the son of Rance and Alice McDonald Durham. He was born in Freestone County on 6 October 1879. He inherited land from Grandpa Rance and, like his father, he was a hard-working farmer who spent his entire life in the Butler community. He grew cotton, corn, peanuts, sweet potatoes, greens, "stingy green" tobacco, sorghum cane, and ribbon cane. Like his father, he operated a syrup mill, providing syrup for several communities. There were always large barrels of syrup to be found on his property.[32]

During the fall of the year, Papa Bud would always plant two gardens, one for his family and one for the public. Noted for his generosity, he would encourage people to stop and pick a bag of greens. Traveling gypsies were known to camp on his property for a week or more at a time. He would provide them with food and other assistance.[33]

Papa Bud married Ellen Anna Titus on 21 October 1899. The ceremony was performed by Justice of the Peace C. C. Whitt.[34] Ellen, who was born in Butler on 2 August 1884, gave birth to the following children: Cuny Anderson Durham, Clara Vernetta Durham Peters, Lillie E. Durham Garrietty, Gladys Celia Durham Henry, Copoleon Yale Durham, Chavus Auto Durham, John Wesley Durham, Walter Titus Durham, Katie Mae Durham Tatum, Lonzo O'Neil Durham, and Harold James Durham.[35]

Ellen Titus Durham died on 15 June 1929.[36] Later, Papa Bud married Ruby Manning, the widow of K. L. Manning. To this union was born a son named Willie Roosevelt Durham and a daughter named Easter Lillie Durham.[37]

Papa Bud had a striking physical resemblance to Grandpa Rance. In many ways, he followed in his father's footsteps. However, he was not known for being such a daring entrepreneur. Contrary to Rance, he never employed laborers on his land. The fact that he had such a large family gave him a ready supply of home-grown help and may have made the hiring of unrelated individuals unnecessary. His daughter recalled the family's wood stove and the long table in the kitchen. She said the family always had plenty of food. In keeping with the customs of the time, his wife never worked outside the home. In accordance with traditional gender roles, his daughters worked in the house and in the yard, while his sons worked in the fields.[38]

Papa Bud was a member of Pine Top Methodist Church, but attended only occasionally. His wife and children attended regularly, travelling to church by wagon.[39]

After retirement, Papa Bud lived alone in the house previously owned by his mother and located near that of his son Walter. Although his physical health deteriorated, his mind remained quite sharp.[40] He died on 19 January 1965. He is buried in Pine Top Cemetery on 24 January 1965.[41]

Dr. William Abner Durham, the son of Rance and Alice McDonald Durham, was born in the Butler community of Freestone County, Texas. In 1908, he received the degree of Doctor of Medicine from Knoxville Medical College in Knoxville, Tennessee.[42] On 14 April 1909, he passed the required examination and was granted Oklahoma State License #54 by the Oklahoma Board of Medical Licensure.[43] He married Pinkie Strawther and they moved to Rentiesville, Oklahoma,[44] where he practiced medicine out of their home. He often made house calls. They attended the Methodist Church there.[45] According to the mayor of Rentiesville, he was at one time the only physician in town and also delivered mail on horseback.[46]

Travis Durham, the son of Johnnie Durham, was born on 8 September 1902 and died on 24 June 1933. He was buried in Lone Star Cemetery on 25 June 1933.[47]

Archie Dennis Durham, the son of Johnnie Durham, was the sixth cousin of the writer's wife and a close friend of the writer. He always expressed great enthusiasm for the writer's efforts to preserve the Durham history and heritage. Archie was born on 20 February 1906 in what he fondly called his "beloved woods," located in the Butler community of Freestone County. In 1989, he wrote:

> *I, Archie D. Durham, am the great grandson of Gubbie Durham, the grandson of Allen Durham, the son of Johnnie Durham and Starrie Woodard Simmons.*
>
> *I am the ninth child of twelve children. . . .*
>
> *I was born . . . on my father's farm and am the only child that wanted to come back to the farm and live. . . .*
>
> *As far as I know, I am the oldest Durham in Freestone County.*[48]

Archie grew up in Lone Star Baptist Church and, after his retirement, served this church as chairman of the board of deacons, choir member, and chef. When Lone Star's remodeled edifice was dedicated on 11 January 1981, Archie's article "A Dream Comes True" appeared in the Souvenir Program:

*This began with my mother and father, John and Starrie Durham who had faith in what they believed. When I was very young, my family would always say I would be the only child that would return home in my later years, so here I am, and the only one.*

*When I started out, my father told me to always be fair to everyone. My mother's advice was to stay with the Lord always, trust and believe that He would keep me. This I have done.*

*I left the old farm walking, knowing not where. I went to Palestine, Galveston, Houston, and Waco, where I spent seven years trying to get an education and work. Finally, I quit school, then I thought of my parents' instructions, so I began to trust and lean on the Lord.*

*In 1930, I left Texas and went to Tucson, Arizona, where I went to work in a private home. I began to realize my blessings but still had in mind of going back home. The Lord then blessed me with a job with the Southern Pacific Railroad.*

*I stayed in Tucson 14 years, was then sent to San Diego, California for 8 ½ years, from there to El Paso, Texas for 3 ½ years of service, and then finally back to Los Angeles for 20 years and to retire after 37 years of service. At this age still looking to come home.*

*I retired in 1971, but the Lord still wasn't ready yet. On the 9th day of February, 1971, a terrible earthquake wrecked our church, the Pleasant Hill Baptist Church, to which we were very devoted. We stayed until it was rebuilt and, in July of 1975, we moved home, the happiest day of my life. We built our home, then my dream was to see Lone Star Baptist Church beautified. So I have lived to see this miracle.*

*So as I close, we want to thank each and every one who has been a part in our life, for it to be filled with joy and happiness. Let's love each other more and lean and depend on the Lord. He will open windows of heaven and pour out so many blessings.*

Archie attended Lone Star School. Reportedly, when he left home at the age of nineteen, he had only seventy-five cents in his pocket. He had one daughter, Maurine Starrie Durham, by Hortense Manning. Maurine was the mother of nine. In 1975, he built a home on family property, where he was active in farming and cattle raising. At the time of his death, Archie had 29 great-grandchildren and 35 great-great-grandchildren. In 1949, he married Willa Mae Love.[49]

The only time Archie could remember being late for work was when his faith got him into trouble. He recalled: "I was in church and there was a real good preacher delivering a sermon and I guess the time just got away." One of his favorite sayings was "If I can just help somebody along the way, my life will not be in vain."[50]

Archie was a Master Mason and a life member of the National Association for the Advancement of Colored People (NAACP). He also held membership in the Texas Cattle Raisers Association and the Butler Lions Club. He performed much community service for the Retired Senior Volunteer Program (RSVP), the Butler Community Center, Butler Coordinating Council, and the Butler Water Supply.[51] In 1982, Judge Sam Bournias presented to him the second place award for the Lone Star, Lakeport, and Wildwood communities at the County Extension-4H Awards Banquet.[52] In 1995, he received a community service award from the E. E. Wheat Chapter of the NAACP at the 27th Annual Freedom Fund Banquet at the Teague Community Center. Over 150 people attended this event. The speaker was Gary Bledsoe of Austin, president of the Texas State Conference of the NAACP.[53]

Willa Mae Durham, the wife of Archie Durham, was born on 19 January 1918 in Wellington, Kansas to William and Minnie B. White Love. After moving with Archie to Butler, she became an active member of Lone Star Baptist Church, the NAACP, and Heroines of Jericho Court #109. She died on 26 June 1994 at her home. Her funeral was held at Lone Star Baptist Church on 29 June 1994, with Rev. Larry Raven officiating. Burial was at Inglewood Park Cemetery in Los Angeles, California, under the direction of Emanuel Funeral Home in Palestine.[54]

Archie died on 10 March 2001 at the age of 95. His funeral was held on 16 March 2001 at Lone Star Baptist Church, with his long-time pastor, Rev. Larry Raven, delivering the eulogy. The writer attended this celebration of Archie's homecoming and victory. He was greatly encouraged by the family's enthusiasm for his research. He hopes this family history is an adequate tribute to Archie's memory.

Evelyn L. Durham McClure, the daughter of Richmond and Anna Jackson Durham, was born in Palestine, Texas. She graduated from Lincoln High School in Palestine in 1919 and from Bishop College in Marshall, Texas in 1923. She taught school in the Lone Star community, Oakwood, Wichita Falls, and La Marque for a number of years. She was a member of Pilgrim Rest Baptist Church in Palestine until she moved to Texas City and joined the First Baptist Church of La Marque. She married Lonnie McClure. She died in Texas City on Tuesday 29 October 1996. Her funeral was held on Sunday 3 November 1996 at Memorial Cemetery, under the direction of Davis Funeral Home. Rev. R. L. White officiated.[55]

Luke Durham, Jr. was born on 13 October 1952. His first job was mowing lawns. As a teenager, he would go to Dallas for summer jobs or babysit while other family members worked. Whatever money he made he used to buy school clothes. He graduated from Fairfield High School in May 1971 and then went to work in Dallas. Following a two-year marriage and divorce, he joined the U. S. Navy. Following active duty, he spent twenty years in the Naval Reserve. In October 1982, he married a woman named Vickie.[56]

## The Fifth Generation

Cuny Anderson Durham, the son of Willie Anderson and Ellen Titus Durham, was born on 4 February 1901 in Butler, where he attended Pine Top Methodist Church with his family. He worked as a carpenter and a farmer. As a young man, he dated Dollie Gibson.[57] He later married Roma Tatum Banks and to this union was born a daughter named Clara V. Durham and a son named Roe Webster Durham. Cuny and Roma settled in the Freestone County community of Avant, where they grew peanuts, cotton, corn, and sorghum cane on their farm. They were active members of Avant Prairie AME Church. He was also a member of Star Sunlight Lodge #451, Free and Accepted Masons (Prince Hall Affiliation) at Avant. He was shot to death on 21 May 1969 in Mexia, Texas.[58] His funeral, under the direction of Dorsey-Keatts Funeral Home in Mexia, was held on 24 May 1969 at Avant Prairie AME Church, with Rev. L. J. Malone officiating. Graveside services at Avant Cemetery were conducted by Star Sunlight Lodge.[59]

Roma Durham, the wife of Cuny Anderson Durham, was born on 8 March 1905 in Freestone County. She was a member of Avant Prairie AME Church. She died on 25 April 1999 at East Texas Medical Center in Fairfield. Her funeral, under the direction of Moore's Angelic Funeral Home in Teague, was held on 7 May 1999 at Avant Prairie AME Church, with Rev. Clifford E. McIlveen officiating. Burial was in Avant Cemetery.[60]

Clara Vernetta Durham, the daughter of Willie Anderson and Ellen Titus Durham, was born on 5 May 1902 in Butler. She married Prince Peters. They lived for many years in the Butler community. She was a member of the Church of God in Christ. She died on 30 April 1999 in Fairview Manor Nursing Center. Her funeral was held on 3 May 1999 at Capps Funeral Home, with Rev. J. E. Reeves, pastor of Fairfield Church of God in Christ

#1 and District Superintendent, officiating. Pallbearers included James Durham, LaCharles Bass, Roy Durham, Buford Durham, Munson Durham, and Roland Brackens. Honorary pallbearers were Walter Durham and Freddie Brackens. Burial was in Pine Top Cemetery.[61]

Lillie Elliott Durham, the daughter of Willie Anderson and Ellen Titus Durham, was born on 1 September 1904 in Butler. She married a man named Garrietty. She lived for many years in Dallas, where she worked for a Jewish family until retirement. She then returned to Butler to live with her sister Gladys. She was a member of Souls Harbor Church and the Order of the Eastern Star in Dallas. She died on 19 September 1982. Her funeral was at Capps Funeral Home with Revs. J. I. Hemphill, W. E. Henry, and John E. Reeves officiating. Pallbearers were James Durham, Alonzo Durham, Nathaniel Henry, and Freddie Brackens. Burial was in Pine Top Cemetery.[62]

Gladys Celia Durham, the daughter of Willie Anderson and Ellen Titus Durham, was born on 23 July 1906 in Butler. She completed the 8th grade at Butler School. On 16 August 1924, she married Rev. Willie Elbert (W. E.) Henry, Sr. To this union were born nine children: Clyde, Laverne, Coleman, Richmond, Aldessa, Willie E. Jr., Vernetta, Clifton, and Eleanor. The family moved around the area as her husband worked on various farms.[63]

Big Mama—as Gladys was called by her grandchildren—grew up in Pine Top Methodist Church, where she took an active part in both Sunday School and church. As an adult, she joined Pyburn Church of God in Christ in Fairfield, under the leadership of Pastor Glover. She gave much support to her husband, who held pastorates at Malone and Hubbard and concluded his ministerial career at Lakeport Church of God in Christ on Highway 84 in Butler. She was for many years an active member of her denomination on both the local and district level.[64]

As a farm woman, Big Mama canned fresh vegetables from her garden. She also worked as a seamstress, making dresses and other items of clothing. She was quite talented when it came to painting, crocheting, knitting, and millinery work. She tatted and made rag rugs. However, she was especially gifted at quilting. This was only natural because she came from a family of quilters, which included her mother Ellen Titus and her grandmother Patsy Reddick Manning. Her legacy of quilting is still carried on by her daughters and granddaughters. Her 1993 quilt Iowa State Medallion was on display at the High Museum of Art, 30 John Wesley Dobbs Avenue, Atlanta, Georgia, between 28 September 1996 and 1 February 1997. This display coincided with the 1996 Olympic Games.[65] Big Mama died on 9 April 1996 at her Butler home. Her funeral was held on 12 April 1996 at Capps Memorial Chapel in Fairfield. The eulogy was delivered by Rev. J. E. Reeves. She was buried in Pine Top Cemetery. She was preceded in death by sons Clyde (1981) Coleman (1982), and Richmond (1995); and an infant daughter, Eleanor (1944).[66]

Capoleon Yale Durham was born on 26 April 1908. He lived for many years in California and married a woman named Molly. They separated and he lived alone. He had experience as a construction worker and retired from Coors Brewing Company in Golden, Colorado. In his later years, he became ill and lived with his sister Katie Mae Durham Tatum and her husband Henry in Denver. In 1977, he moved back to Texas with her. On 16 January 1988, he died at the Fairview Manor Nursing Center in Fairfield.[67] His funeral was held at Capps Memorial Chapel in Fairfield, with Revs. W. E. Henry and John E. Reeves officiating. Special music was played by organist Frank O'Banion. Archie Durham sang "Precious Lord Take My Hand." Pallbearers included Bobby Durham, James Durham, Walter Durham, Freddie Brackens, Monson Durham, and McClenon Brackens. Interment was in Pine Top Cemetery.[68]

Chavus Auto Durham, the son of Willie Anderson and Ellen Titus Durham, was born on 28 January 1910 in Butler. He married Willie Delois Luckett, who was born on 29 March 1916. He died in May 1973 in Washington State. His widow died on 14 February 1999.[69]

Walter Titus ("Nit") Durham, Sr., the son of Willie Anderson and Ellen Titus Durham, was born on 14 July 1914 in the Butler community of Freestone County, Texas. He was educated in the Freestone County schools. As a young man, he followed the tradition inherited from his father Anderson, his grandfather Rance, and his great grandfather Allen and became a hard-working and dedicated farmer. He spent his entire life tilling the soil where he was born and raised.[70]

Nit married Ovena "Sis" Simmons on 7 February 1935. The following results came from their sixty-year marriage:

> *Together they have produced and reared ten children, Bobby Jean, Betty Jo, James Artis, Oneida, Lela Mae, Gene Autry, Walter Jr., LaWanda JoAlander, and Janet Gail. Eight of the ten were sent away to college at Mary Allen, Bishop, and Prairie View A&M University. As a result there are now two elementary school principals, one in the DISD (Dallas Independent School District) and one in the PAISD (Port Arthur Independent School District) systems, a registered nurse, who now works for Columbia Record*

*Company in Dallas; three educators (teachers) for the DISD systems, one fireman, Houston Fire Department, one taxicab driver—Houston had a furniture moving specialist. He also had seventeen grandchildren and six great grandchildren.*[71]

Uncle Nit's personality has been described as a "cool breeze that blew your way on a hot scorching day." From his Crossroads farm, he demonstrated much character, compassion, and love for people. During his lifetime, he wore many "hats" besides farmer. Such included school trustee, caretaker for summer homes and private lake property at Red Lake, friend, counselor, husband, father, and grandfather.[72] His daughter-in-law wrote:

*There were times when he seems so tall*
*That he towered high above.*
*His words of praise and quick smile*
*Filled his children with love*
*His was the arm on which one*
*Could trustingly lean,*
*His footsteps led past many dangers,*
*That to them were unseen*
*When problems came for them,*
*Large, or small,*
*He was right there.*
*And no matter what he'd advise,*
*He always showed his care*
*His was the major responsibility*
*To sustain and mold the family*
*When the children were smaller*
*And younger*
*And sat upon his knee*
*Since the young ones are now grown,*
*To them he's still a guide*
*Cause he's number one. He's FATHER,*
*The man who stands by a mother's side.*[73]

On 6 April 1985, Uncle Nit and Aunt Sis again exchanged wedding vows on the occasion of their fiftieth wedding anniversary at the Butler Community Center.[74]

Sis died on 24 April 1995. Nit died on 11 December 1998 at the Manor Care Professional Health Care Center in Dallas. His funeral was held on 16

December 1998 at Lone Star Baptist Church in Butler. They were buried at Lone Star Cemetery.[75]

Nit's funeral program included a poem called "Fulfillment," which well described his life:

*I have worked in the fertile earth*
*And planted a garden,*
*So I know what faith is.*

*I have listened to the birds*
*Caroling in the morning and at sundown,*
*So I know what music is.*

*I have seen the morning without*
*Clouds after showers,*
*So I know what beauty is.*

*I have sat before a woodfire*
*With old friends and my family,*
*So I know what companionship is.*

*I have walked the path of quietness*
*Along the fence row in the pasture,*
*So I know what peace is.*

*I have seen the miracle of Spring*
*The fruition of Summer;*
*And the beauty of Fall,*
*Followed by the chill of Winter,*
*So I know what life is.*

*And because I have perceived*
*All of these things,*
*I know who God is.*[76]

Katie Mae Durham Tatum was born on 18 August 1917 in the Freestone County community of Butler, between Fairfield and Palestine. She received her education in the Butler School. She married Henry Tatum of Teague (who was born on 19 November 1912) on 26 February 1933. They lived in the Avant community of Freestone County from 1933 to 1939. They then moved to Austin, where they remained from 1939 to 1943. Uncle Henry worked at the University of Texas Sorority House while Aunt Katie Mae worked at the lunch counter of Woolworth's Department Store at 6th and Congress. They then moved to Denver, Colorado, where Uncle Henry was employed at the Rocky Mountain Arsenal during World War II and for one year as a doorman at the Cosmopolitan Hotel. He then was employed in construction work until 1969, when he retired due to a back injury. Aunt Katie Mae worked for Woolworth's and in various private homes in Denver. They moved back to Butler in April 1977.[77] Uncle Henry died on 9 April 1986 at Fairfield Memorial Hospital. His funeral was held at Avant Prairie AME Church, with Revs. J. E. Reeves, Willie K. McDonald, L. J. Manning, W. E. Henry, and Jessie Jones officiating.[78]

Aunt Katie Mae grew up in Pine Top Methodist Church in Butler. After her marriage, she joined Avant Prairie African Methodist Episcopal (AME) Church. In Austin, she joined Grant Chapel AME Church but later moved her membership to the Church of God in Christ (COGIC), a denomination to which she contributed much. In Denver, she was active in Odom Memorial COGIC, serving as Sunday School Superintendent, District Secretary of the Women's Department, District Missionary, State Treasurer of the Women's Department, and State Sunday School Treasurer. She was well acquainted with Bishop Chester E. Morgan, State Overseer of Colorado. Through him, she met Bishop Charles Harrison Mason, the founder of the denomination; and Bishop James Oglethorpe Patterson, the founder's son-in-law and long-time Presiding Bishop. Between 1945 and 1976, she attended practically all of the annual Convocations at Mason Temple COGIC in Memphis, Tennessee. She also attended her church's National Women's Convention in Cleveland, Ohio; Minneapolis, Minnesota; Detroit, Michigan; San Antonio, Texas; Washington, D. C.; Los Angeles, California; Fresno, California; Oakland, California; Atlanta, Georgia; and Albany, New York. The convention in the latter city took place in 1964. At that time, she crossed over to Canada for a visit.[79]

After her return to Freestone County in 1977, Aunt Katie Mae became quite active at Fairfield COGIC #1, where she was known as "Mother Tatum" and taught the women's Sunday School class until her health failed. She served in this capacity under Pastors John E. Reeves and David Algood. She developed a reputation as a great Bible teacher. She was also known far and wide as a master quilter. As a child, she was taught quilting by her mother. During an interview, when she was asked for an estimate on the number of quilts she had made, she said: "That's like asking me how many times I have brushed my teeth."[80] On Sunday 19 August 2001, her 84th birthday was celebrated at Butler Community Center, with many family and friends in attendance. Although she had no children of her own, many nieces, nephews, and others regarded her as their grandmother.

Aunt Katie Mae died on Monday 25 September 2011. Her funeral was held on Saturday 1 October at True Vine DOXA Center in Fairfield. Pastor David Algood officiated at the service. The eulogy was delivered by Evangelist Estelle McIlveen. Revs. Gale Durham, Harold Durham, Charles Brigham, and Kenneth Prox, along with this writer, assisted with the service. Interment was in Pine Top Cemetery.[81]

Alonzo O'Neil ("Uncle Lonzo") Durham was born on 6 March 1921 to Willie Anderson and Ellen Anna Titus Durham. His father was the son of Rance and Alice McDonald Durham. His mother was the only child of Walter and Patsy Reddick. Uncle Lonzo lived in and around the Butler community all of his life. He was very proud to be from Butler. When asked where he was from, he always said "Butler" rather than "Fairfield." A born agriculturalist, he often had truck patches as a child and later became a sharecropper. Eventually, he acquired his own farm, which he worked for more than fifty years. At various times, he raised cattle, horses, and pigs; and grew cotton, peas, corn, watermelons, and sweet potatoes. He enjoyed riding on his tractor, breathing fresh air, and experiencing nature's best. He first worked on a public job only after he had raised his family. He retired from Traylor and Sons in 1984.[82]

Uncle Lonzo married Juanita Henry on 28 December 1941. To this union the following five children were born: Beauford L. Durham (born 25 November 1942), Joyce Helen Durham Robinson (born 21 December 1944), Monson Lee Durham (born 1 October 1946), Earnestine V. Durham Williams (born 3 July 1950), and Ilene B. Durham Harrison (born 3 July 1950). They had ten grandchildren and ten great-grandchildren.[83]

Uncle Lonzo was widely known as the black attorney of Butler. While he never attended law school or took the bar exam, he always kept up with things around him. He frequently visited all segments of the community, providing information on tax breaks, Social Security, land leases, etc. He helped with the distribution and delivery of commodities and other products and services to the citizens of his community. He served as Chair of the Board of Pine Top Cemetery Association for over 25 years. He was a member of the Owens Chapel/Pine Top Community Council and a volunteer for the Butler Senior Citizens.[84]

On Thursday 17 May 1990, Aunt Juanita received the Outstanding Senior Citizen Award for her volunteerism and involvement in the community. This award was presented at a luncheon at the Fairfield Senior Center and sponsored by the Texas Agricultural Extension Service, the Freestone County Extension Home Economics Committee, and the Freestone County Senior Services.[85]

Uncle Lonzo was a long-time active member of Union United Methodist Church on Highway 84 in Butler. He served as a trustee and in many other capacities until his health failed in 2003. This church was formerly known as Pine Top Methodist and formerly located across from Pine Top Cemetery. Lonzo's father Anderson and grandfather Rance were members of this congregation.[86]

Uncle Lonzo died on 24 March 2006 at Hillcrest Baptist Medical Center in Waco following a lengthy stay at Mya Health Care and Fairview Manor Nursing Home. His funeral was held on Sunday 26 March 2006 at Union United Methodist Church. Rev. George Hancock, Jr. officiated. Revs. Estell McIlveen, Gale Durham, and Harold Durham; and this writer participated in the service. The eulogy was delivered by Union pastor Rev. David Daviss, Sr. Active pallbearers were Alfred Alonzo Durham, Tryone Lamon Robinson, Altovis Terrance Harrison, Sr., Richard Hardridge, Norwood Turner, Jeremy Timothy Williams, Beauford Isodore Durham, Derek O'Neal Coleman, Norris Henry, and General Lee Henry. Honorary pallbearers were Alton Henry, Wilson Henry, Benard Henry, James Durham, Guy Manning, Countee Woodard, Dorsey Strawther, and Walter Durham, Jr. Services were under the direction of the Emanuel Funeral Home in Palestine. Interment was in Pine Top Cemetery. Uncle Lonzo's family placed the following on his funeral program:

> *After losing his mother at a very young age, life sometimes seemed miscued and truly uncertain—he always knew what he needed to do—work, become the best citizen of his community and provider for his family. With guidance from his beloved father, Anderson (Papa Bud) and older sister, Katie Mae—he labored for many years as a farmer and rancher which taught him and he taught others the intricate values of hard work with a "can do attitude" that should never be confused or replaced.*
>
> *Real men know that wisdom is true strength, that gentleness is a virtue— not because they act and talk tough. Real men don't blame anyone and everything for what doesn't go their way. Real men accept life's challenges and use them to grow.*
>
> *You covered us as an eagle—with love and protection, and showed us how a good man, a real man, leads and cares for his family.*
>
> *To commemorate you today with pride and honor—we're proud to be a*

*part of your legacy.*[87]

Harold James Durham, the son of Willie Anderson and Ellen Titus Durham, was born in Butler on 19 October 1923. He served in World War II, receiving an honorable discharge. He worked in law enforcement and was employed for a number of years at a chemical plant. He married Mamie Bernice Laws, who was born on 25 August 1936 in Bryan, Texas. They had the following children: Harold Glenn, Helen Rene, Gale Lynn, Frankie Michelle, Patricia Yvonne, and Deborah Rochelle. He died in 1981.[88]

Willie Roosevelt Durham, the son of Willie Anderson and Ruby Durham, was born on 28 June 1933 in Butler. He attended the Butler schools and served in the United States Navy. He married Doris Willis and had two daughters—Willie Jean and Tempie. He lived for a number of years in Corsicana. He died on Saturday 26 September 1987 at a Waco hospital. His funeral was held on Wednesday 30 September 1987 at Union United Methodist Church, with Rev. W. E. Henry officiating. Burial was in Pine Top Cemetery. Arrangements were handled by W. H. Littles and Sons Mortuary in Waco.[89]

## The Sixth Generation

Clara Durham McIlvene, the daughter of Cuny Anderson Durham, was born on 18 October 1928. She has lived all of her life in Freestone County. She grew up in Avant and has lived near Fairfield for many years. She graduated from Dogan High School in May 1946 and married Clifford Lincoln McIlveen on 30 June 1946. She retired from twenty-two years as an operator for Continental Telephone Company. Her husband is a retired barber. The following children were born to this union: Clifford Estell McIlveen (23 April 1947), Linda Jean McIlveen (30 September 1948), Sandra Elaine McIlveen (24 October 1951), and Gary DeGaulle McIlveen (4 February 1964). They have nine grandchildren and nine great-grandchildren.[90]

Clyde Henry, the son of Gladys Durham Henry, was born on 15 November 1925 in Fairfield. He was educated in the Fairfield Independent School District. At an early age, he moved to Fort Worth, where he married Hazel Crenshaw. He died in Fairfield on 25 July 1981. His funeral was held on 27 July 1981 at Kibler-Capps Chapel in Fairfield. He was buried in Pine Top Cemetery. The writer delivered the eulogy.[91]

Laverne Arella Henry Brackens, the daughter of Gladys Durham Henry, was born on 13 April 1927 in Fairfield. She recalls: "My mother whose skills were many was an avid dressmaker who also pieced quilts. . . . As a child, having quilts in many stages of completion was an almost daily event. I would on occasion have to help my mother piece or tack a quilt. I never really took an interest in quilting in childhood."[92]   Later, however, all of this changed.

Laverne worked for thirty-five years as a cook at local restaurants and for fourteen and a half years at Mexia State School. Upon retirement, Laverne developed a passion for quilting and soon began pursuing this activity full-time. She said: "I don't go by patterns. I make it up out of my head. When you pick up the material and start working with it (that's when you know what it will be)." She uses a sewing machine for some of her quilts but other must be hand-pieced. A machine made quilt takes her about a week to piece and another two weeks to quilt. Handmade quilts take one to two months. When she sent several quilt tops to California, these were seen and shown by Eli Leon and this was the beginning of her recognition as a quilter. She was later contacted by Pat Jasper of the Texas Folklife Resources in Austin, Texas and, thus, began statewide showing of her quilts. This brought greater recognition. Her quilts have been displayed in *Four Generations of African-American Quilt Makers in Atlanta*, Georgia (1996); *No Two Alike/ African-American Improvisations on a Traditional Patchwork* at the South Carolina State Museum (1998); "Fiber Art: The Stuff of Dreams," in *The International Review of African-American Art*, vol. 15, no. 4 (1999); *Quilts of Color* in Austin (August 1999); *Fairfield Recorder* (1999 and 2000); *Three Generations of Quilters in an Afro-Texan Family* (1999); "Passed on Family Quilts of Color: One Family's Journey" in *Quilt World* (November 2000); *Southern Living* (November 2000); and University of Texas at Austin Museum (Spring 2002).[93]

Coleman Henry, the son of Gladys Durham Henry, was born on 7 March 1929 in Freestone County. He graduated from Dogan High School. He later moved to Fort Worth, where he met and married Lula Mae Brown. He had two daughters, Carolyn Roberts and Gladys Henry. He died on 3 March 1982. His funeral was held on 8 March 1982 at Nat Clark Funeral Home in Dallas. He was buried in Lincoln Memorial Cemetery in Dallas.[94]

Richmond Henry, the son of Gladys Durham Henry, was born on 3 August 1931 in Fairfield. He graduated from Dogan High School and served in the Korean War. He worked at a number of country clubs in the Dallas area. During his youth, he professed faith in Christ at the Pyburn Church of God in Christ in Fairfield. In his later years, he attended Truevine Interdenominational Church. In 1967, he met and married Shirley Davies. He had a daughter named Jackie Stanfield. He died in Fairfield on 6 July 1995. His funeral was held on 9 July 1995 at Capps Memorial Chapel in Fairfield. He was buried in Pine Top Cemetery.[95]

Aldessa Alice Henry Bass, the daughter of Gladys Durham Henry, was born on 6 September 1933 in Fairfield. She married Kenneth Duncan ("K. D.") Bass on 8 April 1951. They were active members of Fairfield Church of God in Christ #1 for many years. They celebrated their 50th anniversary wedding anniversary with a gala event at the Veterans of Foreign Wars (VFW) Hall in Fairfield on 7 April 2001. They celebrated their 60th anniversary with a similar event at Truevine Interdenominational Church on 15 April 2011. K. D. died on 8 April 2011. To this union were born the following children: Debra Diana Bass Uzzel (26 July 1953), Kenneth Laclaire Bass (8 September 1954), Celia Marketta Bass Strickland (26 May 1957), Cilkaye Varenesser Bass Jessie (8 April 1959), Teresa Marie Bass Haynes (5 November 1960), and LaCharles Michael Bass (30 May 1962).[96]

On Saturday 7 September 2013, Aldessa's 80th birthday was celebrated at the Fairfield VFW Hall. Our daughter Ericha Bass Prox served as mistress of ceremonies for this wonderful occasion. I presented the welcome and read Psalm 90. Our son Rob Uzzel played the National Anthem on his guitar--something not unusual at a VFW Hall. However, his performance resembled that of Jimi Hendrix at Woodstock. A number of songs and praise dances were performed by Aldesa's great-granddaughters Kendra and Kayla Prox and Destani and Dena Burns. Her great-grandson Derrick Burns II did a mime. Her granddaughter Gladys Burns conducted a court summons. Cilkaye Jessie read a poem written by her son Coach Gary Jessie (formerly of Ennis). Various friends and relatives presented flowers to Aldessa while she can still smell them. Remarks were made by each of her six children, accompanied by their spouses. Debra expressed hope that Aldessa will be able to join in celebration of her (Debra's) 80th birthday in 2033. Words of encouragement were given by the Rev. Melvin Gatson and the benediction was pronounced by the Rev. Daniel Gatson.[97] On 14 February 2014, Aldessa officially retired from many years of service as a nurse at the local hospital in Fairfield.[98]

Willie Elbert Henry, Jr., the son of Gladys Durham Henry, was born on 23 September 1937 in Fairfield. He later married Annie Mae Williams. To this union, the following children were born: Kevin Bernard Henry, Clifton

Oneal Henry, Della Ruth Henry, and Helen Henry. He lived for many years in Austin, Texas before returning to Fairfield.[99]

Vernetta Lee Henry, the daughter of Gladys Durham Henry, was born on 18 August 1941 in Fairfield. She married Nathaniel Henry (no relation). To this union, the following children were born: Reginald Henry, LaChelle Henry, Chystella Henry, and Thelma Henry. She lived in Houston for many years before returning to Fairfield, where she owns and operates a beauty shop.[100]

Clifton Artell Henry, the son of Gladys Durham Henry, was born on 27 November 1948 in Fairfield. After living for a number of years in California and Louisiana, he returned to live in the Butler community. He is employed in the printing department of a newspaper in Palestine. He married a woman named Pamela and has five daughters: La Tisha, Chrystal, Cheryl, Tara, and Priscilla.[101]

Bobby Jean Durham, Sr., the son of Walter Titus Durham, Sr., was born on 17 August 1935 in Fairfield. On 1 April 1956, he married Eddie Marie Jones, the step-daughter of Luke Durham, his great-great uncle. To this union were born the following children: Bobby Jean Durham, Jr.; Larry Durham; James Lee Durham; and Kenneth Wayne Durham. Bobby graduated from Prairie View A&M University in 1957 and worked as director of student activities at his alma mater from 1957 to 1959. He later received a master's degree from Prairie View. He and his wife moved to Port Arthur, Texas in 1959 and were employed in the Port Arthur Independent School District until retirement in 1991. He served as a teacher and later as a principal. They continue to reside in Port Arthur, where they are long-time members of Progressive Missionary Baptist Church. They make regular visits to Freestone County, where Bobby looks after his late father's farm at Butler.[102]

James Artis Durham, the son of Walter Titus Durham, Sr., was born on 9 March 1939. He graduated from Butler High School in 1957 and attended Mary Allen College in Crockett, Texas and Houston Community College. He served two years in the U. S. Army and received an honorable discharge. He worked for 25 years for the Houston Fire Department, working as a pipe and ladder man, paramedic, and chauffeur. In 1990, he retired and returned to Freestone County. He lives in Butler, where he owns and operates D&D Tractor/Auto Care. He also owns a number of cattle ranches. He serves on the Freestone County Soil and Conservation Commission and on other committees related to farming and ranching in Freestone County. His love for agricultural life is fully in line with the Durham family tradition extending back over one hundred and fifty years. He enjoys sitting under the peach tree with family and friends and sharing knowledge and encouragement to others. At meetings and seminars, he shares his knowledge of farm and ranch law. He is always ready to share his knowledge related to "life" to anyone seeking his guidance.[103] By his first wife, Delores Butler, James has two children: Rodney Durham and Deanna Rebecca Durham. By his second wife, Thelma, he has a son, Jeffrey Durham.[104]

Oneida Durham, the daughter of Walter Durham, Sr., was born on 30 April 1943 in Fairfield. She married Clyde Steen in December 1965. To this union was born a daughter, Senequa Denise Steen, on 9 September 1956. Lela married Harold Wayne Parks on 21 December 1972. Her second husband was born on 25 November 1945 in Pine Bluff, Arkansas. To this union was born a daughter, Halisa Denise Parks, on 4 July 1975 in Dallas. Halisa died in Dallas on 2 July 1995.[105]

Gene Durham, the son of Walter Durham, Sr., was born on 7 March 1946. He married a woman named Rita. To this union was born Marcus Durham and Latonya Durham.[106]

Walter Titus Durham, Jr., the son of Walter Titus Durham, Sr., was born in Fairfield on 29 June 1949. He married Lucy Ann Watkins on 15 July 1968. His wife was born on 18 June 1949. To this union were born on 11 July 1968 Calvin Dyane Durham, who now lives in San Antonio and has a delivery service; and on 9 April 1973, Roderick O. Durham, who now lives in Houston, where he does income tax. For many years, he worked as a delivery driver at Foley's in Houston. He eventually returned to live in Butler, where he raises cattle. He is employed as a supervisor at Wal-Mart in Palestine.[107]

LaWanda Durham, the daughter of Walter Titus Durham, Sr., was born in Fairfield on 19 October 1951. She married Larry Mitchell and to this union was born Steven Titus Mitchell in Dallas on 21 July 1987.[108]

Jo Lander Durham, the daughter of Walter Titus Durham, Sr., was born on 29 June 1954 in Palestine. She married Salter Mitchell, Jr., on 14 June 1976 in Dallas. Her husband was born on 12 April 1955 in Galveston. To this union was born a daughter, Montice Verlena Mitchell, on 21 July 1980 in Dallas.[109]

Beauford Durham, the son of Lonzo Durham, was born on 25 November 1942. He grew up in Butler and graduated from Butler High School in 1960. He attended Texas Southern University in Houston for two years, majoring in sociology. He then moved to Tulsa, Oklahoma, where he worked for four years as a city bus driver and two and a half years for Transcon Freight Lines. He then returned to Houston, where he operates an Exxon service station and garage on Reed Road. He has taken courses in upholstery and refrigeration at Houston Community College. He enjoys camping, fishing, and boating. His love for camping has taken him to various sites in Texas and Louisiana.[110] He married Julia E. Parker, who was born on 21 June 1943. To this union were born three children—Joseph Calvin Durham (born 3 July 1964), Alfred Alonzo Durham (born 22 April 1966), and Beauford Isadore Durham (born 16 September 1967). In 1999, he married his second wife, Pamela.[111]

Helen Durham Robinson, the daughter of Lonzo Durham, was born on 21 December 1944. She married John Robinson. They have one child—Tyrone Lamont Robinson (born 3 June 1971).[112]

Monson Lee Durham, the son of Lonzo Durham, was born on 1 October 1946. He graduated from Butler High School in 1966 and attended Prairie View A&M University, where he majored in plumbing and received his license. He currently lives in Waller, Texas, where he raises cattle. He operates an Exxon service station in Houston, about five miles from the station owned by his brother. He enjoys traveling and "playing farmer." He married a woman named Archie. To this union were born two children: Reed LaDesa Durham (born 12 September 1966 in Tulsa, Oklahoma) and Monson Lee Durham, Jr. (born 5 August 1968 in Palestine). He later married Linda Lenese Cook, who was born on 23 July 1950. To this union was born one daughter: Nekisha Evette Durham (born 25 October 1976).[113]

Earnestine Vernetta Durham Williams, the daughter of Lonzo Durham, was born on 3 July 1950. She graduated from Butler High School with honors in 1968. While in high school, she was active in Future Homemakers of America and participated in Interscholastic League competition in math and spelling. She also sang in the school choir. She attended Prairie View A&M University, where she received a certificate in secretarial science.[114]

Earnestine moved to Houston in 1970 and went to work for Humble (later Exxon and now Exxon Mobil) Oil Company. While in Houston, her company presented her with a service award. In 1990, she transferred to Exxon's corporate headquarters, which had recently moved from New York to Dallas. She is still employed by Exxon Mobil as an administrative secretary in the Public Affairs Contributions Group. She attends many seminars, workshops, and training programs each year.[115]

Earnestine married Doyle Richard Williams on 20 October 1972 in Houston. Her husband was born on 29 July 1949 in Houston. Their son, Jeremy Timothy Williams, was born on 2 December 1977. She now resides north of Dallas in Lewisville, Denton County, Texas.[116] Her son attended R. L. Turner High School in the Farmers Branch/Carrollton District, where he was in the honors program, a star running back, and a member of the Youth Leadership Team for Metropolitan Dallas.[117]

In 1996, Earnestine was instrumental in arranging for a $1,000.00 contribution from the Exxon Community Service Fund to the Butler Community Improvement Coordinating Council, for the purchase of audio-visual equipment to be used by the area's senior citizens center. Such equipment included a TV/VCR combination, typewriter, cassette player/recorder, and table tennis set. She said: "This will hopefully enhance the activities for the council and also serve as a pivotal point for future activities and contributions for them. The center is a great service to the community and should be held in high esteem. This, of course, is just a small token of what should be done for such a dynamic place. Personal sacrifices and reaching out help not only an individual but also a great number of people. There's not enough hours in the day for one to give of himself. Don't forget—always volunteer." She expressed the determination to never quit working for a place that she cherishes and would like to see grow. She also renders volunteer services to the Alameda Heights Outreach Foundation, the Bethlehem Foundation, the Dallas Black Dance Theater, and the Senior Adult Services for Addison, Carrollton, Coppell, and Farmer's Branch.[118]

Ernestine grew up in Pine Top (now Union) United Methodist Church. She was active in Sunday School, Methodist Youth Fellowship, choir, and other activities. Although she no longer lives in Butler, she still participates at Union, serving as mistress of ceremonies at homecoming and other special occasions. While in Houston, she was an active member of Trinity Missionary Baptist Church, where she served on the Nurse's Board, worked with the children, and participated in special programs.[119]

Ilene B. Durham Harrison, the daughter of Lonzo Durham, was born on 3 July 1950. She married Geronie M. Harrison, Jr., who was born on 21 January 1948. To this union were born two children—Elissa Denise Harrison (born 7 September 1969 in Harbor City, California) and Altovis Terrance Harrison (born 5 September 1974). She currently lives in Carson, California.[120]

Harold Glenn Durham, the son of Harold James Durham, was born on 9 January 1959 in Fort Worth. He graduated from Polytechnic High School in 1977 and later took courses at Texas Christian University. He has worked in the restaurant business, in meat processing, and for United Parcel Service. He has the following children: Robert Durham (born 1 June 1983), Tiffany Durham (born 6 May 1984), and Donnell Durham (born 19 October 1987). In 2003, he received his Bachelor of Science degree in Organizational Management at Paul Quinn College in Dallas. The writer served as his academic advisor and senior thesis director. Since then, he has earned Master's and Doctoral degrees from the School of Scripture. He is currently working on a degree in Counseling at Amberton University. In 2004, he became an Anderson and Anderson Certified Anger Management Facilitator. In 2006, he received a Master of Christian Counseling and a Doctorate in Biblical Studies from the School of Scripture.[121]

Harold became a Christian in November 1974 under the ministry of Rev. Mark Hanby at the First Pentecostal Church of Fort Worth. He accepted the call to the Gospel ministry in January 1980. He was inspired to start a radio program called Better Way Ministry and, one year later, a weekly cable television program. In June 1997, he organized BetterWay Apostolic Church in Arlington, Texas. This congregation, which is affiliated with the Pentecostal Assemblies of the World, now operates both a child care center and a resale store. He has served as chair of his denomination's Northern District Fellowship. He continues to serve as his conference's couples' marriage speaker. He is also a religious volunteer mentor for prisoners ages 17-21 for the Texas Department of Criminal Justice.[122]

Harold and his wife Shirley Givens Durham, have one daughter, Porschia G. Durham (born 25 September 1994). Shirley is the director of Better Way Childcare Center associated with the church. In May 2004, she received her Bachelor of Science degree in Organizational Management at Paul Quinn College. As was the case with her husband, the writer served as her academic advisor and senior thesis director.[123] She has since earned Master's and Doctoral degrees in Christian Counseling. She is the author of the following books: of *Pastoring From Scratch* and *Marriage: Better with Time.*[124]

Helen René Durham, the daughter of Harold James Durham, was born on 11 December 1959 in Fort Worth. She grew up in Fort Worth and graduated from Polytechnic High School. She attended college for several years, majoring in Liberal Arts. She enlisted in the U. S. Air Force and served several years as an inventory management specialist. Her tours of duty included Norton Air Force Base in San Bernadino, California; Lowery Air Force Base in Denver, Colorado; Clark Air Force Base in San Antonio. She is currently employed at Watson, Inc. as an accounting clerk. She attends Mount Moriah Baptist Church, where she is president of the Young Ushers and serves as Mission Evangelist at Sycamore Care Center. She married Lewis McCloud on 18 June 1987 in Fort Worth. Her husband was born on 6 January 1959. Their daughter Venicia D'Money McCloud was born on 15 May 1994.[125]

Gale Lynn Durham, the son of Harold James Durham, was born on 14 May 1961 in Fort Worth. He graduated from Polytechnic High School in 1979 and from Tarrant County College, South Campus, in 1981. He also has taken some courses at the University of Texas at Arlington. He has served as manager of Rodeo Steakhouse in downtown Fort Worth and currently works for United Parcel Service. He served as pastor of Mount Gaza Baptist Church and, on 19 June 2002, was called as pastor of El Bethel Baptist Church. Both congregations are located in Fort Worth. Every August, he conducts the annual revival, which climaxes with the homecoming celebration, at Butler's Lone Star Baptist Church, the spiritual home of so many members of the Durham family. His son Matthew Gale Durham was born on 29 January 1991. He married Debra Kay Boone on 12 September 1997.[126]

Frankie Michelle Durham, the daughter of Harold James Durham, was born on 22 June 1962 in Fort Worth. Her son Christopher Tavares Durham, was born on 16 August 1980. She married Gary Wayne Donison on 24 August 1985 in Fort Worth. Her husband was born on 22 June 1959 in Fort Worth. They have the following children: Michelle Lashon Donison (born 15 August 1985), Linda Zmonique Donison (born 14 September 1987), and Rachel Yanette Donison (born 7 September 1997). Patricia Yvonne Durham, the daughter of Harold James Durham, was born on 1 June 1963. She married Clarence Jones, who lived from 9 April 1972 to 7 August 1997. She later married Louis Driver. She has the following children: Tamey Rene Durham (born 11 July 1981) and Aubrey Deshun Durham (born 28 December 1985). Deborah Rochelle Durham, the daughter of Harold James Durham, was born on 13 June 1964 in Fort Worth. By Terry Lyn Green (born 6 December 1964) she has a daughter named Dieterrickia Lynchelle Green (born 26 April 1991).[127]

## The Seventh Generation

Freddie Oneal Brackens, Sr., the son of Laverne Henry Brackens and the grandson of Gladys Durham Henry, was born on 3 September 1946. He married Alvianna McElroy. To this union were born the following children: Freddie Oneal Brackens, Jr.; Debbie Brackens; Cynthia Renae Brackens, and Chris Brackens.[128]

McLenon Lee Brackens, the son of Laverne Henry Brackens and grandson of Gladys Durham Henry, was born on 16 January 1948 in Fairfield. He attended Dogan High School and grew up in the Church of God in Christ. He died on 22 November 2000. His funeral was held on 25 November 2000 at Capps Memorial Chapel in Fairfield, with Rev. Dorsey Strawther officiating. Interment was in the Methodist Cemetery in Fairfield.[129]

Sherry A. Brackens Byrd, the daughter of Laverne Henry Brackens and granddaughter of Gladys Durham Henry, was born on 4 March 1951 in Fairfield. She received many and varied awards in the Fairfield public schools, including valedictorian of her eighth-grade class. She attended Dogan High School through the eleventh grade. She graduated from Fairfield High School in 1969 as part of the first completely integrated class. She was in the top percentile of her graduating class. At Dogan High, she had served as secretary of the Student Council and as secretary of Future Homemakers of America. At Fairfield High, she was nominated for Homecoming Queen. In 1972, she received a Bachelor of Arts degree in history and art at Sam Houston State University. She was nominated for inclusion in the 1972 edition of *Who's Who Among College Students*. She was the first member of her immediate family to graduate from a four-year institution of higher learning.[130]

Sherry described her upbringing as being raised in a religious home by parents who were firm believers in hard work and education. She grew up in the Church of God in Christ. In 1977, she was baptized into Jehovah's Witnesses.[131]

Sherry married Curtis Byrd, Sr., who was born on 25 November 1952. They have the following children: Curtis Byrd, Jr. (born 7 August 1974), Baralelessa D. Byrd (born 10 September 1975), Catherine R. Byrd (born 1 March 1977), Leah R. Byrd (born 28 July 1978), Miriam O. Byrd (born 19 June 1980), Sarah E. Byrd (born 13 September 1982), Micah Byrd (stillborn 1984), Ornan Micah Byrd (born 6 February 1986), and Cephas Byrd (born 10 May 1988).[132]

While in high school, Sherry worked at York's, Awalt's, Rockett's Drive In, and Sam's Restaurant. At the latter, she was a bus girl, dishwasher, and cook's helper. She also helped her mother in working for Athel Ivy, loading poultry on trucks. She later worked as a maid at Ramada Inn and in the mail order department of Sakowitz Department Store in Houston.[133] For six months, she taught history and art to sixth through eighth grade students at Willis Junior High School in Willis, Texas. Since 1989, she has helped her husband with his recycling business.[134]

Sherry lived for twenty-three years in Richmond, California. She later moved to Teague, 10 miles west of Fairfield; and finally back to Fairfield. Like her mother and grandmother, she is a master quilter. She has observed that the ideas for quilts can come from anywhere and it is sometimes as simple as playing with colors or shapes. She said: "You just start with pieces and build it till it goes across the bed." When her cousin Bill Titus traced the African roots of the Titus family, Sherry immortalized his findings in a family history quilt. While she normally uses a layer or two of fluffy cotton batting between layers of quilt, she knows how to substitute other things during lean times. She recalled: "My grandmother couldn't afford cotton or batting, so she used old clothes. I would love it when the fabric would start tearing and I could see what was inside." She is currently working on two books on the art of quilt-making in Freestone County and one on quilting in the Titus family.[135] Her hobbies include visiting good book stores, browsing through libraries, flea marketing, visiting thrift shops and garage sales, hanging out with her husband and children, and creating "quilts and more quilts."[136]

Lillie Elizabeth Brackens, the daughter of Laverne Henry Brackens and granddaughter of Gladys Durham Henry, was born on 8 February 1953 in Fairfield. She married Jimmy Rogers Gipson, Sr. and to this union was born two children: Jimmy Rogers Gipson, Jr.; and Tamara Gipson. She later married Harvell Mayes.[137]

Betsy Evelyn Brackens, the daughter of Laverne Brackens Henry, was born on 1 October 1955 in Fairfield. She married X. Johnson and to this union were born the following children: Connie Earl Brackens, Michael Johnson, and Tanika Brackens.[138]

Roy Lee Brackens, the son of Laverne Henry Brackens and grandson of Gladys Durham Henry, was born on 19 July 1964 in Fairfield. He married Eleanore Herrera, a native of Guam. To this union were born the following children: Nikisha Brackens, NaTishia Brackens, LaCharles Brackens, Lofton Brackens, and Lebo Brackens.[139]

Debra Diana Bass Uzzel, the daughter of Aldessa Henry Bass and the granddaughter of Gladys Henry Durham was born on 26 July 1953. She graduated from Fairfield High School in 1971 and earned her certificate as a Licensed Vocational Nurse at Navarro College. She married this writer on 19 February 1977 at Fairfield Baptist Church. The ceremony was performed by Rev. W. M. Johnson. Our family consists of the following children: Ericha Diana Bass (born 15 June 1970 in Fairfield), Eric LaClaire Bass (born 7 August 1972 in Fairfield), and JoAnna Elaine Bass (born 25 September 1974 in Corsicana), and Robert Elton ("Rob") Uzzel (born 12 June 1981 in Kaufman). Debra worked as a nurse at Fairview Manor Nursing Center in Fairfield Chester Clinic in Dallas, Presbyterian Hospital in Kaufman, and Hillcrest Baptist Medical Center in Waco. She currently does private-duty nursing in Corsicana. She has done a wonderful job as first lady at the following churches pastored by her husband: Emmanuel AME Church in Dallas, Macedonia AME Church in Kaufman, Tyree Chapel AME Church in Blooming Grove, Brown Chapel AME Church in Maypearl, Forest Hill AME Church in Fort Worth, and Wayman Chapel AME Church in Ennis. She is a member of Zakat Court #133, Daughters of Isis, the ladies auxiliary to Zakat Temple #164 of the Ancient Egyptian Arabic Order of Nobles of the Mystic Shrine, to which this writer belongs.[140] Ericha married Kenneth Wayne Prox and has the following children: Kendra Denise Prox (born 9 October 1997) and Kayla Leigh Prox (born 3 April 2001). Eric married Cheryl Young and has the following children: Richard James Walker (born 31 October 1989) and Kayleigh Young (1 October 2006).[141] JoAnna married Charles Parker and has the following children: Dominique Jubar Bass-Parker (born 4 September 1991), Alicia Denise Bass (born 14 September 1993), and Charles Daveon Bass-Parker (born 4 March 1998). Alicia gave birth to our first great grandchild Chaz Anthony Grogan on 21 January 2014.[142] Rob married Audrey Wise on 12 December 2013. The writer officiated at Ericha's wedding and co-officiated at Rob's wedding.[143]

Kenneth LaClaire Bass, the son of Aldessa Henry Bass and the grandson of Gladys Durham Henry, was born on 8 September 1954 in Fairfield. He worked for sixteen years for Drilco, one year for Klein Independent School District, and twelve years for John Moore Services. He is now retired. On 5 January 1974, he married Beverly Joyce Dorham (born 12 March 1955). The following children were born to this union: Kevin Jabar Bass on 7 October 1974; Kimberly Bass on 15 November 1975; and Karen Shanell Bass on 6

June 1978.[144]  Kevin married Joi Albert on 23 May 1997. They were divorced on 11 March 2011.  He has four children:  Allegra Elisha Jackson (born 18 October 1999); Ellis Leon Jackson, III (born 25 March 2001); Ka'Niya Ayanna-La Sun Bass (born 1 May 2012); and Alijiah Mari Bass (born 5 December 2013).  He married Alicia Spriggs on 5 July 2014.[145]  Kim married Donald Brown, Jr. on 25 April 1998.  She has the following children:  Travon De-Ray Brown (born 17 September 1995); Dajay Le Ann Brown (born 28 June 2007); and Issac DeVon Brown (born 12 November 2009).  Kim and Don were divorced on 15 April 2011.[146]  Karen married Jasmahn Marcel ("Jazz") Dabney ((27 July 1974-18 October 2011) on 12 August 2000. To this union was born Empress Renee' Dabney on 24 December 2003. Following her first husband's death, Karen married Anre' "AJ" Jones (born 13 December 1964) on 26 May 2012. To this union was born Hannah Lee Jones on 19 September 2013.[147]

Celia Marketta Bass Strickland, the daughter of Aldessa Henry Bass and the granddaughter of Gladys Durham Henry, was born on 26 May 1957 in Fairfield. She married Sam Hawthorne, a native of Wortham, Texas. To this union was born a daughter, Gladys Maxine Nicole Hawthorne, on 9 August 1976 in Corsicana. This marriage was dissolved. Celia married Lonnie Roynell Strickland I on 18 November 1978 at Emmanuel AME Church, 2627 South Marsalis, Dallas. The writer, then pastor of Emmanuel, performed the ceremony. To this union was born a son, Lonnie Roynell Strickland, II, on 24 July 1981, in Corsicana. They currently reside in Cedar Hill, Texas. Celia is employed as a physician's assistant. Lonnie is self-employed in carpentry, plumbing, and electrical work. He is also a disc jockey. His company is called Strick-9. Nicole married Derrick Burns Sr. on 25 December 1995 and has the following children: Destani Burns (born 5 September 1997); Dana' Burns (born 25 February 1999); and Derrick Burns, Jr. (born February 18, 2000). Lonnie II married Kim Myers (born 13 September 1981). Lonnie and Kim have two daughters: C'Andra (born 22 June 2000); Jadyn (born 13 November 2002). Kim also has a son named Isayah (born 24 November 2009). Lonnie has two other children: Karly Stogin (born 21 December 2007); and Quintin Stogin (born 5 April 2013).[148]

Cilkay Varenesser Bass Jessie, the daughter of Aldessa Henry Bass and the granddaughter of Gladys Durham Henry, was born on 8 April 1959 in Fairfield. She married Cedric Michael Jessie, Sr. on 22 July 1980 in Dallas. They currently reside in Corsicana. Cedric was employed by K-Mart for twenty-two years and now works for Gander Mountain. Cilkay graduated from Fairfield High School in 1977 and Navarro College in 1978. She worked as an operating room technician at Chester Clinic in Dallas from 1978 to 1980 and at Navarro Regional Medical Center from 1980 to 1998. She has worked as an electronic scheduler for D&D Media Group, a Christian Publicity organization; and a clerk at Hometown Pharmacy. She has been an active member of the First Baptist Church of Corsicana since 1987. She has worked as an after-school coordinator for her church and has been involved in a number of summer youth camps. She surrendered to the call to the Gospel ministry in 2002. They have the following children: Gary Charles Jessie (born 24 February 1976); Cedric Michael Jessie, Jr. (born 25 July 1980); and Kendal D'Nique Jessie (born 3 April 1990). Gary married TaShena Shareese Moss (born 3 August 1979) and has the following children: Kasey Jessie (born 5 May 1994). Trinity J'Sean Jessie (born 28 October 2001); and Zion Kaedric Jessie (born 16 November 2004). Cedric married Jessica Darleen Chatman (born 10 July 1981) and the have the following children: Cedric Michael Edward Jessie III, nicknamed "Tre" (born 26 March 2000); Dakota Isaac Shelton Jessie (born 9 November 2001); and Jacobi Kenneth Jessie (born 8 June 2003). Cedric is also the father of Caylin Monique Jessie (born 18 November 2008); and Dominic DeSean Jessie (born 17 February 2014). Kendal married Ashely Elisa Black (born (born 7 March 1990) and has the following children: Zaida U'nique Jessie (born 19 January 2010); Serenity A'nique Jessie (born 19 June 2012); and Kaylene Ly'Nique Jessie (born 9 July 2014.)[149]

Teresa Maria Bass Haynes, the daughter of Aldessa Henry Bass and the granddaughter of Gladys Durham Henry, was born on 5 November 1960 in Fairfield. She graduated from Fairfield High School in 1979. She married Clyde Anthony Haynes (born 20 May 1957). Their family includes the following children: LaToya Renee ("Toy") Bass-Haynes (16 January 1977-2 October 2008), LaTanya Bass Haynes (born 5 June 1979), Marcus and Jhonna Haynes (11 March 1983-6 September 1983), Jason Haynes (born 26 September 1984), Joshua Lance Bass (born 5 June 1985), and Aaron Haynes (born 8 May 1988). Their grandson Nicholas Haynes was born on 20 January 2010. They currently reside in Houston.[150]

LaCharles Michael Bass, the son of Aldessa Henry Bass and the grandson of Gladys Henry Durham, was born on 30 May 1962 in Fairfield. He graduated from Fairfield High School in 1980. He later attended Texas State

Technical Institute in Waco and graduated from Navarro College in Corsicana. He married Glenda Gibson, a native of Fairfield. They have two sons—Michael Bass (born 17 February 1983), who is married to Shantarica Teal-Bass; and Gavan Bass (born 29 April 1990), who is married to April Hawkins-Bass. After living in Cedar Hill for several years, they moved back to Fairfield. Charles is employed by TU Electric at the Big Brown Power Plant and serves on the Fairfield Independent School District (FISD)'s Board of Trustees. Glenda is employed as a FISD police officer. Charles and Glenda have the following grandchildren: Mikayla (born 20 February 2004); Jamaria (born 24 March 2008); Sanaa (born 28 April 2009), Jamichael (born 25 February 2010); Zoie (born 6 November 2013); Faith (born 19 June 2010); and Zayne (born 5 September 2013).[151]

The Luke Durham Family

The Durham sisters: Gladys Durham Henry, Clare Durham Peters, Katie Mae and Durham Tatum.

Willie Anderson Durham

Lillie Durham Garrietty

Gladys Durham Henry

Rev. W. E. Henry was married to Gladys Durham Henry, great granddaughter of Allen Durham.

# In Loving Memory

## Evangelist Missionary
## Katie Mae Tatum

**August 18, 1917 ~ September 25, 2011**

# No Two Alike
# African American Improvisational Quilts
## September 28, 1996 – February 1, 1997

Come see 40 spectacular examples of the quilter's art. Organized by the High Museum of Art, Atlanta, *No Two Alike* features the work of 21 contemporary African American quiltmakers whose tradition of improvisation transforms conventional quilt patterns into startling new creations. All of the quilts are drawn from the vast collection of quilt scholar Eli Leon of Oakland, California.

Also on view: *Recent Acquisitions in Photography.* See examples of the High's rapidly growing photography collection including works by Annie Leibovitz, Richard Misrach, Cindy Sherman, William Eggleston and many others.

Of special interest are recently commissioned views of Atlanta and the South by Sally Mann, Alex Webb and Dawoud Bey.

Gladys Henry, *Iowa Star Medallion*, 1993. Photograph by Sharon Risedorph

**HIGH** museum of art
folk art and photography galleries

30 John Wesley Dobbs Avenue, Atlanta, Georgia 30303
Monday-Saturday, 10 a.m.-5 p.m. Free Admission. Call (404) 577-6940.

The Galleries are a partnership of Fulton County Arts Council, High Museum of Art, Metropolitan Life Insurance Company and Georgia-Pacific Corporation

This Gladys Durham Henry quilt won a prize at the Iowa State Fair.

Gladys Durham Henry with Five Generations

The 80th birthday party for Aldessa Henry Bass at the VFW Hall in Fairfield, Tx. (L-R) Bob Uzzel, Aldessa Henry Bass and Debra Uzzel.

K.D. and Aldessa Bass

Bob and Debra Uzzel

Aldessa Henry Bass at her retirement reception at East Texas Medical Center (formerly Fairfield Memorial Hospital).

Richard Walker — Domino Champion at Isaac Durham Reunion on 5 July 2014.

JoAnna Bass-Parker, Rob Uzzel, Eric Bass, and Ericha Bass-Prox

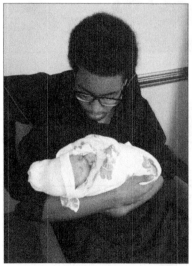

Daveon Bass-Parker holding nephew Chaz.

Alicia Bass

Dominique Bass Parker at 2012 Graduation from ATI. NOTE: In 2001, Dominique accompanied his grandfather to various events at the Fairfield Sesquicentennial.

(L-R) Bob, Kayla and Debra at the George W. Carver High School Reunion held at the American Legion Hall in Ennis, Tx.

Walter and Lucy Durham

Chaz Grogran, descendant of Allen Durham.

Kayleigh Young, descendant of Allen Durham.

Harold Durham, Pastor of Better Way Apostolic Church, Arlington, Tx.

Children of K. D. and Aldessa Bass. Left to right: Debra Bass Uzzel, Kenneth "Buck" Bass, Celia Bass Strickland, Cilkaye Bass Jessie, Teresa Bass Haynes, and LaCharles Bass.

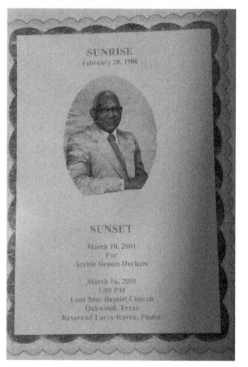

Archie Durham

Alonzo and Juanita Durham

Capole and Eula Durham

Chavus Auto Durham

Walter and Ovena Durham

Cuny and Roma Durham

# Chapter VIII
## *Minor Durham and His Descendants*
### The Second Generation

Minor Durham, the son of the African Gobi and Mary Allen Durham, was born on 1 December 1845 in Fairfield County, South Carolina. He moved with his master to DeSoto Parish, Louisiana and settled in Freestone County, Texas after the Civil War. He worked as a farmer in the Butler community. He had a reputation as a good man who always had something to give to somebody. He was known as a "ring maker" who made rings out of pennies and dimes.[1] He attended Lone Star Baptist Church and is buried in Lone Star Cemetery. He is listed in the U. S. Census for 1920 but not 1930.[2]

Minor Durham married Charlotte Lyle, who was born in 1848 in South Carolina. They were married about 1862. Their son Saylor was born in DeSoto Parish, Louisiana in 1853. The rest of their children were born in Texas. Such included: Henry (1865); Becky (1866); Sillimon (1867); Mary Ann (1868); Minor, Jr. (March 1871); Sally Ann (July 1873), Isabella (1875), and Kate (1878). Charlotte was baptized at Lone Star Baptist Church about 1871.[3]

### The Third Generation

Saylor Bee Durham was born in DeSoto Parish, Louisiana in 1853. He married a woman named Beckie in September 1886.[4] She preceded him in death. He worked as a farmer. He died on 23 May 1937 and was buried in Lone Star Cemetery.[5]

Sillimon Durham was born in Freestone County, Texas in 1855. He married a woman named Laura and to this union were born the following children: Chloe (1914) and Jeff (1917).[6] He worked as a farmer. He died on 7 May 1920 and was buried on the following day at Oakwood, Texas.[7]

Harry Durham was born in Freestone County, Texas in 1865. He married Ellen Rhodes on 10 November 1892.[8] He died in Freestone County on 6 April 1937.[9]

Mary Ann Durham married Willie Jackson, but the date of the marriage is unknown.[10]

Minor Durham, Jr. was born in Freestone County, Texas in March 1871. He married Delia Turner on 27 December 1894. The ceremony was performed by Mason Durham, an ordained minister of the Gospel.[11] He later married Lizzie Simmons.[12] He raised a step-daughter named Artillery Wilson, who was born in 1904.[13] Minor, Jr. has been described as a "feisty old guy." His nickname was "Piggy." Like his father, he was a farmer in Butler. His daughter Octavia married Edell Johnson. Their son Bobby Dale Johnson is a resident of Butler today.[14] Minor, Jr. died on 13 March 1963 of "natural causes due to old age." He was buried on 17 March 1963 in Lone Star Cemetery, under the direction of Updack Funeral Home of Palestine.[15] His wife Lizzie, who lived from 1880 to 1951, is also buried in Lone Star. Lizzie had a daughter named Artillery Wilson.[16]

Sally Ann Durham was born in Freestone County, Texas in July 1873. She married Butler Woodard, Jr., the son of Butler and Easter Roberson Woodard, around 1889. Her husband was born on 24 December 1869. The following children were born to this union: Bessie (22 January 1893-8 June 1980), Commie (22 April 1894-14 October 1987), Laura (22 July 1895-10 November 1990), Isabella (9 December 1896-?), Georgia (September 189?), Robbie Faye (17 September 1901-1958), Arrutha (20 May 1904-23 January 1997), Carl Arthur (13 June 1906-25 May 1961), General (1907), Utie Mae (10 July 1908-2 November 1993), and Edgar Dale (20 February 1910-20 April 1989). Sally Ann died on 23 November 1939. Her husband died on 25 October 1948.[17]

Isabella Durham married Henry Jones. To this union were born nine children; Pervey, Eva, Quannah Lee, Ozie, Careen, Taft, Casey, Josephine, and Pocahontas.[18] Sally Ann died on 23 November 1939 and was buried in Lone Star Cemetery.[19]

Kate Durham married Haywood Jackson but the date of the marriage is unknown.

## The Fourth Generation

Bessie Woodard, the daughter of Sally Durham Woodard, was born on 22 January 1894. She married Frank Sumuel and had the following children: Mattie, Bessie, Coleman, Ozell, Rosa Lee and Frankie Lee. They moved from Butler to Wortham, another Freestone County community, where she spent the rest of her life. She died on 8 June 1980.[20]

Utie Mae Woodard, the daughter of Sally Durham Woodard, married Governor D. Palmer. To this union was born Alice Palmer Jarmon.[21]

## The Fifth Generation

Rosa Lee Quarles, the daughter of Bessie Woodard Sumuel and granddaughter of Sally Durham Woodard, was born on 4 August 1914 in Butler. Her family moved to Wortham when she was a small child. Her husband, Porter Quarles, preceded her in death. She had one daughter, Bessie Louise Williams. She was active in Beulah Baptist Church, Lilies of the Field Court of the Heroines of Jericho, the Wortham Black Cemetery Association, and the Blind Lemon Jefferson Blues Foundation.[22] She died on 17 July 2003. Funeral services were held on 21 July 2003 at Beulah Baptist Church followed by interment at Wortham Black Cemetery.[23]

Frankie Lee Carter, the daughter of Bessie Woodard Sumuel and granddaughter of Sally Durham Woodard, was born on 29 September 1920 in Wortham. At the age of 16, she graduated as valedictorian from F. W. Wheeler, also known as Wortham Colored High School. She was the first African American graduate of Wayland Baptist College (now Wayland Baptist University) in Plainview, Texas, where she received a Bachelor's degree in Education. She taught for 27 years in public schools in Lubbock and Plainview. After retirement, she worked for 17 years as a substitute teacher. She eventually returned to Wortham. She was a member of Delta Kappa Gamma, the Retired Teachers Association, the Plainview Cultural Arts Center, and the Wortham Garden Club. She did volunteer work at nursing and rehabilitation centers in Wortham and Teague. She was a member of Beulah Baptist Church in Wortham and later of Sardis Primitive Baptist Church in Mexia. She died on 28 April 2014. Funeral services were held on 3 May 2014 at Sardis Primitive Baptist Church. Rev. Claude Jackson officiated, with the eulogy delivered by Rev. Lester Brown. Interment was in the Blind Lemon Jefferson Cemetery. Final arrangements were entrusted to Dorsey and Keatts Funeral Home in Mexia.[24]

Alice Palmer Jarmon, the daughter of Utie Mae Woodard Palmer and granddaughter of Sally Ann Durham Woodard, was born on 11 September 1929. She has lived all of her life in Freestone County. She worked many years as a maid. She married Billy Joe Jamon and to this union four children—Elvin Wayne; Billy Joe, Jr.; Diane; and Larez were born. She resides in the Butler community and is a member of Lone Star Baptist Church.[25]

## Chapter IX
## *Chris Durham and His Descendants*
### The Second Generation

Christopher Columbus ("Chris") Durham, the son of the African Gobi and Mary Allen Durham, was born in slavery in Fairfield County, South Carolina in September 1848.[1] He moved with his master to DeSoto Parish, Louisiana and settled in the Butler community of Freestone County, Texas after Civil War. On 30 March 1872, Chris married Jessie Brown. The ceremony was conducted by W. B. Jose, Justice of the Peace.[2] Following Jessie's death, he married Josephine Manning on 8 February 1881. This ceremony was conducted by R. P. Anderson. His third wife was named Ofelia. She was born in 1872.[3] Chris' daughter Vira was born in 1877. He had the following sons: Christopher Jr. (March 1888), Julious (September 1889), J. W. (1903), Mitcheola (1909), Booker T. (1910), Major (1911), and Thomas Lamar (1916).[4]

Chris was employed by Bond Daniels as a fireman at the Lakeport Cotton Gin. While on the job, he lost a leg and an eye in a boiler accident.[5] He cut down a tree and made his own peg leg. He did a lot of fishing in the Trinity River.[6] In his later years, he was listed among the paupers maintained by Freestone County at a monthly cost of $147. The custodian of his funds was W. W. Harding.[7] He died on 24 June 1930.[8]

### The Third Generation

Julious (nicknamed "Pius") Durham, the son of Chris Durham, was born 10 September 1889 in Butler. He later moved to Red Oak, Ellis County, Texas, where he met and married Teaner King. To this union, six children were born. They lived most of their lives around Italy, Ellis County, Texas, where Julious was employed as a farm worker. They moved to Dallas in 1978. Julious died on 1 May 1980. Teaner died on 21 August 1982. Both were buried in Saint Mary's Cemetery at Avalon, Ellis County, Texas (between Italy and Ennis). Three of their children preceded them in death. They were survived by their daughter Pearline, sons Isiah and Ike, and many grandchildren, great-grandchildren, and great-great-grandchildren.[9]

Thomas Durham, the son of Chris Durham, grew up in Butler. He married Ruby Jo Compton, the daughter of Bill Compton. His wife was born on 3 June 1924. Three sons were born to this union. Thomas worked at the John Day Burleson Funeral Home in Fairfield. He later moved to Texas City, Texas, where he worked and died on the dock on 16 April 1947.[10] The circumstances of his death are, thus, described:

> *A giant explosion occurred during the loading of fertilizer onto the freighter Grandcamp at a pier in Texas City, Texas, on this day in 1947. Nearly 600 people lost their lives and thousands were injured when the ship was literally blown to bits.*
>
> *Ammonium nitrate was used as an explosive by the U.S. Army in World War II and, after the war ended, production of the chemical continued as its use as a fertilizer became accepted. However, the precautions used in its transport became far more lax in the post-war years.*
>
> *On April 16, the Grandcamp was being loaded with ammonium nitrate as well as tobacco and government-owned ammunition. Cigarette smoking, although officially banned, was a common practice by longshoremen on the docks. Just two days prior to the explosion, a cigarette had caused a fire on the docks. On the morning of April 16, smoke was spotted deep within one of the Grandcamp's holds.*
>
> *Some water and an extinguisher were used to fight the fire, but hoses were not employed for fear of ruining the cargo; there were already 2,300 tons loaded on the ship. While the ammunition was removed from the ship, the crew attempted to restrict oxygen to the hold in hopes of putting out the fire. Apparently they did not realize that because of ammonium nitrate's chemical composition, it does not require oxygen in order to burn.*
>
> *By 9 a.m., flames had erupted from the hold and within minutes it exploded. The blast was heard 150 miles away and was so powerful that the ship's 1.5- ton anchor was found two miles away. The force of the explosion lifted another ship right out of the water. People working at the docks were killed instantly.*
>
> *Pieces of flaming debris damaged the oil refineries in the area. A nearby Monsanto chemical storage facility also exploded, killing 234 of the 574 workers there. Nearly all of the survivors were seriously injured. A residential area of 500 homes was also leveled by the blast. Another ship, the High Flyer, which was carrying similar cargo, was pushed completely across the*

harbor. *The crew fled when it came to rest, failing to notice that a fire had started and the next day their ship also exploded. Two people died.*

*In all, 581 people died and 3,500 were injured. The explosion caused $100 million in damages. A long-disputed court case over the cause of the blast was resolved when Congress granted compensation to 1,394 victims. They received a total of $17 million in 1955. The port was rebuilt to handle oil products only.*[11]

Mitcheola Durham, the son of Chris Durham, was born in Butler on 23 April 1909. He spent most of his life in Freestone County, living in both Butler and Teague. He joined Lone Star Baptist Church and later Lakeport Church of God in Christ. He picked cotton in West Texas for four months and lived for five years in Muskogee, Oklahoma, where he washed dishes at the Shevers Hotel. He settled in Teague in 1971. He lived his last years at the McGee Nursing Home.[12] He died on 23 May 1994 at Navarro Regional Medical Center in Corsicana. His funeral was held at Lone Star Baptist Church on 26 May 1994. Burial was in Lone Star Cemetery. Services were conducted by Emanuel Funeral Home of Teague.[13]

Booker T. Durham, the son of Chris Durham, was born in Butler in 1910. He died on 7 May 1931 and was buried in Lone Star Cemetery.[14]

Major Durham, the son of Chris Durham, was born in Butler in 1911. He died on 26 March 1942.[15]

## The Fourth Generation

Isiah Durham, Sr., the son of Julious Durham and the grandson of Chris Durham, was born on 14 July 1923 in Red Oak, Texas. He was educated in the public school system of Oakwood, Texas. In 1944, he entered the U. S. Navy, serving in World War II. On 15 December 1942, he married Lillie Mae Brackens and to this union ten children were born. They lived in Avalon, Texas, where they were faithful members of Saint John Baptist Church. Isiah served as a deacon, while Lillie Mae served as a deaconess, mission president, usher board president, and financial clerk. They truly loved their church and were always willing to do whatever they could to further God's Kingdom. They opened their home and kitchen to everyone who graced their doorstep. Isiah died on 6 December 1996 at the Veterans Medical Center in Dallas. Lillie Mae died on 7 September 1998. They are both buried in Rankin Cemetery at nearby Rankin, Texas. They were survived by sons Isaac, Eddie, Billy, and Jimmy; by daughters Teaner, Karen, Lynda, and Diana; and by many grandchildren, great-grandchildren, and great-great-grandchildren.[16]

John Durham, the son of Ruby Jo Durham, the wife of Thomas Durham, was born on 11 August 1949 in Fairfield, Texas. He died on 3 January 2005. His funeral was held at Hemphill Temple Church of God in Christ, where he was a member. Rev. J. J. Manning officiated. Pallbearers were David Brackens, Micky Hargrove, Randolph Daniels, Jimmy Daniels, and M. J. Daniels. He was survived by his children Pam Brackens, Bridget Durham, John "Jeff" Durham, Jr., brothers Tommy Durham, Ike Durham, Rickey Durham, and Ike Durham, sister Sandra Kay Harrison, and two grandchildren.[17]

Ike Durham, the son of Ruby Jo Durham, the wife of Thomas Durham, was born on 11 November 1957 in Fairfield, Texas. He attended Dogan and Fairfield High Schools and graduated from Los Angeles High School in 1976. He went to Jamestown College in Jamestown, North Dakota on a basketball scholarship. He received a Bachelor of Business Administration from Jamestown in 1980. He has worked in banking for 25 years. His employers have included the Old Pacific Coast Stock Exchange, Wells Fargo, City National Bank of Los Angeles, and Equitable Insurance Company. From the latter, he received his securities license. He has much experience as a college basketball referee.[18]

## The Fifth Generation

Isiah Durham, Jr., the son of Isiah Durham, grandson of Julious Durham, and the great-grandson of Chris Durham, was born on 14 May 1944. He married Betty Joe Jackson. He was the father of a daughter named Ternissa. He died in November 1985 at Methodist Central Hospital in Dallas. Funeral services were conducted at Saint John Baptist Church in Avalon, with Rev. R. L. Wingham officiating. Burial was in Rankin Cemetery under the direction of Jones Funeral Home.[19]

Isaac Durham, the son of Isiah Durham, grandson of Julious Durham, and great grandson of Chris Durham, was born on 14 May 1944. He graduated from Stafford High School in Italy, Texas on 21 May 1964. Following graduation, he joined the U. S. Air Force, serving active duty from 1964 to 1967 and serving in the reserves from 1973 to 1983. He was employed at Texas Envelope, American Petrofina, Arrow Foods, and Goodyear Tire and Rubber Company." He is now retired and living in Dallas. He married Dorothy Echols on 9 February 1967. They have three children—Robert Wayne (born 17 January 1967), Teresa Renee (born 5 January 1968), and James Bernard (born 27 June 1970). They also have six grandchildren.[20]

Eddie Lee Durham, the son of Isiah Durham, grandson of Julious Durham, and the great-grandson of Chris Durham, was born on 18 November 1947 in Rankin, Ellis County, Texas. He worked as a plumber. He is a disabled veteran, having done two tours of duty in Vietnam. He married Katherine Bruce.[21] Katherine Bruce Durham holds a Master of Christian Studies degree from School of Scripture in Dallas. They live in Avalon.[22]

Teaner Annie Durham Johnson, the daughter of Isiah Durham, granddaughter of Julious Durham, and the great-granddaughter of Chris Durham, was born on 14 January 1951 in Lancaster, Dallas County, Texas. She has two children: Sandra Jones (born 3 August 1970) and Regina Henderson (born 20 May 1972). In 1987, she obtained a certificate in Cosmetology at Hill College in Hillsboro. In 1996, she competed training as a Certified Nurse's Aide. In 2009, she received a Bachelor of Christian Studies degree at the School of Scripture in Dallas. She currently lives in Avalon.[23]

Billy Ross Durham, Sr., the son of Isiah Durham, grandson of Julious Durham, and the great-grandson of Chris Durham, was born on 25 September 1952. At an early age, he united with the Austonia Baptist Church in Rankin. He married Diedra Massey. He was the father of three sons, Raystell McGowan, Preston Massey, and Billy Durham, Jr.; and three daughters, Angela Laury, Tenisha Shepard, and Christy Massey. He died on 17 April 2000. Funeral services were held on Saturday 22 April 2000 at Saint John Baptist Church in Avalon, with Rev. W. E. Cook, Sr. officiating. Burial was in Rankin Cemetery under the direction of Jones Funeral Home.[24]

Karen Elaine Durham Bailey, the daughter of Isiah Durham, granddaughter of Julious Durham, and the great-granddaughter of Chris Durham, was born 18 April 1957. She married Elbert Bailey and they have three children: Geneise, Jacque, and Drakus. She has worked at Bank I and currently serves as office manager at a facility serving disabled persons in Dallas. She lives in Bardwell, where she is active at Saint Mary's Baptist Church.[25]

Lynda Kay ("Katie") Durham Collins, the daughter of Isiah Durham, granddaughter of Julious Durham, and the great-granddaughter of Chris Durham, was born on 10 December 1958 in Ennis, Ellis County, Texas. She married Billy Eugene Collins, Sr. They live in Waxahachie. She has three children: Jerome DuPree Durham (born 1 November 1979), Lakeshia N'Tay Durham (born 20 September 1981), and Billy Eugene Collins, Jr., (born 23 May 1984). She currently lives in Waxahachie.[26]

Jimmy R. Durham, the son of Isiah Durham, grandson of Julious Durham, and the great-grandson of Chris Durham, was born on 22 April 1963 in Waxahachie, Ellis County, Texas. He has the following children: Ashley U. Durham (born 26 June 1985) and Justin J. Durham (born 27 September

1986). His son Damien P. Durham was born on 25 February 1989 and died on 5 November 1994. He lives in Waxahachie and works as a custodian for Ennis Independent School District.[27]

Diana Faye Durham Massey, the daughter of Isiah Durham, granddaughter of Julious Durham, and the great-granddaughter of Chris Durham, was born on 19 July 1964. She lives in Waxahachie and does office work for a home health care agency.[28]

Isiah and Lillie Mae Durham

Isiah and Lillie Mae Family; (front left to right) Teaner, Issac and Karen; (middle row) Lillie, Isiah, Diana and Lynda; (back row) Billy, Eddie and Jimmy.

# Chapter X
## *Anderson Durham and His Descendants*
### The Second Generation

Anderson Durham, the son of the African Gobi and Mary Allen Durham, was born on 4 May 1849 in slavery in Fairfield County, South Carolina. He moved with his master to DeSoto Parish, Louisiana and settled in Freestone County, Texas after the Civil War. He spent his life as a farmer in the Butler community. His mother Mary was living with him at the time of the 1880 Census.[1]

Anderson married Ellen Calhoun on 13 July 1870. The ceremony was conducted by Rev. George W. Solomon.[2] The following children were born to this union: Pinkey J. (1871) and Liza (1872).[3]

After Ellen's death, Anderson married Laura Ann Rhodes on 10 September 1874. The ceremony was performed by Parson Jesse Davis.[4] Laura was born in Texas in 1855. The following children were born to this union: Matilda (1878), Minnie (1879), Monica (March 1880), Jerome (November 1881-12 May 1941), Emmanuel (11 March 1883), Anna (March 1884), Bettie (January 1887), Sylvester (February 1891-16 July 1935), Asa (13 March 1892), Eugene (May 1895), and Hilery (November 1896).[5]

On 1 October 1895, some property was deeded to Anderson by John H. Reagan of Palestine, Texas. This deed was filed on 20 January 1896.[6]

Anderson died on 14 June 1928. His wife Laura died on 6 January 1928.[7]

### The Third Generation

In 1902, Matilda Durham, the daughter of Anderson Durham, gave birth to a son named Houston. The father of this child was her first cousin Richmond Durham, the son of Allen Durham. Houston—who used the surname of "Slaughter"—recalled hearing his grandfather Anderson say he was born in the Carolinas and that he was a teenager when he received his freedom.[8] Matilda later married a man named Woodard.[9]

Jerome Durham, the son of Anderson Durham, was born in November 1881. He married Matilda Simmons on 18 December 1901. The ceremony was performed by Rev. George W. Solomon.[10] They had one son, Watson Durham; and three daughters: Lee Frankie (1908), Ellen (1912), and Lillie P. (1917).[11] He died on 12 May 1941 and was buried in Lone Star Cemetery on 18 May 1941.[12]

Emmanuel Durham, the son of Anderson Durham, was born on 11 March 1883 and was, for many years, a farmer in the Butler community. He was a member of Lakeport Church of God in Christ under the pastorate of Rev. W. E. Henry. He spent his last years in Oakwood, Texas. He died in March 1965 and is buried in Lone Star Cemetery. By his first wife, Pearl Turner, he had one daughter, Pinkie J., who was born in 1909 and later married a man named Brooks. By his second wife, Bertha Garrett, he had no children. By his third wife, Lela Lewis, he had one son, Emmanuel Durham, Jr., who was born on 24 May 1934. His fourth wife, Etta Mae Plummer, had a son named Johnny Richardson from her first marriage. The following children were born to this union: Anderson, Jerome, Joe Earl, Joe Louis, Minnie (who married a man named Burroughs), Ruby Faye (who married a man named Jones), Clara (8 July 1942), James King (November 10, 1944), and Arthur (1949).[13]

Sylvester Durham was born in February 1891. His wife, Callie Woodard Durham, the daughter of General and Anna Johnson Woodard, was born on 4 March 1897.[14] They had the following children: Sylvester T. (23 December 1918-January 1980), Zenobia, Leola, J. T., Johnny, JaVan (1917), Willie, Eugene, and General.[15] Callie died on 16 August 1928 and was buried in Lone Star Cemetery on 17 August 1928.[16] Sylvester died on 16 July 1935 and was buried in Lone Star Cemetery on 17 July 1935,[17] Eugene Durham was born in 1896. His wife Nora was born in 1899. Their daughter Clara was born in 1917.[18]

## The Fourth Generation

Watson Durham, the son of Jerome and Matilda Simmons Durham, was born on 15 October 1902.[19] He spent his life as a farmer in the Butler community and was a member of Lakeport Church of God in Christ. He married Emma Lee Carter. To this union were born four sons: L. C. Durham (21 December 1927); Hubert Durham (17 January 1932); J. W. Durham (17 January 1936); and Watson Durham, Jr. (1948); and five daughters: Barbara Durham Rock; Edna Mae Durham Anthony (6 November 1933) Mary Edna Durham Rabb (3 November 1935); Minnie Lee Durham Young (5 May 1942); and Zyronia Durham Young (1946).[20] He died on 1 October 1973 and was buried by Dorsey-Keatts Funeral Home.[21]

Sylvester T. Durham, the son of Sylvester and Callie Durham, was born in Freestone County on 23 December 1918. He had two daughters: Ruby Durham Gatewood and Shirley Durham Ford. He died in Freestone County in January 1980.[22]

General Durham, the son of Sylvester and Callie Durham, spent most of his life in Butler. He worked there as a farmer and as a school bus driver and also as a janitor at Sam's Barbecue in Fairfield. He married Bertha Henry. To this union was born the following children: Gennelle Durham Moseley, Brenda Joyce Durham Sapp, Hellen L. Durham-Jones, General D. Durham, Cathy Durham Lewis, Mary J. Durham Barrett, Anna L. Durham, Donnie R. Durham, Jerry L. Durham, Lester R. Durham, Terri Y. Durham, Tony D. Durham, and Donald W. Durham. He died in an automobile accident on 8 October 1982. His wife died in September 1983.[23]

Javan Durham, the son of Sylvester and Callie Durham, grew up in Butler. He worked as a farmer but his main occupation was truck driving. He loved driving big rigs. He was raised in Lone Star Baptist Church. He married Helen Smith and to this union were born the following children: Javan, Jr.; Jimmy; Maurice; Milton; Kenneth; Cathy; and Patrick. He also had a daughter named Evelyn Durham. He died in 1998 and is buried in Laureland Cemetery in Dallas.[24]

Clara Durham Page, the daughter of Emmanuel and Etta Mae Durham, was born on 8 July 1942 in the Butler community. She lived for a number of years in Oakwood and now lives in Palestine with her husband Walter Page. She is an active member of Pilgrim Hill Baptist Church.[25]

Hubert Durham, the son of Watson and Emma Lee Carter Durham, was born on 17 January 1932. He was a life-long resident of Butler and was involved in farming and ranching all of his life. He was educated at Dunbar Public School. For seventeen years, he drove a school bus and also catered parties for Gilbert Daniel. He owned a ranch for many years. On 10 October 1957, he married Bertha B. Smith. They had one son, Hubert Durham, Jr. (who preceded him in death) and one daughter, Bernice Durham Terry.[26] He accepted Christ at an early age and joined Rocky Mount Baptist Church. He was later active at Pilgrim Rest Community Church. He died in Palestine on 15 May 2010. Services under the direction of Emanuel Funeral Home were held on 22 May 2010 at Lone Star Baptist Church. Interment was in Oakwood Cemetery.[27]

## The Fifth Generation

Watson Durham, Jr., the son of Watson and Emma Lee Carter Durham, was born on 28 November 1948 and died on 12 December 1948. He lived only fifteen days. His death certificate states that he was "too weak to make it." He was buried in Lone Star Cemetery on 13 December 1948.[28]

Gennelle Durham Moseley, the daughter of General and Bertha Henry Durham, was born on 5 October 1948. She grew up in Butler and graduated from Dunbar HighSchool in Oakwood. She lived in San Diego, California for ten years and came to Dallas in 1979. She has done various types of work and has been employed by the U. S. Postal Service since 1998.[29]

Hellen L. Durham Jones, the daughter of General and Bertha Henry Durham, was born on 8 December 1950. She grew up in Butler and graduated from Oakwood High School in 1969. She married Roy Washington of Kerens, Texas in 1970. They lived in New Mexico; Alexandria, Louisiana; Idaho; and on an Indian reservation in the state of Washington. They were divorced in 1981. Hellen worked at Texas Instruments for five years and has been employed by the U. S. Postal Service since 4 April 1981. She married Eddie Jones of Ennis, Texas in 1989. She has two daughters: Jessica Durham, who was born on 20 June 1986; and Jennifer Jones, who was born on 23 March 1988. Both attended Lancaster High School.[30]

Maurice Durham, the son of Javan and Helen Smith Durham, was born on 7 September 1954 in Dallas, Texas. He graduated from Wilmer-Hutchins High School in 1973. He worked for eleven years for Employers Insurance of Texas. Like his cousin Hellen, he has been employed by the U. S. Postal Service since 1981. He married Cassandra Ross, who died of asthma at the age of 33. His second marriage was to Debbie McAfee and his third to Sandra Menoy. He has four children: Onterrio, Morris, Lameysha, and Bryant. He has written columns in *The Dallas Morning News* and has written a screenplay which is set in 1947 on the farm of General Woodard at Butler.[31] He has directed two films. The first, released in 2009, was *Secrets and the Restaurants*. This is the story of a newspaper reporter investigating a serial rapist case who ends up closer to the investigation than she anticipated. In this story, a man's and woman's connections to a restaurant changes their lives forever.[32] The second, released in 2012, is *A Race Against Time: The Sharla Butler Story*, the true story of a Texas track star whose short life inspired an entire community.[30]

# Chapter XI
## *Isaac Durham and His Descendants*
### The Second Generation

Isaac N. Durham, the youngest son of the African Gobi and his wife Mary Allen Durham, was born on 15 August 1860 in Freestone County, Texas. His five older brothers—Belton, Allen, Minor, Anderson, and Christopher—were born in South Carolina. Apparently, Mary was pregnant at the time of Gobi's brutal murder in South Carolina and gave birth to Isaac shortly after her arrival in Texas.[1]

In the 1880 Freestone County Census, Isaac—also known as "Ike"—is listed as an engineer. He acquired some land and donated a portion of it for the building of Lone Star Baptist Church, where he served as a deacon.[2] He was a Master Mason. On 11 June 1877, he married Easter Benjamin, who was born in Texas in 1861 and whose parents had been slaves in Alabama. At the time of the 1900 Census, Easter's 86-year-old mother, Abbie Benjamin, was living with them. Isaac died on 10 September 1921 and was buried in Lone Star Cemetery.[3]

### The Third Generation

On 15 January 1879, Thomas A. Durham, the son of Isaac Durham, was born. On 27 December 1899, Thomas was united in marriage with Allee Jackson, the daughter of John and Susan Jackson. Allee was born in Texas in January 1878.[4] The ceremony was performed by Rev. G. W. Solomon. Two sons—Albert and Hobart—were born to this union. Thomas followed in his father's footsteps in serving as a deacon at Lone Star.[5] He died on 16 July 1914.[6] On his tombstone in Lone Star Cemetery appears the inscription "He died as he lived—a Christian."

### The Fourth Generation

Albert Durham, the son of Thomas Durham, was born in April 1896.[7]

Hobart Durham, Sr., the son of Thomas Durham, was born on 26 October 1900. He was not quite fourteen years old at the time of the death of his father Thomas. Thus, he lived the remainder of his teenage years with his grandfather Isaac. He attended Boyd's Industrial College at Oakwood, taught in the Brown Creek Community School and drove a bus for the Bethel Independent School District.[8]

When he was about twenty-five, Hobart, Sr.—who had a son named Dorris with a woman named Ida Johns--became involved in a common-law marriage with Rebecca Washington. Two children—Thelma Lee and Thomas Arthur (T. A.)—were born to this union. The relationship was stormy and they eventually went their separate ways.[9]

In 1937, Hobart, Sr. married Fannie Mae Tippens, who had a son named Therman. Eventually, their family grew to thirteen children. In order of birth, these children were: Dorris Jim, Thelma Lee, Thomas Arthur, Therman Rogene, Hobart, Jr., Texanita, LaRue, George Douglas, Isaac Newton, Richard Eugene, Allie Faye, Bascom, Gerald and James Ronnie.[10]

Hobart, Sr. raised all of his children on his farm. They always ate at the same table. At times, it was necessary to take out mortgages in order to get the necessary resources to produce crops. During one bad year, everything he owned was auctioned off. However, a friend came to his aid and saved his farm. The family managed to remain on the farm throughout the years of the Great Depression. The family never went hungry. He never had to bail any of his children out of jail.[11]

Hobart, Sr. united with Lone Star Baptist Church at an early age. He served his church in various capacities, including secretary, chairman of deacons, chairman of trustees, and president of ushers. He often represented Lone Star at the meetings of the Lebanon District Association.[12]

Hobart, Sr. served as Worshipful Master of East Lake Lodge #247, Free and Accepted Masons, for 39 years. He initiated most of his sons into the lodge.[13]  He was also a member of the NAACP and served as chairman of the Community Council. His political activities included involvement in voter registration and in the struggle to abolish the poll tax.[14]

Hobart, Sr. died in Palestine on 30 July 1979. He was buried on 4 August 1979 in Lone Star Cemetery.[15]

## The Fifth Generation

Dorris "Jim" Durham, the son of Hobart Durham and Ida Johns, was born on 25 November 1922. He grew up in Butler and attended both Butler High School and Dogan High School in Fairfield. He majored in Political Science at Wiley College in Marshall, Texas. In 1938, he entered the Civilian Conservation Corps, working at a camp along the Navasota River between Mexia and Groesbeck. He was drafted into the U. S. Army following the bombing of Pearl Harbor on 7 December 1941. He served in both World War II and the Korean War. He was stationed many places prior to his discharge in May 1956. He received the World War II Victory Ribbon, the American Theater Ribbon, the AP Ribbon, and the Bronze Service Star. He worked briefly for the Mexia Police Department, then moved to Dallas, where he lived for the rest of his life. For many years, he worked in security for such companies as Wells Fargo, Wackenhut, and a company owned by the late Dallas City Councilman James Fantroy, a native of Fairfield. He grew up in Lone Star Baptist Church in Butler and later joined True Gospel Ministries, which is located at 1734 Ann Arbor in Dallas.[16] He married Roberta Ray in 1988. He died on 29 May 2010 in Dallas. Services, under the direction of Golden Gate Funeral Home, were held at True Gospel Ministries on 5 June 2010. He was survived by his wife Roberta, six brothers, five sisters, and his goddaughter Rosezena Smith. At this service, Rev. Donald Hooks, pastor of Loving Kindness Ministries in Waco, officiated. The Old Testament Scripture was read by Rev. Willis Durham and the New Testament Scripture was read by Rev. Henry Williams. Prayer was delivered by Minister Bishop Cooper. Special remarks were made by Rev. James Foster, pastor of Celestial Haven Baptist Church in Dallas. The eulogy was delivered by Rev. D. L. Washington, pastor of True Gospel Ministries. Active pallbearers included Bryan Douglas Durham, Eddie Ray Durham, Jansen Johnson, Richard Durham, Jr., Margin Hooks, Jr., and Minister Derrick Brown. Honorary pallbearers included Therman R. Durham, Bascom G. Durham, Isaac Durham, O. D. Washington, George D. Durham, Richard E. Durham, Frederick Perry, and Morris J. Washington. Interment was at Lone Star Cemetery, with reception following at the Butler Community Center.[17]

Thelma Lee Durham Roquemore, the daughter of Hobart Durham and Rebecca Washington, was born on 16 February 1926. She grew up in Butler and attended Butler High School. She married Cullen Davis on 4 May 1944. Their only child, Janet Hill, was born on 27 January 1945. They moved to Houston in 1946. She worked as a maid for a while. After graduation from cosmetology school, she worked at a number of beauty shops. She also studied hat-making and was self-employed in this field for five years. She was divorced from Cullen Davis in 1948 and married Larry Roquemore in 1954. Her second husband died in 1995. She was an active member of the Second Pleasant Grove Baptist Church in Houston but, until the end of her life, she would returns to her home church—Lone Star—every chance she got. She enjoyed being with loved ones and friends, to whom she imparted many words of wisdom and interesting stories.[18]   She died on 1 May 2014.  Her funeral was held at Pentecostal Missionary Baptist Church and was followed by burial at Paradise North Cemetery in Houston.[19]

Thomas Arthur Durham, the son of Hobart Durham and Rebecca Washington, was born on 12 September 1929 in Butler.  He joined Lone Star Baptist Church at an early age.  He worked for Flemming Food Supply in Houston.  He died on 9 March 1998.  His funeral was held on 14 March 1998 at the Second Pleasant Grove Missionary Baptist Church, followed by burial in Houston Memorial Gardens.  He was survived by his wife Elma Joyce Durham; three sons:  Wayne Holcome and Ronald Evans of Houston and Earl Whitmire of California; and seven daughters:  Karen Holcome, Carolyn Parks, Gloria Moore, Yvonne Flowers, Verna Evans, Sharon Evans, and Cheryl Brigham.  He was preceded in death by a step-daughter Jacqueline Jones.[20]

Therman Rogene Durham, the son of Fannie Tippens and Willis McDonald, was adopted by Hobart Durham, whom his mother married when he was six months old.  He was born on 28 June 1936.  He grew up in the Butler community and graduated from Butler High School in 1955.  He worked in Houston during the summer of 1955.  He then moved to Waco, where he attended Paul Quinn College for three years, majoring in Business Education.  He married Archie Mae Haliburton on 16 April 1960.  To this union, five children were born: Eddie Ray (1 October 1960), Herrold Gene (May 1962), Terrye Lynn (30 June 1963-December 20, 2003), Melissa (25 March 1967), and Willis Rogene (12 December 1970).  This marriage ended in divorce in 1975.  Therman married Julia Randall on 31 December 1977.  They adopted three children—Joanne Jackson, Darrell Jackson, and Fujimi Jackson.  Therman eventually had twenty-three grandchildren and one great-grandchild.  He worked for 23½ years as a baker at Mrs. Baird's Bakery, retiring on 1 July 1991.  He later worked at Mercury Tool and Machine Shop at the Waco Airport.  He established residence in the Waco suburb of Elm Mott since 1970.  Although he, like many other Durhams, grew up in Lone Star Baptist Church, he joined the Cumberland Presbyterian Church in the Waco area and was involved with this denomination for seventeen years.  Beginning in 1981, he became involved with Mount Lebanon Seventh-day Adventist Church in Waco.[21]  Therman died on Sunday January 5, 2014.  A wake was held at 7:00 p.m. on Friday January 10 at W. H. Littles & Sons Funeral Home in Waco.  His funeral was held on Saturday January 11 at Mount Lebanon Seventh-day Adventist Church, which is now located in the Waco suburb of

Lacy Lakeview. Interment was in Lone Star Cemetery.[22]

Hobart Durham, Jr., the son of Hobart Durham, was born on 14 December 1937. He graduated from Butler High School in 1957. Shortly after graduation, he moved to California. He was drafted into the military, receiving his basic training at Fort Ord, California and doing active duty in Germany, where he worked for replacement recruits. On 15 November 1962, he was discharged. He returned to California, where, on 1 January 1963, he met actor Richard Crenna and actress Shirley McClain. They told him of the need for Nubian extras in the movie *John Goldfarb, Please Come Home*. Thus began a twenty-one-year career as a television and movie extra. He worked in *Blazing Saddles, Mission Impossible, Laverne and Shirley, McHale's Navy, Gomer Pyle, Daktari: A Cowboy in Africa, Hill Street Blues, Mandingo*, and *Roots*. The latter television miniseries was based on the book by Alex Haley, which inspired much genealogical research, including this book. Hobart, Jr. had the pleasure of meeting not only such *Roots* stars as Lavar Burton and James Earl Jones but also Alex Haley himself. He had many fond memories of listening to Alex tell stories about his family.[23]

Hobart, Jr. married Jean Joiner Williams on 7 December 1962. One child was born to this union. On 9 December 1967, he married Fayeleece Byrd. One child was born to this union. At an early age, he united with Lone Star Baptist Church. While living in California, he sang in the choir and served on the usher board of Saint Andrew's Baptist Church. In his later years, he returned to Butler. Like many members of the Durham family, he loved farming. He entered eternal rest on 27 December 2008. His funeral was held at Lone Star Baptist Church on 3 January 2009, with Lone Star's pastor Rev. Larry Raven officiating. Revs. Patrick Benson, Luster Shannon, and Willis Durham participated in the service. The eulogy was delivered by Rev. Donald Hooks. Active pallbearers included Bryan Douglas Durham, Keith I. Durham, Anthony Woods, Richard Durham, Jr., Joseph H. Lewis, Lance D. Hicks, Nathan R. Durham, and Robert Durham. Honorary pallbearers included Dorris Jim Durham, George D. Durham, Richard E. Durham, Therman R. Durham, Isaac N. Durham, Bascom G. Durham, and James R. Durham. Interment was in Lone Star Cemetery.[24]

Texanita Durham Bluitt, the daughter of Hobart and Fannie Tippens Durham, was born on 11 July 1939 in Butler. As a child, she picked cotton but did not like it. Sometimes, while working in the field, she would hear a train whistle in the distance and fantasized about having a ticket out of the area. Following graduation from Butler High School in 1957, she applied to the Homer G. Phillips School of Nursing in Saint Louis, Missouri.[25] Butler native and Palestine physician Dr. J. Don Jackson had done a residency in Saint Louis and encouraged her to apply at Phillips School. She was picking cotton for "Uncle Sherman" Jackson—Dr. Jackson's father—when her letter of acceptance arrived in the mail. Her family was not well off financially and 1957 turned out to be a bad year for crops. Her father did not have the $392.00 required in advance for three years of tuition and fees. Thus, he placed $60.00 in an envelope, along with a three-page letter pleading for her acceptance and promising to send more money once he sold his first bale of cotton. He took her to a train station in Palestine. Since the family could not afford to pay her fare, a friend employed by the Southern Pacific Railroad let her use his pass. As the train approached Little Rock, Arkansas, she hid under the seat, after hearing that federal troops were occupying Little Rock to enforce court-ordered desegregation of Central High School.[26]

Texanita made excellent grades at Homer G. Phillips. As a result, she received a full scholarship and her father did not have to pay anything beyond the initial $60.00. She was able to bring her mother to Saint Louis to witness her graduation in September 1960.[27]

After passing the examination administered by the Missouri State Board of Nursing Examiners, Texanita worked for a year as a psychiatric nurse at Malcolm Bliss Hospital in Saint Louis. As a result of this experience, she was able to reflect on things back home, recalling that, during her childhood, her mother had disappeared for about six months and she did not know her whereabouts. She later learned that her mother was then a patient at Rusk State Hospital and remembered the hallucinations that prompted her admission to the latter psychiatric facility. By 1960, her mother's condition was much better and Texanita was able to talk with her about her history of mental problems. Throughout her career, she has had much experience in working with psychiatric patients and substance abusers.[28]

In 1961, Texanita's grandmother, Allie Durham Releford, became ill. As a result, Texanita returned to Texas and went to work at G. L. Prince Hospital in Crockett.[29] Shortly after her arrival there, the building was split in half by Hurricane Carla. The hospital received a steady stream of patients from an area stretching from the Texas Gulf Coast to Oklahoma. Dr. J. Don Jackson helped Dr. James Hilliard, Jr., the medical director at Prince Hospital, in dealing with the overflow of patients. In addition to performing her duties at the hospital, Texanita also taught classes in nursing at Mary Allen College across the street.[30]

In 1962, Texanita married a Baptist preacher named Arthur Chester Parker III. They moved to Tyler, Texas, where Rev. Parker was a pastor and Texanita worked at the Texas Medical Center. Three sons and one daughter were born to this marriage, which ended in divorce in 1972. Texanita married Lonnie Bluitt, Sr. in 1988.[31]

When Texanita first came to Tyler, the hospital was segregated, with white and black patients housed on different floors. After the passage of the 1964 Civil Rights Act, a committee from the U. S. Department of Justice visited the hospital and announced to the administration that they must integrate the facility within twelve hours. Texanita was the head nurse of the black section at the time. She was involved in the integration process. She noticed that her next paycheck was considerably higher and soon learned that her raise came as a result of an audit which revealed a long pattern of lower pay for black employees performing the same duties as their white counterparts.[32]

In 1964, Texanita moved to California and went to work at the Southern Pacific Railroad Hospital in San Francisco. While employed at this facility, she re-connected with her fourth cousin, Archie Durham, a long-time employee of Southern Pacific. She returned to Tyler in 1966 and worked there as public health nurse until 1969, when she moved back to California and went to work for Kaiser Permenente, a health maintenance organization. She remained with Kaiser until 1981, when she took a teaching position at the Merritt Hospital School of Nursing. She held the latter position for 10 ½ yeas. After leaving Kaiser, she went to work as director of patient care services for Rubicon, a nonprofit organization serving the homeless, the mentally deficient, substance abusers, etc.[33]

In 1964, Texanita received her Bachelor of Science degree in Nursing from the University of San Francisco. Following graduation, she went to England, where she studied midwifery at the Royal College of London. In 1966, she received her Master of Science degree in Nursing at the University of California at San Francisco. For the latter degree, she wrote a thesis on Labor Relations in the Health Care Industry. She has served on the board of directors of the California Nurses Association. In 1974, she played a key role in the largest nursing strike in California history.[34]

Since 1979, Texanita has lived in Richmond, California. She owns property in a number of California cities and some acreage in her home community of Butler. Despite her childhood desires to leave the cotton fields, she maintains a fondness for the people of Butler and tremendous appreciation for the Durham legacy.[35]

LaRue Durham Hooks, the daughter of Hobart Durham, was born on 8 October 1940. She graduated from Butler High School in 1958. She moved to Waco shortly after graduation and remains there today. She was a head start teacher for the Economic Opportunities Advancement Corporation (EOAC) from 1964 to 1978. She graduated from Paul Quinn College in 1978 and was a second grade teacher for Waco Independent School District. She married Margin E. Hooks, Sr. and they have the following children: Donald W. Hooks, Darryl D. Hooks, Cynthia Hooks Young, Carlos O. Hooks, LaSonya Hooks Russell, and Margin E. Hooks, Jr. They have seven grandchildren and seven great-grandchildren. She grew up in Lone Star Baptist Church. After moving to Waco, she joined Wesley United Methodist Church and later Carver Park Baptist Church. She is now involved in Love and Kindness Ministries, where her son Donald W. Hooks serves as pastor.[36]

George Douglas Durham, the son of Hobart Durham, was born on 22 February 1942. He graduated from Butler High School in 1959 as salutatorian and attended Texas Southern University in Houston from 1959 until 1962, majoring in criminal justice. He then worked for seven years for the Houston Fire Department and for thirty years for the Harris County Sheriff's Department. In the latter department, he worked for four years as a jailer and then was promoted to sergeant and later to lieutenant. After ten years at the jail, he was transferred to the warrant division as a detective. In this capacity, he traveled to all fifty states and some foreign countries bringing fugitives to justice. In March 2001, he retired from a long career in law enforcement. He and his wife Linda have a daughter named Rachell Durham Shannon who has had a long career with the Houston Police Department, including service on the mayor's protection detail; and a son named Bryan Durham who has worked for many years for the Harris County Sheriff's Department. While George continues to reside in the Houston area, he maintains strong ties to Freestone County, where he serves as recording secretary of the Ike Carden Rodeo Association, a non-profit charitable organization which sponsors a rodeo in Fairfield during each second weekend in July.[37] He is a Freemason, having been brought into the craft by the late Judge Thomas H. Routt, the eighteenth Grand Master of the Prince Hall Grand Lodge of Texas and a friend of the writer.[38]

Isaac Newton Durham, the son of Hobart Durham, was born on 19 October 1943. He lived in Butler from 1943 until 1961, when he graduated from Butler High School. He then moved to Houston, where he lived until he joined the U. S. Army in 1963. His military career included nine years in Germany, one year in Vietnam, and two years in Korea. While stationed in California, he received his Associate in Arts degree from Los Angeles Community College. He retired in 1985 and moved to Austin, where he worked for the next seven years for the U. S. Postal Service.[39]

"Isaac married Marilyn Sue Edwards on 11 March 1991. He has the following children: Ramona Yvette Durham Benson (born 1 March 1964); Keith Isaac Durham (born 11 July 1965); and Amy Durham (born 12 March 1981). He also has the following step children: Gerald Hicks (born 24 September 1968); and Lance Hicks (born 24 September 1979). He has fifteen grandchildren." In July 1992, Isaac built a house on some heir property at Butler and moved back home. He became involved in community activities, distributing commodities from Palestine to senior citizens at Butler. In January 1995, he completed the Freestone County Sheriff's Academy. He became a Deputy Sheriff and was promoted to sergeant. He worked in patrol and later criminal investigations.[40]

In December 2003, at the annual Freestone County Sheriff's Christmas Dinner at Fairfield VFW Post 5872, he was promoted to Lieutenant and named "Deputy of the Year." In announcing this award, Sheriff Ralph Billings said: "I try to pick out the person who gives out a good year's work. He has a great interest in youth and has high morals and ethics."[41]

Isaac retired from the Sheriff's Department on 31 March 2007. He said: "I love the work I do, but I feel it is time to spend more time with my wife and grandkids." He spoke of plans for travel and tending the cows and horses on his Butler ranch.[42] Retirement, however, did not last long. Within a year, he went to work as a Freestone County Security Officer. In this position, he patrols the courthouse, all county annexes and the office of the Justice of the Peace in Teague.[43]

In June 2000, Isaac was appointed to the Fairfield Independent School District's Board of Trustees to complete an unexpired term. During his 2001 campaign, he said: "We need to get parents involved in the education of their children. I would like to be the vehicle to get voices to the board. We must give the very best education today if we are going to require our children to lead in the future." He vowed to take a greater part in school and youth activities.[44] He attended the Texas Association of School Boards Summer Governance Seminar in Arlington, Texas on 13-14 July 2001. The focus of this session was on boardmanship, teamwork, and school law, including open meetings, conflict of interest laws, and employment issues.[45]

Isaac has served as president of the Freestone County Chapter of the NAACP in 1997-98. He has also served on the U. S. Marshal Task Force out of Waco. He works part-time for Emanuel Funeral Home in Palestine. He is a long-time member of Lone Star Baptist Church. In 1971, he was raised to the sublime degree of Master Mason by his father, Hobart Durham, who was then Worshipful Master of East Lake Lodge #247. He later received the 32nd degree of the Scottish Rite in Aniston Consistory #202 in Aniston, Alabama and was made a Noble of the Mystic Shrine in Aswan Temple No. 115 in Stuttgard, Germany.[46]

Richard Eugene Durham, Sr., the son of Hobart Durham, was born on 1 July 1947. He graduated from Butler High School in 1965. He received an Associate in Arts degree in Business Administration from Tyler Junior College in Tyler, Texas in February 1968. He then joined the U. S. Air Force, serving until February 1972. Upon discharge, he moved to Dallas and went to work for Dial Finance Company, serving as a loan officer and later promoted to branch manager. Eventually, he was transferred by Dial to Houston. He resigned from Dial in 1980 and moved back to Dallas, where he managed Dallas Premium Carriers, which finances insurance policies for various companies and agencies, until 1998. He then went to work as director of disaster services for the American Red Cross, covering Dallas, Ellis, and Rockwall counties. He traveled all over the country, working natural disasters and teaching classes on disaster management. He held this job until 1995, when he returned to Butler and obtained employment as laundry manager at the Coffield Unit of the Texas Department of Criminal Justice at Tennessee Colony, near Palestine, Texas. He retired on 30 September 2008.[47]

On 25 January 1978, Richard Sr. married Dianne Houston Session in Dallas. Dianne was the daughter of Katie J. Davis Houston and the late Edward O. Houston. Richard had an adopted son Nathan Ray Durham, who was born on 9 September 1964; and a daughter, Cecelia, from a previous marriage, who was born on 14 April 1971. On 15 August 1980, their son, Richard Eugene Durham, Jr., was born—exactly 120 years after his great-great grandfather Isaac. In 1982, Richard and Dianne were divorced. Today, Dianne lives in Dallas and Richard lives in Butler, where he raises cattle and horses. On 1 September 1991, Richard married Karen Parker Worthy, who has a daughter named Kimberly Dromgoole.[48]

Richard Sr. serves as chairman of the deacon board at Lone Star Baptist Church. He is a member of East Lake Lodge #247. He is quite active in the

Butler community. He sees his mission as helping people, especially the widows of the community.[49]

Allie Faye Durham Moore, the daughter of Hobart Durham was born on 4 December 1949. She grew up in Butler and graduated from Butler High School in 1968. She attended Henderson County Junior College in Athens Texas for one year and later resumed her studies at Prairie View A&M University. In 1975, she withdrew from Prairie View one semester short of obtaining a Bachelor of Science degree in nursing. She moved to California in 1976. She is now a Certified Echocardiograph Technician and has been employed at Kaiser Hospital in Richmond, California for many years. On 23 June 1980, she married Alvin Moore, a native of Wascom, Texas who played for the Chicago White Sox and Atlanta Braves and later worked for AFLAC Insurance. She has the following children: Michael Cornell Durham (who was born on 8 December 1969 and has worked for Southwestern Bell Telephone Company in Richmond, California); Darien Arvetta Moore (who was born on 29 June 1978 and has worked at the Dallas campus of the University of North Texas); and Alvin Earl Moore, Jr. (who was born on 5 July 1982 and is interested in music and baseball.). Allie Faye, her husband, and her son live in Fairfield, California.[50]

Bascom Gerald Durham, the son of Hobart Durham, was born on 6 September 1951. He recalls:

> *I received an early introduction to work and responsibilities at age 4. It became my responsibility to gather two five-gallon buckets of small woodchips and place them in the kitchen before sunset. These woodchips had to be available for one of the other older siblings to start the fire in the kitchen stove at about 6 a.m. . . .*
>
> *On September 1st, 1956 I started school at Butler High School in Oakwood, Texas. After only one month in school, eager to learn, I had a brush with state and federal government. The law, at that time, was for one to start school if they were born prior to September 1st 6 years earlier. Being born on the 6th, I was born 5 days too late.*
>
> *At age 10 my responsibilities around the farm increased to providing drinking water for the house that had to be drawn from a 64-foot deep well located about 1,200 yards from the house. Using a two gallon pail attached to a rope, I would lower this pail into the well and when it made contact with the water there was a 2-pound rock attached to the top of the pail which would cause it to flip over and begin to take in water. Once it became full, the bucket then hung perpendicular to the rope and one could fill the*

*weight. This rope was attached to a pole which was lying parallel attached to two poles that were standing 6 feet apart and perpendicular to each other. . . Also at age 10, my duties included (prior to catching the school bus for a 45 minute to an hour and a half ride to school) feeding the pigs and milking 6 cows by hand.*[51]

Bascom graduated from Butler High School on 23 May 1970. He was president of a class of 23 with the 4th highest grade point average. On 13 September 1970, he enrolled at Prairie View A&M University. He declared a major in political science and a minor in history and was a distinguished member of the Reserved Officer Training Corps (ROTC). In January 1973, he accepted the offer of the professor of military science to take a slot in the United States Airborne School at Fort Benning, Georgia. He was the first student from Prairie View to do so. In late May 1973, he enrolled in three weeks of intense training at Fort Benning. In mid June 1973, after completing two static line parachute jumps from a C-13 airplane and one static line from a C141 airplane and graduated from Jump School. During the first week of July 1973, he attended summer camp at Fort Riley, Kansas. This was the final phase of his military training before being commissioned as a Second Lieutenant. He was the first Prairie View A&M student to enter airborne school and receive such a commission. He graduated from Prairie View on 21 December 1973.[52]

Bascom was promoted to the rank of captain in 1978. During his career, he was stationed at Fort Knox, Kentucky; Fort Hood, Texas; Fort Benjamin Harrison, Indiana; Fort Bragg, North Carolina; Patrick Air Force Base, Florida; and Vicenza, Italy. His military career was marked by completion of a number of courses, including airborne school, armor school, personnel administrative officer advanced training, and equal opportunity staff officer training. He was awarded the Meritorious Service Medal, the Army Commendation Medal, the Army Achievement Medal, the Army Reserve Components Medal, the National Defense Service Medal, the Army Service Ribbon, the Parachuter's Badge, and the Overseas Service Ribbon. His active duty ended on 4 September 1986. He joined the New York Army National Guard as a sergeant in May 1989. Since then, he was been promoted three times, reaching the rank of chief warrant officer. He has served as a personnel technician at the headquarters in Albany County, New York.[53]

Bascom was called to active duty at the Pentagon. His tour of duty lasted from 1 November 1999 to 30 September 2000. This assignment ended less than one year before the terrorist attacks on the World Trade Center and the Pentagon on 11 September 2001. He later was involved in the cleanup of "Ground Zero" in New York City. He still becomes very emotional when talking about this.[54]

In civilian life, Bascom was employed as a civil rights compliance specialist with the New York State Department of Transportation in Poughkeepsie since 4 September 1986. He began work as a regional compliance specialist grade 18. In September 1987, he was promoted to minority business specialist. He is now retired from the State of New York.[55]

Bascom grew up in Lone Star Baptist Church in Butler and later became a deacon at Beulah Baptist Church in Poughkeepsie. Like most of his brothers, he was initiated into East Lake Lodge #247 by his father. He is now a member of Paul J. Cooper Military Lodge in Fort Drum, New York and of both the Scottish Rite and York Rite Bodies in Utica, New York.[56]

Bascom married Estella Marie Dunn on 15 December 1972. This union produced three children—Robert Lemont Christopher Durham (born 8 September 1972), Sophia Natasha Chrystal Durham (born 18 August 1978), and Katherine Elaine Durham McAleer (born 28 September 1981)—were born to this union. They were divorced in January 1985. He married Virginia Burrow on 11 September 1993. He has seven grandchildren and two great-grandchildren.[57]

Bascom resigned his commission as chief warrant officer, effective 1 December 2003. His future plans include development of his land at Butler and dividing his time between New York and Texas.[58]

James Ronnie Durham, the son of Hobart Durham, was born on 30 May 1953. He was past of Butler High School's last graduating class in 1971. He worked for eighteen years as a chemical engineer for Shell Oil Company in Richmond, California and for six years as a custodian for Dallas Independent School District. He retired in 2005 and currently lives in Houston. His daughter Daydrian Durham was born on 6 August 1980.[59]

## The Sixth Generation

Rachel Durham Shannon, the daughter of George Douglas and Annette S. Durham, was born on 6 November 1962. Like her father, she has pursued a career in law enforcement, working for the Houston Police Department since 1981.[60]

Bryan Douglas Durham, the son of George Douglas and Annette S. Durham, was born on 4 October 1963 in Houston, Texas. He graduated from Jack Yates High School in 1983 and attended Houston Community College. Like his father, he has pursued a career in law enforcement, working for the

Houston Police Department and later for the Harris County Sheriff's Department. He is a member of Windsor Village United Methodist Church in Houston. His son Dae-reon D'Von Durham was born on 1 January 2007.[61]

Ramona Yvette Durham, the daughter of Isaac Newton Durham and Mattie Lean Lewis, was born on 1 March 1964 in Germany. She is married to Patrick Benson and has two children: Dominique Durham (born 26 May 1991) and Kiara Benson (born 13 January 1993).[62]

Keith Isaac Durham, the son of Isaac Newton Durham and Mattie Lean Lewis, was born on 11 July 1965 in West Germany. He graduated from Hempstead High School in Hempstead, Texas in 1983. He served in the U. S. Army. He was stationed at Fort Polk, Louisiana; Fort Leonard Wood, Missouri; and Korea. In 2009, he had a tour of duty in Iraq. He reached the rank of staff sergeant. Since leaving the military, he has done security work. He currently lives in Monaville, Texas and works with patients at the Brenham State School in Brenham, Texas. On 15 September 1989, he married Sandra Kennedy. They have a son, Keith Isaac Durham, II (born 19 October 1991) and a daughter, Kendra Roshell Durham (born 4 January 2003).[63]

Melissa Durham, the daughter of Therman Durham, was born on 25 March 1967 in Waco, Texas. Her daughter, Angelique Derek Brown Green, was born on 8 December 1989.[64]

Michael Cornell Durham, the son of Isaac Culbreath and Allie Faye Durham Moore, was born on 8 December 1969 in Richmond, California. He is married to Trenese Danielle LaFrance Durham. They have two children: Monye Abnese Durham (born 21 August 1993) and Taylor Amina Durham (born 21 January 1998).[65]

Cecilia Rena Durham Woods, the daughter of Richard Eugene Durham, Sr. and Mae Frances Lewis, was born in San Antonio, Texas on 14 April 1971. She is married to Anthony Woods and is the mother of the following children: Christen Danielle Johnson (born 9 January 1993), Ciara Denise Johnson (born 3 April 1997) who is a varsity tennis player, David Durham Johnson (born December 26, 1998) who plays basketball, and Daniel Durham Johnson (born 26 December 1993), who plays basketball and runs track. All are on the honor roll.[66]

Robert Lemont Christopher Durham, the son of Bascom Durham and Estella Mae Dunn, was born on 8 September 1972. He currently works as a line operator for Caterpillar in Raleigh, North Carolina. He married Norah Burns Durham and they have the following children: Raquella Victoria Durham (born 31 October 1991), Janelle Durham (born 7 September 1996), Ashley Durham (born 20 December 1999), Aaron Durham (born 19 May 2000), Alyssa Durham (born 10 July 2002), and Preia Durham (born 13 June

2005), and Robert Durham (born 4 October 2006).[67]

Sophia Natasha Chrystal Durham, the daughter of Bascom Durham and Estella Mae Dunn, was born on 18 August 1978. She graduated from 71st Senior High School in Fayetteville, North Carolina. She is employed in Information Technology in Houston, Texas.[68]

Daydrian Durham, the daughter of James Ronnie Durham and Karen Roberts, was born on 6 August 1980. She graduated from South County Technical High School in Saint Louis, Missouri in 1998. She received a Bachelor of Science in Health Information Management at Rend Lake College in Mount Vernon, Illinois. She has done graduate work at Walden University. She currently lives in Mount Vernon and is employed as a corporate specialist by SSM Health Network. Her daughter, Myrikle Williams, was born on 16 June 2004.[69]

During the fall of 1999, the writer had the pleasure of having Richard Eugene Durham, Jr.—the son of Richard Eugene Durham, St. and Diane Houston Durham-Roberson—as a student in his U. S. History class at Navarro College in Corsicana, Texas. Richard wrote an excellent paper on his branch of the family tree. He was amazed to learn that his birth on 15 August 1980 occurred exactly 120 years after that of his great-great grandfather, Isaac Durham. Richard, Jr. was born in Houston, Texas and currently resides in Dallas, Texas. He is a teacher in the Dallas Independent School District. He is married to Ericka Nichole Durham. Their son Willie Edward Durham was born on 3 September 2008.[70]

Amy Durham, the daughter of Isaac Newton and Eva M. Durham, was born on 12 March 1981 in Austin, Texas. She graduated from Red Oak High School in 1991 and from Prairie View A&M University in 2004. She currently teaches special education for Dallas Independent School District. She has a daughter named Adyson Grace Birdow, who was born on 19 May 2008.[71]

Katherine Elaine Durham McAlear, the daughter of Bascom Durham and Estella Mae Dunn, was born on 28 September 1984. She currently lives in Louisville, Kentucky, where she works as a state social worker.[72]

## The Seventh Generation

Raquella Victoria Durham, the daughter of Robert and Norah Durham, was born on 31 October 1981. She has two children: Ronald Durham (born 7 October 2010) and Victoria Durham (born November 13, 2011).[73]

### *Old Durham Spirit*

At a reunion of descendants of Isaac Durham, the following song has been sung to the tune of "Old Time Religion":

*Give me that good old Durham spirit*
*Give me that good old Durham spirit*
*Give me that good old Durham spirit*
*It's good enough for me.*

*It was good for Hobart and Fannie*
*It was good for Hobart and Fannie*
*It was good for Hobart and Fannie*
*And it's good enough for me.*

*Give me that good old Durham spirit*
*Give me that good old Durham spirit*
*Give me that good old Durham spirit*
*It's good enough for me.*

*Give me that good old Durham spirit*
*Give me that good old Durham spirit*
*Give me that good old Durham spirit*
*It's good enough for me.*

The writer has attended a number of reunions of the Isaac Durham Family over the years. On 5 July 2014, he spoke to the gathering about this book. He was accompanied by his grandson, Richard James Walker, who won a trophy in the domino tournament. Those in attendance agreed that, although Richard's last name is "Walker," he is still a Durham. Richard is descended from Allen Durham.

Hobart and Fannie Durham

James Ronnie Durham with Daughter and Granddaughter.

George Durham

Therman Durham and Family

Richard Durham, Sr., Richard Durham, Jr,
and Family Members

Larue Durham Hooks and Family

(L-R) Donald Hooks, Richard Durham, Bascom Durham, and Gail Russell

Isaac Newton Durham

Robert and Norah Durham
and Family

# Chapter XII

## *The Durhams and the Strawthers*

"Strawther"[1] is the name of a black family in the Butler community who have lived near the Durhams for many years. Reportedly, their ancestor Philip Strawther was at one time owned by the same master as Gobi, the ancestor of the Durhams. Philip Strawther married Matilda Manning. They lived in the Bethel and Pine Top areas of Butler. Some of their children became active at Pine Top (now Union) Methodist Church. Such included Philip Strawther, Jr. Matilda was probably once a slave to the Manning family. In 1860, John, Reuben, and Hillary Manning were listed among the slaveholders of Freestone County. Reportedly, Mandy Durham, the wife of Belton Durham and daughter-in-law of Gobi, was a cousin to the Strawther family. Dorsey Strawther has lived near the Durhams not far from the Crossroads Store at Butler for many years.[2]

In the 1880 Anderson County Census, R. Strawther, age 50, is listed. Like the Durhams, he was born in South Carolina.[3]

In the 1880 Freestone County Census, there is a black family named Straw listed. Such included Violet Straw, the servant of W. E. Day; Lucy Straw, the niece of Bob Miles; Mary Straw, the sister-in-law of Giles Smith; and Adelia Straw, the servant of F. R. Huckaby. Oree Straw and Frank Straw are listed as farmers and heads of households. The roots of this family are in Alabama rather than South Carolina. Thus, the possibility of a connection between the Straws and Strawthers appears remote, although certainly possible.

## Chapter XIII
## *Other Durhams*
### Rev. J. J. Durham, M.D.

J. J. Durham was born in slavery in Spartanburg County, South Carolina. As a young man, he worked as a blacksmith and mastered reading and writing. In 1868, he was ordained as a Baptist minister. For eighteen months, he served as pastor of a small congregation in Spartanburg County, receiving for his services about eighteen dollars.[1]

Rev. Durham moved to Greenville, South Carolina, where he studied for three years. He hired a tutor in Latin and Greek to help him prepare for admission to the senior preparatory class of South Carolina University. He enrolled in 1874 and stayed until the school was closed by the "Redeemer" government elected in 1876. He transferred to Atlanta University in Atlanta, Georgia and, in 1880, graduated from Fisk University in Nashville, Tennessee.[2]

After a brief pastorate in Columbia, South Carolina, Rev. Durham returned to Nashville, where he enrolled at Meharry Medical College. In 1882, he received the degree of Doctor of Medicine and the designation of valedictorian of his class.[3]

After medical school, Rev. Dr. Durham moved to Society Hill, South Carolina, where he served the community as both pastor and physician. He then served eight years as missionary of the American Baptist Publication Society and as secretary of the state Baptist convention. He eventually returned to the pastoral ministry.[4]

### Dr. Bartlett Durham's Cook

When the writer first began research on the Durham family, he suspected that they came from North Carolina, in view of the city of Durham, North Carolina, the site of Duke University, which was a product of the philanthropy of the Duke family, who made millions of dollars in tobacco, textiles, and electric power. This hypothesis proved incorrect, as all of the sources pointed to South Carolina and Louisiana. He also looked for a connection with Bull Durham tobacco, but found none.[5]

Bartlett Durham

Dr. Bartlett Leonidas Snipes Durham (November 3, 1824-February 2, 1859) was an American physician and entrepreneur whose land, donated for a railway station, became the location of Durham, North Carolina, named for him.[6] The community was originally called Durhamville Station, then Durham's Station, and finally, Durham.[7]

According to an article in the *Durham Herald-Sun*:

*Bartlett Durham, who gained a spell of immortality for donating 4 acres of land for a railroad station around which a city arose, grew up 12 miles west of Chapel Hill. Born Nov. 3, 1824, to William L. and Mary Snipes Durham, Bartlett was a fourth generation of Orange County Durhams.*

*Legend has it he studied medicine first with a family acquaintance - perhaps Dr. James Webb of Hillsborough - and then in Philadelphia, maybe at Jefferson Medical College, maybe the University of Pennsylvania - no record survives, in any case. And in any case, in 1847 or 1848 Durham apparently bought about 100 acres of land in the vicinity of the present Durham Bulls Athletic Park and American Tobacco ruin and relocated himself and his practice there. . . .*

*Lore has it Durham had a two-story home called Pandora's Box, near the present intersection of Corcoran Street and the Loop. The site would have been across the track from the depot he provided for; in later years, it would be the site of Julian Carr's grandiose Carolina Hotel, then of the Durham Hosiery Mill. Today, it's a parking lot.[8]*

Dr. Durham was a very popular physician, with patients in a number of counties. When he died of pneumonia during the very cold winter of 1859, he was buried in the Snipes burial ground at Antioch Baptist Church, on White Cross Road eight miles west of Chapel Hill near the Orange-Chatham County line.[9] On 27 June 1933, his remains were exhumed. Hundreds of persons attended a memorial service at Antioch Church. Apparently his corpse had frozen because no decomposition had taken place in the seventy-five years since his death. Thousands viewed his remains at the Hall-Wynne Funeral Chapel. On 1 January 1934, he was reburied in Maplewood Cemetery in a plot donated by the grateful city of Durham.[10] On his tomb appear the following words: "Country physician and public-spirited citizen who donated land for a railroad station and thereby became founder of a city. . . . The merit belongs to the beginner should his successor do even better."[11]

Dr. Durham never married. It appears that he developed a reputation as a womanizer. After his death, Susan Ann Clements brought a "bastardy suit" against his estate, claiming that he was the father of her son Romulus. She lost the suit.[12]

At the 1933 memorial service, the principal address was delivered by S. B. Turrentine, president of Greensboro College and a native of southwest Orange County.

The crowd included at least three persons who had attended Dr. Durham's funeral in 1859. One of these was "Uncle Mabane" Edwards, an 87-year-old African American, who made a short talk which included details of the funeral service which he had attended as a 10-year-old slave. He had the following recollections of Dr. Durham's cook: "She was dressed in green silk from her head to feet and she sure was pretty."[13]

Who was Dr. Durham's cook? More than likely, she was a slave. In 1850 Slave Schedules for Orange County, North Carolina list Bartlett Durham as the owner of one slave—a 17-year-old female. If this was the same person, she would have been twenty-five at the time of his death. In view of the un-limited control of masters over slaves, one wonders if there was a sexual rela-tionship between the doctor and his cook. Slavery continued until 1865—six

Bull Durham Tobacco

120

years after Dr. Durham's death. Did she have another master? What was her first name? After freedom, did she use the surname of Durham? Perhaps later research will discover and bring to light the answers to these intriguing questions.[14] Even though we presently know little about her, there can be no doubt that this unnamed cook in green silk deserves mention in any study of black Durhams.

## Tempe Herndon Durham

During the 1930s, many former slaves were among the Americans from various walks of life who were interviewed by the staff of the Federal Writers Project (FWP), a division of the Works Progress Administration (WPA), an

Tempe Hendon Durham

agency created as part of the "New Deal" of President Franklin Delano Roosevelt.

In 1937, FWP worker Travis Jordan interviewed 103-year-old Tempe Herndon Durham at 1312 Pine Street in Durham, North Carolina. Ms. Durham, probably the oldest African American in Durham at the time, said to Jordan:

*I was thirty-one years ole when de surrender come. Dat makes me sho nuff ole. Near bout a hundred an' three years done passed over dis here white head of mine. I'se been here, I mean I'se been here... I'se been here so long dat I done forgot near 'bout as much as dese here new generation knows or ever gwine know.*

*My white fo'ks lived in Chatham County. Dey was Marse George an' Mis' Betsy Herndon. Mis Betsy was a Snipes befo' she married Marse George. Dey had a big plantation an' raised cawn, wheat, cotton an' 'bacca.... Dey was a big weavin' room whare de blankets was wove, an' dey wove de cloth for de winter clothes too. Linda Herndon an' Milla Edwards was de head weavers, dey looked after de weavin' of da fancy blankets. Mis' Betsy was a good weaver too....*

*When I growed up I married Exter Durham. He belonged to Marse Snipes Durham who had de plantation 'cross de county line in Orange County. We had a big weddin'. We was married on de front po'ch of de big house. Marse George killed a shoat an' Mis' Betsy had Georgianna, de cook, to bake a big weddin' cake all iced up white as snow wid a bride an' groom standin' in de middle holdin' han's. De table was set out in de yard under de trees, an' you ain't never seed de like of eats. Dat was some weddin'. I had on a white dress, white shoes an' long while gloves dat come to my elbow, an' Mis' Betsy done made me a weddin' veil out of a white net window curtain. When she played de weddin' ma'ch on de piano, me an' Exter ma'ched down de walk an' up on de po'ch to de altar Mis' Betsy done fixed. Dat de pretties' altar I ever seed. Back 'gainst de rose vine dat was full or red roses, Mis' Betsy done put tables filled wid flowers an' white candles. She spread down a bed sheet, a sho nuff linen sheet, for us to stan' on, an' dey was a white pillow to kneel down on. Exter done made me a weddin' ring. He made it out of a big red button wid his pocket knife. He done cut it so roun' an' polished it so smooth dat it looked like a red satin ribbon tide 'roun' my finger. Dat sho was a pretty ring. I wore it 'bout fifty years, den it got so thin dat I lost it one day in de wash tub when I was washin' clothes.*

*Uncle Edmond Kirby married us. . . . After Uncle Edmond said de las' words over me an' Exter, Marse George got to have his little fun: He say, 'Come on, Exter, you an' Tempie got to jump over de broom stick backwards; you got to do dat to see which one gwine be boss of your househol'.' Everybody come stan' 'roun to watch. Marse George hold de broom 'bout a foot high off de floor. De one dat jump over it backwards an' never touch de handle, gwine boss de house, an' if bof of dem jump over widout touchin' it, dey won't gwine be no bossin', dey jus' gwine be 'genial. I jumped fus', an' you ought to seed me. I sailed right over dat broom stick same as a cricket, but when Exter jump he done had a big dram an' his feets was so big an' clumsy dat dey got all tangled up in dat broom an' he fell head long. Marse George he laugh an' laugh, an' tole Exter he gwine be bossed 'twell he skeered to speak less'n I tole him to speak. . . . We had eleven chillun. Nine was bawn befo' surrender an' two after we was set free. So I had two chillun dat wuzn' bawn in bondage. I was worth a heap to Marse George kaze I had so many chillun. De more chillun a slave had de more dey was worth.*

*When de war come Marse George was too ole to go, but young Marse Bill went. He went an' took my brother Sim wid him. Marse Bill took Sim along to look after his hoss an' everything. . . .*

*(De Yankees wuzn' so bad. De mos' dey wanted was sumpin' to eat. Dey was all de time hungry, de fus' thing dey ax for when dey come was sumpin' to put in dey stomach. An' chicken! I ain' never seed even a preacher eat chicken like dem Yankees. I believes to my soul dey ain' never seed no chick-*

*en 'twell dey come down here. An' hot biscuit too. I seed a passel of dem eat up a whole sack of flour one night for supper. Georgianna sif' flour 'twell she look white an' dusty as a miller. . .*

*After we was free we lived right on at Marse George's plantation a long time. We rented de lan' for a fo'th of what we made, den after while we bought a farm. We paid three hundred dollars we done saved. We had a hoss, a steer, a cow an' two pigs, 'sides some chickens an' fo' geese.[15]*

## William J. Durham

William J. Durham, civil-rights activist and attorney, was born on a farm near Sulphur Springs, Hopkins County, Texas, in 1896.[16] After completing one semester at Emporia State College in Kansas, he served in the United States Army in France during World War I, after which he studied law in the office of Ben F. Gafford, a white attorney in Sherman, Texas. After passing the bar examination in 1926, Durham established his practice in Sherman and began taking on civil-rights cases, even though in the Sherman riot of 1930 a lynch mob burned the black business district, including his office. Though such lawsuits were rarely profitable, Durham had a lucrative practice as legal counsel to an insurance company and could therefore spend part of his time fighting for equal rights. By 1940 he was recognized as the leading black lawyer in Texas.[17]

William J. Durham

In 1943, Lawyer Durham moved from Sherman to Dallas, where he became known not only as a civil-rights champion and the most effective leader of the National Association for the Advancement of Colored People (NAACP), but also for his effectiveness in court and pretrial strategy. He took part in more than forty civil-rights cases involving such causes as school integration, voting rights, and equalization of teachers' salaries.[18]

Lawyer Durham and other attorneys fought successfully to enroll Herman M. Sweatt at the University of Texas Law School. He knew that there was no law school for African Americans in the state at that time and that UT would consequently be particularly vulnerable to a lawsuit if the school rejected Sweatt on the basis of race. He became best known for the school-integration cases in which he and his associates went to court to implement the 1954 Supreme Court rulings. Additionally, he served on the national board of the NAACP and assisted in directing its education and legal-defense fund. He also helped organize the Texas Council of Voters.[19]

Lawyer Durham died in Dallas on 22 December 1970. His funeral was held at Good Street Baptist Church, where he served as a trustee on 26 December 1970. He was buried in Greenville Cemetery in Greenville, Hunt County, Texas. He was a trustee of Good Street Baptist Church.[20] After his death, Good Street honored their distinguished member by the establishment of the W. J. Durham Library.

## Eddie Durham

Eddie Durham, one of the most important Swing Era composer–arrangers, was born in San Marcos, Texas, on 19 August, 1906. He was the son of Luella Rabb and Joseph Durham, Sr. In addition to their African-American ancestry, his father was also part Irish and Mohawk, and his mother was part Cherokee. His father played the fiddle at square dances, and his oldest brother, Joe, who played cello briefly with Nat King Cole, took correspondence lessons and in turn taught Eddie and his other brothers to read and notate music. Joe Jr. also served as musical director for Teddy Roosevelt's Rough Riders Cavalry Band during World War I. Joe Jr., with his brothers Eddie, Earl, and Roosevelt, formed the Durham Brothers Orchestra in the early 1920s. The brothers were occasionally accompanied by their sister Myrtle, a pianist. Their cousins Allen and Clyde Durham later joined them.[21]

According to his own account, Eddie began as a professional musician at  age ten; at eighteen he was with the 101 Ranch Brass Band playing for circuses in the Southwest and traveling as far as New York City, where he performed in Yankee Stadium. In 1926 he joined a jazz group and toured the Southwest before joining the Blue Devils, who were based in Oklahoma City, in 1928. He then played with Benny Moten out of Kansas City from about 1929 to 1933. He moved to New York in

Eddie Durham

1934.[22]

Eddie Durham's early training in music theory led to his work during the 1930s and 1940s as a jazz composer–arranger for four important bands from Oklahoma, Missouri, and Tennessee: the Blue Devils, Bennie Moten, Count Basie, and Jimmie Lunceford. The tunes he composed or arranged for these bands include such classics as "Moten Swing," "Swinging the Blues," "Topsy," "John's Idea," "Time Out," "Out the Window," "Every Tub," "Sent for You Yesterday," "One O'Clock Jump," "Jumpin' at the Woodside," "Lunceford Special," "Harlem Shout," and "Pigeon Walk." In addition, he arranged music for Artie Shaw and Glenn Miller, among other white big bands of the Swing Era; he contributed to one of Miller's greatest hits, "In the Mood." He is primarily considered a key figure in working out arrangements in the famous Kansas City riff style.[23]

Eddie Durham is regarded as an influence on fellow Texan Charlie Christian, probably the most important guitarist in jazz history, who recorded electric guitar the following year. In 1938 Durham was the leader for a historic combo recording session with Lester Young, Count Basie's star tenor saxophonist. In the 1940s, he organized his own band, directed an all-girl orchestra, the International Sweethearts of Rhythm, and brought together a number of important Texas jazzmen from the Kansas City era, including Joe Keyes, Hot Lips Page, and Buster Smith. During the 1950s and 1960s he performed less but still worked as an arranger for various groups. Durham and Smith appear in conversation on a 1979 video entitled "The Last of the Blue Devils," on which Durham also plays a trombone solo. He was heralded for his non-pressure technique on the trombone. In England, albums were released under Eddie Durham's name in 1974 and 1981; on the latter he can be heard in impressive form at age seventy-five, in particular on "Honeysuckle Rose," where he plays single string guitar solos in the southwestern style. In the 1980s he toured Europe with the Harlem Blues and Jazz Band. He died in New York City on 6 March, 1987. His hometown of San Marcos declared August 19th as "Eddie Durham Day" and, in 2003, began an annual Eddie Durham Day Musical Tribute and Festival with the long-term goal to establish a Durham Family Archival Museum and Memorial Park.[24]

Major General Archer L. Durham

## Major General Archer L. Durham

Major General Archer L. Durham is the grandson of Hanzel Durham, who was born in Woodstock, a suburb of Marietta, Georgia, and came to California in the 1920s.[25] The official U. S. Air Force Website provides the following biography of General Durham:

*Major General Archer L. Durham is director of deployment, U.S. Transportation Command, MacDill Air Force Base, Fla.*

*General Durham was born in Pasadena, Calif., in 1932, where he graduated from high school. He earned a bachelor of science degree in political science from Utah State University in 1960 and a master of science degree in international affairs from The George Washington University in 1975. He completed Squadron Officer School in 1960, Air Command and Staff College in 1961, Industrial College of the Armed Forces in 1973, National War College as a distinguished graduate in 1975, the advanced management program at Columbia University, and the program for senior executives in national and international security at the John F. Kennedy School of Government, Harvard University.*

*He began his military career in January 1953 as an aviation cadet and in April 1954 received his commission and pilot wings at Laredo Air Force Base, Texas. In August 1954 he was assigned as a pilot with the 744th Troop Carrier Squadron at Charleston Air Force Base, S.C., and in October 1955 he transferred with the squadron to Kadena Air Base, Okinawa.*

*From June 1956 to June 1958 the general was assigned to the 2720th Maintenance Group, an Air Force Logistics Command unit, at Clark Air Base, Philippines, as a flight test maintenance officer. He then served with the 28th Logistics Support Squadron at Hill Air Force Base, Utah, as an aircraft commander and squadron plans and mobility officer. The squadron was redesignated as the 28th Air Transport Squadron and assigned to the Military Airlift Command in 1962.*

*In August 1963 General Durham transferred to the 162nd Support Squadron in Paris, France, where he performed duties as an airlift command post controller until the squadron was disestablished in June 1964. From July 1964 to September 1966 he was assigned to the 322nd Air Division at Chateauroux Air Station, France, as a plans officer in the Directorate of Plans and Programs.*

*Returning to the United States in October 1966, he served at Headquarters Military Airlift Command, Scott Air Force Base, Ill., as chief of the Advanced Programming and Policy Division, Office of the Deputy Chief of Staff for Plans, until December 1968. General Durham was assigned to Headquarters U.S. Air Force, Washington, D.C., in the Directorate of Plans, Office of the Deputy Chief of Staff for Plans and Operations, in January 1969. During this tour of duty, he served as a plans action officer and as assistant deputy director for plans and policy for Joint Chiefs of Staff matters. From June 1973 to June 1974 he was assigned to the 314th Air Division at Osan Air Base, South Korea, as director of plans and programs for U.S. air forces in Korea. He then returned to the United States to attend the National War College.*

*General Durham transferred to McGuire Air Force Base, N.J., in August 1975, as deputy base commander and became base commander in February 1976. He commanded the 1606th Air Base Wing, Kirtland Air Force Base, N.M., from July 1977 to February 1979, when he transferred to Dover Air Force Base, Del., as commander of the 436th Military Airlift Wing - the only all-C-5 wing in the Air Force. In February 1980 the general assumed command of the 76th Military Airlift Division, Andrews Air Force Base, Md. In February 1982 he was assigned as vice commander of the Military Traffic Management Command, Washington, D.C. General Durham became the director of plans, programs and policy, J-5, and inspector general, U.S. Readiness Command, MacDill Air Force Base, in March 1984. He was assigned as director of deployment, Joint Deployment Agency, at MacDill in April 1985. He assumed his present duties in June 1987.*

*The general is a command pilot with more than 6,000 flying hours. His military decorations and awards include the Defense Superior Service Medal, Legion of Merit with two oak leaf clusters, Meritorious Service Medal with oak leaf cluster, Air Force Commendation Medal with oak leaf cluster, Air Force Outstanding Unit Award with three oak leaf clusters, Good Conduct Medal, National Defense Service Medal with service star, Armed Forces Expeditionary Medal, Air Force Longevity Service Award Ribbon with six oak leaf clusters, Armed Forces Reserve Medal and Small Arms Expert Marksmanship Ribbon.*

*He was promoted to major general June 1, 1984, with date of rank Sept. 1, 1980.*

*He retired on July 1, 1989.*[26]

# Epilogue
## *The Durham Legacy*

The Durhams of Fairfield truly have a great legacy. So much has happened since the capture of Gobi in Africa and his enslavement in Fairfield County, South Carolina. Following his violent death, his five older sons went with their masters to DeSoto Parish, Louisiana while his pregnant widow went directly to Freestone County, Texas and gave birth to their youngest son Isaac shortly after arrival. The end of slavery in 1865 opened the way for Mary Allen Durham's five older sons to join her and Isaac in the Butler community.

Belton, Allen, Minor, Christopher, Anderson, and Isaac Durham were six outstanding brothers. Their achievements and that of several generations of descendants would make Gobi and Mary proud indeed!

The Durhams of Fairfield continue to make their mark. The Durham name is well known in Freestone County, but especially in the Butler community. Durhams with roots in Butler are now scattered throughout the United States, involved in many businesses and professions and contributing much to their communities and to the world as a whole.

Circumstantial evidence indicates the existence of a distant relationship between the Durhams who came to Texas and the African Americans with the same surname who remain in Louisiana and South Carolina. The remote possibility of a connection with the "Other Durhams" discussed in this book needs to be explored. There can be no doubt that members of this outstanding family to whom the writer is related by marriage will always make their mark. It is my prayer that this book will inspire the present generation and generations to come to do all they can to preserve the Durham legacy.

# *Notes*
## Chapter I

1. Ouida Watter Nelson and Edward Kenneth Nelson, *The Nelsons and Scotts of DeSoto Parish, Louisiana and Related Families (Shreveport, La., 1969), iv-v.*

2. As early as 1777, the settlement was known as "Winnsborough." The town was named for Richard Winn, who was born in Fauquier County, Va., in 1750 and moved to Fairfield County in 1768. Winn served as a clerk in a counting house; engaged in cotton buying and other mercantile pursuits, and worked as a land surveyor. He entered the Revolutionary Army as a lieutenant and attained the rank of colonel of State militia. After the war, he was promoted to the rank of major general of militia. He held a number of offices, including member of the State assembly, 1779-1786; superintendent of Indian affairs for the Creek Nation in 1788; member of Congress from March 4, 1793 to March 3, 1797 and again from January 24, 1803, to March 3, 1813. He moved to Tennessee in 1813, becoming a planter and continuing in the mercantile business until his death on his plantation at Duck River, Maury County, Tennessee on December 19, 1818. He is buried in Winnsboro; see ioguide.congress. gov/scripts/biodisplay.pl?index=W000637, 1.

3. "Fairfield County, SC--History,"http.www.fairfieldsc.com/secondary.aspx?pageID=176, 1. According to Dr. J. Chapman Milling, South Carolina physician and historian: "The country east of the Santee River was the early home of the Catawba and their allied tribes, including Wateree, Caongaree, Peedee, Sara or Cheraw, Santee, Waccamaw, Winyah, Kadapau, Sugaree, and in North Carolina the Eno, Shakoree, KIeyauwee, Saxapahaw, Cape Fear and others"; see Fitz Hugh McMaster, *History of Fairfield County, South Carolina, From "Before the White Man Came" to 1942 (Spartanburg, S. C., 2003),* 5.

4. Ibid. The name was probably was probably inspired by the words of Isaiah 61:1-3: "The Spirit of the Lord God is upon me; because the Lord hath anointed me to preach good tidings unto the meek; he hath sent me to bind up the brokenhearted, to proclaim liberty to the captives, and the opening of the prison to them that are bound; To proclaim the acceptable year of the Lord, and the day of vengeance of our God; to comfort all that mourn; To appoint unto them that mourn in Zion, to give unto them beauty for ashes, the oil of joy for mourning, the garment of praise for the spirit of heaviness; that they might be called trees of righteousness, the planting of the Lord, that he might be glorified," see ibid., 96.

5. Ibid., 62. William Porcher DuBose (11 April 1836-18 August 1918) served as a Confederate chaplain and spent most of his career as a professor at the University of the South in Sewanee, Tennessee. He is remembered on 18 August on the Episcopal Calendar of Lesser Feasts and Fasts. He had a vested belief in the Confederacy as the bearer of the Spirit in history. His faith was transformed by the Confederate defeat into devotion to the church as the extension of the Incarnation (God's becoming man in Jesus Christ) in history. Reportedly: "Between the ages of seventy and eighty, the old theologian who had spent forty years teaching in the mountains of east Tennessee, reached out in five new books, in an important series of articles, and through the growing influence of his students, to make his southern theology available to the nation and the world," see Ralph E. Luker, "William Porcher DuBose and a Southern Theological Tradition, 1840-1920," in Samuel S. Hill, ed., *Varieties of Southern Religious Experience* (Baton Rouge, La.: Louisiana State University Press, 1988), 162-63. In March 1913, *The Constructive Quarterly* was established as an international ecumenical journal. The editorial board included DuBose, Archbishop of Canterbury William Temple, Swedish Lutheran Bishop Nathan Soderblom, and Baptist theologian and Social Gospel advocate Shailer Matthews; see ibid., 166.

6. Ibid., 62.

7. Ibid., 65-66.

8. Ruth M. Stevenson. Letter to author. 3 January 1984. Mrs. Stevenson, a staff member at the Fairfield County Museum in Winnsboro, also wrote: "We know of no connection with the Texas Fairfield. We do know that many of our ancestors went to Texas, Mississippi, and Louisiana."

9. According to the record of Mills Statistics (1826), p. 537: "By the County Court Act (the work of the late Judge Pendleton, the upper country was divided into counties. At that division, the name of Fairfield was given to this section of country in all probability it owes its name to the author of that act," see The News and Herald. 11 July 1935.

10. Fairfield County, SC--History,"http.www.fairfieldsc.com/secondary.aspx?pageID=176, 1.

11. McMaster, *History of Fairfield County, South Carolina*, 78-79.

12. Ibid., 127-33.

13 Fairfield County, SC--History,"http.www.fairfieldsc.com/secondary.aspx?pageID=176, 1.

14. McMaster, *History of Fairfield County, South Carolina*, 157.

15. Ibid.

16. McMaster, *History of Fairfield County, South Carolina*, 81-83.

17. Ibid.

18. McMaster, *History of Fairfield County, South Carolina*, 47-49.

19. Ibid., 51. It has been estimated that, as a result of emancipation, a Fairfield County planter might have lost 75% of his accumulated wealth in 1865; see John I. Sanders, "The Significance of Mr. Will Durham and His Country Store" (Winnsboro, S. C., 2007), 3.

20. Ibid.,45.

21. "Winnsboro Cotton Mill Blues," http://labornotes.org/2011/01/winnsboro-cotton-mill-blues, 1-2.

22. Fairfield County, SC--History,"http.www.fairfieldsc.com/secondary.aspx?pageID=176, 2.

23. Ibid.

24. McMaster, *History of Fairfield County, South Carolina*, 28.

25. Ibid., 36.

26. Tom Blake,"Fairfield County, South Carolina: Largest Slaveholders from 1860 Census Schedules and Surname Matches for African Americans on 1870 Census," http://freepages.genealogy.rootsweb. ancestry.com/-ajac/scfairfiled.htm, 2.

27. McMaster, *History of Fairfield County, South Carolina*, 38.

28. Ibid., 39.

29. Blake,"Fairfield County, South Carolina: Largest Slaveholders from 1860 Census Schedules and Surname Matches for African Americans on 1870 Census," 2.

30. Emilia Gay Griffith Means and Liz Chrysler, *Images of America: DeSoto Parish* (Charleston, S. C.: Arcadia Publishing, 2011), 7-10. Society Hill, South Carolina is located in Darlington County, two counties east of Fairfield County.

31. Judy Baugh, "Mansfield Female College," http://www.countygenweb.com/DeSotoParishLA/mansfield_female_college.htm., 2.

32. Sally Moss Bannerman, "Reminiscing About the First Commencement of the Mansfield Female College, http://www.countygenweb.com/DeSotoParishLA/commencement.htm, 2-3. This cornerstone was probably laid by DeSoto Lodge #55, which was chartered by the Grand Lodge of Louisiana, F.&A.M., in 1847. Dr. Thweatt, the first president of Mansfield Female College was a member of this lodge; see "Masonry in Mansfield, DeSoto Plume 1:1(February 1966): 109-10. Today, Mansfield Lodge #250 operates in Mansfield. There is also Star Light Lodge #111, F.&A.M. (Prince Hall

Affiliation) whose membership is predominately black. The author stopped by the latter lodge hall during his visit to Mansfield on 11 March 2013. For more information about the grand lodge under which Star Light operates, see Joseph A. Walkes, Jr., *Jno. G. Lewis, Jr.—End of an Era: The History of the Prince Hall Grand Lodge of Louisiana, 1842-1979* (Baton Rouge, La., 1986)

33. Baugh, "Mansfield Female College," 2.

34. Ibid. A legend developed about the ghost of "Old Peg-leg," a Confederate soldier whose leg was amputated and who later died at the college during its time as a military hospital; and who returned to the college on a certain night of each year in search of his missing leg.

35. Michael Stotts, "History of the Mansfield Female College: The Oldest Female College West of the Mississippi River, 1855-1930."

36. "Mansfield Female College Museum," http://cityofmansfield.net/photo_gallery/mansfield_female_college_museum.html.

37. Ibid. The author conducted research at this museum on 11 March 2013.

38. Nathaniel P. Banks (30 January 1816-1 September 1894), former governor of Massachusetts, was appointed as one of the first major generals of the volunteers by President Abraham Lincoln. During the 1862 Peninsula Campaign the two divisions under the command of Banks were assigned the task of preventing Confederate commander, Thomas "Stonewall" Jackson, from reinforcing the defenses of Richmond, Virginia. Banks and his men were unsuccessful. On 25 May 1862, Banks lost the Battle of First Winchester to the Jackson Brigade. On 9 August, Banks met Jackson for a second time in the Shenandoah Valley at the Battle of Cedar Creek. Both sides claimed victory in this battle, but there was no real outcome. In December 1862, Banks traveled to New Orleans, Louisiana to command the Department of the Gulf. From New Orleans, he traveled up the Mississippi and, on 27 May 1863, he began to attack Port Hudson, Louisiana. This was the first time that African American troops participated in a Civil War battle. The 1st and 3rd Louisiana Native Guard fought under the Banks' command suffering numerous casualties. After an unsuccessful first attempt the Union troops attacked again on 14 June 1863. This too ended unsuccessfully. However, Banks was determined to break through because of the need to join General Ulysses S. Grant's siege on Vicksburg, Mississippi. The initial attacks had now progressed into a siege with strong artillery bombardment. On 9 July 1863 the Confederate forces surrendered, having run out of supplies and receiving word that Vicksburg had also surrendered. During the Red River Campaign of 1864, he was ordered to capture Mobile, Alabama. However, he never made it to Mobile. Following his loss at the Battle of Mansfield, he and his men were forced to retreat. Arriving in Alexandria, Louisiana, Banks' army attempted to continue their retreat on Dixon Porter's fleet. With water levels low in the channel, the men were forced to build dams under heavy fire. In two days the dams were completed raising the water level high enough to continue the retreat. With the Confederates holding the Red River until after General Robert E. Lee's surrender in 1865, the Red River Campaign was considered a failure. Following the Red River Campaign, Banks was removed from command and sent back to Washington, DC on leave for the remainder of the war; see www.civilwar.org/.../biographies/nathaniel-banks.html. General Banks was a Freemason, holding membership in Monitor Lodge in Massachusetts; see Allen E. Roberts, *House Undivided: The Story of Freemasonry and the Civil War* (Richmond, Va.: Macoy Publishing & Masonic Supply Co., Inc., 1990), 333.

39. General Taylor

40. "The Old Val Verde Cannon," http://www.fairfieldtx.com/cannon.html, 1-2. Richard Strother Taylor (27 January 1826 – 12 April 1879) was the son of United States President Zachary Taylor. His sister Sarah Knox Taylor was the first wife of Confederate President Jefferson Davis. His victories at Mansfield and Pleasant Hill received the thanks of the Confederate Congress and a promotion to Lieutenant General. After the war, he wrote his memoirs, *Destruction and Reconstruction*, which is one of the most credited reports of the Civil War. He was active in Democratic Party politics, interceded on behalf of Jefferson Davis with President Andrew Johnson, and was a leading political

opponent of Northern Reconstruction policies. He died in New York City and is buried in Metairie Cemetery, New Orleans. Lt. General Richard Taylor Camp #1308, Sons of Confederate Veterans in Shreveport, Louisiana, is named for General Taylor. The camp was chartered in 1971; see "Richard Taylor: Confederate General," http://www.civilwarreference.com/people/index.php?peopleID=1199. In *House Undivided*, Masonic historian Allen E. Roberts listed no Masonic membership for General Taylor. The librarian at the Grand Lodge of the State of Louisiana, F.&A.M., searched the records and concluded that he was never a member of any Louisiana lodge; see Andi Grindle. Telephone conversation with author. 3 April 2014. The librarian of the Grand Lodge of Mississippi, F.&A.M., searched the records and had similar results; see Mickey McMahan. Telephone conversation with author. 12 November 2014. Nevertheless, while a student at Yale University, Gen. Taylorwas reportedly a member of the Skulls and Bones Society.

41. Means and Chrysler, *Images of America: DeSoto Parish*, 9.

42. Irbie Palmer Lawrence, "John Franklin Durham (II): Courier for Battle of Mansfield in Nelson and Nelson, eds. *The Nelsons and Scotts of DeSoto Parish, Louisiana and Related Families*, 171.

43. Donald Smith Durham. Interview by author. 15 September 2001.

44. Means and Chrysler, *Images of America: DeSoto Parish*, 9. In 2000, the population of Pleasant Hill was 786. Pleasant Hill was the bloodiest battle of the Civil War west of the Mississippi River. Every April, a reenactment of the battle is held. It is one of the few reenactments staged at the actual battlefield of the engagement. see http://www.battleofpleasanthill.com/default.asp, 1. Pleasant Hill is the birthplace and burial site of the legendary Shreveport minister D. L. Dykes, Jr., who served as pastor of the First United Methodist Church there from 1955 to 1984. Dykes was a pioneer of television ministry and a voice for racial harmony during the civil rights movement; see "About D. L. Dykes, Jr." *D. L. Dykes Jr. Foundation for Faith and Reason*, http://faithandreason.org/index.php/about.

45. Means and Chrysler, *Images of America: DeSoto Parish*, 9.

46. Eric J. Brock, "Honoring a Black Man Who Offered His Services to the Confederate Army: Levy S. Carnine is Remembered Today as a Civil War 'Hero,'" *Shreveport Journal*, www.countygenweb.com/.../carnine.htm, 1-2.

47. Ibid., 3.

48. "The Old Val Verde Cannon," http://www.fairfieldtx.com/cannon.html, 1-2.

49. "Val Verde Cannon, FHS Band to Mansfield," *Fairfield Recorder*, 2 April 1964, 1. No member of the Durham family or any other African American family was then part of the Fairfield High School Band. Fairfield Independent School District, like many other districts, was slow in implementing school desegregation, as required by *Brown v. Board of Education of Topeka* (1954). The high school grades were integrated during the 1968-69 school year. The elementary and junior high grades were integrated during the 1969-70 school year. The students, faculty, and administration of the Butler Independent School District was absorbed into the Fairfield district on 1 June 1971. By the beginning of the 1971-72 school year, school desegregation was complete throughout Freestone county; see Tom Cameron, "The Integration of the Fairfield Independent School District, *History of Freestone County*, vol. II (Fairfield, Tx.: Freestone County Historical Commission, 1989), 25-27.

50. Ibid., 2.

51. Robert L. Uzzel, "Battle of Mansfield Remembered," *Ennis Daily News*, 11 May 2014, 8.

52. John Leffler, *Freestone County Online, Handbook of Texas Online* (http://www.tshaonline.org/handbook/online/articles/hcf09) , 1.

53. Ibid., 2. Freestone County derives its name from indigenous stone found here. No one is sure of the source of the name "Fairfield." It was reported that the town was named for Fairfield, Alabama. This, however, is not possible because the latter was not founded until 1910, when the featured speaker at the dedication ceremony was former President Theodore Roosevelt. It was originally named Corey, after an executive of U. S. Steel Corporation. The name was later changed to the city in which the

president of U. S. Steel lived, Fairfield, Connecticut. It was planned as a model city by the Tennessee Coal, Iron and Railroad Company to house workers in their new Fairfield Works plant, now owned by U.S. Steel similar to its northeastern city of Ensley; see http://www.citytowninfo.com/places/alabama/fairfield.

54. Philip Dale Browne, "Material Prosperity and Slavery," in *History of Freestone County, Texas Vol. 1* (Fairfield, Tx.: Freestone County Historical Commission, 1978), 14.

55. Leffler, *Freestone County Online*, 2-3.

56. Philip Dale Browne was born on 22 December 1899 in Fairfield. He graduated from Fairfield High School in 1916. He received a Bachelor of Arts in Mathematics, with a minor in Spanish, from Baylor University in 1921. He received a Master of Arts in History, with a minor in Educational Administration, from the University of Texas at Austin in 1925. His M. A. thesis was on "The Early History of Freestone County to 1865." He served as principal of Teague High School from 1921 to 1922, principal of Crystal City High School from 1922 to 1924, and superintendent of Fairfield Independent School District from 1925 to 1943. Moving to Waco in 1943, he spent the rest of his life there, serving as associate professor of math and religion at Baylor from 1925 to 1943 and from 1951 to 1971 and as director of the Baylor Retired Professors Center from 1973 to 1978. He was education director and finance officer at Seventh and James Baptist Church from 1944 to 1951. He died in Waco in April 1991. He recalled: "Mine was the bittersweet heritage of vocalized memories of the Old South by its surviving soldiers growing old. Tales told by aging whites and blacks of the days before and during the War Between the States so captured my childhood that, in manhood, I have not regarded the future with hope but have remembered the past with gratitude"; see "Freestone County Historian Dies," *Fairfield Recorder*, 11 April 1991, 1A.

57. Philip Dale Browne, "Social Conditions Before the War of Secession: Pioneer Life," in *History of Freestone County, Texas* 16.

58. Browne, "Material Prosperity and Slavery," 15.

59. Leffler, "Freestone County Online," 3. Early settlers who were Masons petitioned for a Masonic Lodge in Fairfield on 15 July 1851. For a detailed discussion of the contributions of the members of Fairfield Lodge #103, Ancient Free and Accepted Masons, to education in Freestone County, see James David Carter, *Education and Masonry in Texas*, 1846 to 1861 (Waco, Tx.: Committee on Masonic Education and Service for the Grand Lodge of Texas, A.F.&A.M., 1962), 324-31. During the 1850s, Eudora Lodge #43, Independent Order of Odd Fellows was organized in Fairfield. It is quite likely that there was overlapping in membership between the two lodges. In May 1855, while the district court was in session, the Odd Fellows sponsored a social event in which many members and visiting brethren made a full procession from the lodge room to a church, where the lodge's first anniversary was celebrated. That night, a ball was held at the Masonic hall "for the enjoyment of members, visitors, and ladies." Over fifty ladies and more men were present. The dancing continued into the next morning when "All went home in peace and harmony" see Browne, "Social Conditions Before the War of Secession," 15. One may assume that African Americans present were there to provide music or serve refreshments and were not members of either lodge. After the Civil War, a number of black Masonic lodges were established in Freestone County and some continue to operate today. Some are chartered by the Fort Worth-based Prince Hall Grand Lodge of Texas, F.&A.M. and others by the Austin-based Saint Joseph Grand Lodge of Texas, A.F.&A.M. At this writing, neither organization has inter-visitation rights with the predominately white Grand Lodge of Texas.

60. Browne, "Material Prosperity and Slavery," 14-15.

61. Philip Dale Browne, "The War of Secession: Military Forces," in *History of Freestone County, Texas*, 51.

62. Michael Edd Bonner, "Freestone County in the Civil War," in ibid., 38.

63. Ibid.

64. P. D. Browne, "Reconstruction after the Civil War," 51.

65. Ibid.

66. Ibid., 51-52.

67. Ibid.

68. Ibid., 3-4.

69. Ibid., 4.

70. Ibid.

71. Helen Franklin Starnes, "Butler," *History of Freestone County, Texas*, 90. Butler County, Alabama was named for Captain William Butler of the Georgia Militia who was killed in an Indian raid in 1819.

72. Ibid., 91.

73. Ibid. George Washington Baines was born on 29 December 1809 near Raleigh, North Carolina. He moved with his family to a farm near Tuscaloosa, Alabama, in 1818 and lived in Arkansas and Louisiana before moving to Texas in 1850. He held pastorates in Huntsville, Independence, Anderson, Fairfield, Springfield, Florence, and Salado as well as Butler. He served as president of Baylor University at Independence from 1861 to 1862. When he left Baylor, he moved to a farm near Fairfield, where he remained until 1867. He died in Belton on 28 December 1882 and was buried in Salado; see Travis L. Summerlin, "Baines, George Washington, Sr.," *Handbook of Texas Online* (http://www.tshaonline.org/handbook/online/articles/fba14), 1-2. His son Joseph Wilson Baines was the father of Rebekah Baines, who married Samuel Ealy Johnson, Jr. To this union was born Lyndon Baines Johnson; see Judith N. McArthur, "Johnson, Rebekah Baines," Handbook of Texas Online (http://www.tshaonline.org/handbook/online/articles/tj022, 1.

74. Starnes, "Butler," History of Freestone County, Texas, 90. The writer speculates that the "music of the fiddle and the bow" was provided by slaves, perhaps by some members of the Durham family. Slaves may have also served refreshments at such events. Sadly, however, blacks were seldom direct participants in such social events in the Old South.

75. Ibid. During the war, Hillary Manning made arrangements to sell his plantation to a physician named Gibbs, expecting to receive payment in gold. As the southern cause became increasingly hopeless, Dr. Gibbs made full payment in Confederate currency which was legal tender but virtually worthless, leaving Manning destitute; see J. R. Sessions, Jr., "Alderman's Store Cotton Gin," *Freestone County Times*, 2 September 2003, 7-B. The many black Mannings in the Butler community today are probably descended from Hillary Manning's slaves. Dr. Gibbs settled in Mexia, where the Gibbs Library is named for him. His daughter Mary Gibbs married Houston financier Jesse H. Jones, who eventually became the owner of the *Houston Chronicle* and one of the most powerful men in America during the administration of President Franklin D. Roosevelt, who gave him a number of important appointments, including Secretary of Commerce; see Lionel V. Patenaude, "Jones, Jesse Holman," *Handbook of Texas Online* (http://www.tshaonline.org/handbook/online/articles/fjo53), 1.

76. Starnes, "Butler," History of Freestone County, Texas, 90.

77. Ibid., 92.

78. Robert L. Uzzel, *Blind Lemon Jefferson*. The writer met K. M. Williams for the first time on 8 September 2001 when he was performing at the Wortham Blues Festival. Three days later, terrorist attacks occurred in New York and Washington, D. C. Williams expressed it well when he said "The whole country has the blues." Since 2008, they have worked together at Wayman Chapel AME Church in Ennis, Texas; see www.reverbnation.com/kmwilliams.

## Chapter 2

1. Military Records, Bureau of Pensions--V.L.M.--9418. Per John Crowe and Faye Woodard. Dutchman's Creek was located along the Wateree River, where African American Durhams continue to reside today.

2. Captain Charnel Durham (1753-1836), http://freepages.genealogy.rootsweb.ancestry.com/-donny-krun/Durham, 2.

3. "Genealogical Outline of Durham," in Nelson and Nelson, *The Nelsons and Scotts of DeSoto Parish,* Louisiana, 173.

4. Captain Charnel Durham (1753-1836), http://freepages.genealogy.rootsweb.ancestry.com/-donny-krun/Durham, 5-6.

5. Ibid. Winfield Echols Durham was a close relative of General Winfield Scott, who served in both the Mexican War and the Civil War and was the Whig Presidential nominee in 1852; see ibid., 6-7.

6. Molsey Eliza Ross was the daughter of Abner Ross and Mary Whitaker, both of who are buried on the Durham Cotton Plantation in Fairfield County.

7. "Robert Winfield Durham," http://stith.packent.com/ged2/d0000/g0000039.html, 1.
This grave is located seven miles southeast of Winnsboro, one half mile off the road, near a highway extending from Columbia, South Carolina and Charlotte, North Carolina. James Michael Durham. Interview by author. 16 September 2001.

8. Nelson and Nelson, *The Nelsons and Scotts of DeSoto Parish, Louisiana,* 168.

9. *Biographical and Historical Memoirs of Northwest Louisiana* (Nashville, Tenn.: Southern Publishing Co., 1890), 236; submitted by Gaytha Carver Thompson; typed by Trudy Marlow; http:files.usgwar-chives.net/la/Desoto,taxlists/slaves.txt.

10. Nelson and Nelson, *The Nelsons and Scotts of DeSoto Parish, Louisiana,* 168.

11. Ibid. Over 100 years later, Lowndes County, Alabama would play a role in the Civil Rights Movement. Early in 1966, African Americans in rural Lowndes County, aided by activists from the Student Non-Violent Coordinating Committee (SNCC), established an all-black, independent political party called the Lowndes County Freedom Organization (LCFO). The group was formed in part to protest the barriers to black enfranchisement that had for decades kept every single African American of voting age off the county's registration books. Even after the passage of the Voting Rights Act of 1965, most African Americans in this overwhelmingly black county remained too scared even to try to register. Their fear stemmed from the county's long, bloody history of whites retaliating against blacks who strove to exert the freedom granted to them after the Civil War; see Hasan Kwame Jeffries, *Bloody Lowndes: Civil Rights and Black Power in Alabama's Black Belt* (New York: New York University Press, 2010).

12. Ibid., 6.

13. Ibid.

14. Ibid.

15. Ibid.

16. *DeSoto Parish Conveyance Records,* J:232.

17. *Biographical and Historical Memoirs of Northwest Louisiana,* 236.

18. Ibid., M:4.

19. *Nelson and Nelson, The Nelsons and Scotts of DeSoto Parish, Louisiana,* 174.

20. Ibid., 179.

21. *Nelson and Nelson, The Nelsons and Scotts of DeSoto Parish, Louisiana,* 179.

22. *DeSoto Parish Conveyance Records,* I:257.

23. *Biographical and Historical Memoirs of Northwest Louisiana,* 236.

24. *Nelson and Nelson, The Nelsons and Scotts of DeSoto Parish, Louisiana,* 179.

25. Ibid.

26. *Biographical and Historical Memoirs of Northwest Louisiana,* 236.

27. Donald Smith Durham. Letter to author. 24 February 1983.

28. *Records of Louisiana Confederate Soldiers and Commands* (Baton Rouge, La.; La Commission of Military Records), 1.

29. James Michael Durham. Interview by author. 16 September 2001.

30. Nelson and Nelson, *The Nelsons and Scotts of DeSoto Parish, Louisiana,* 139.

31. Ibid., 140. It is interesting to note that this wedding took place five hours late and there were two reasons for the delay. First, Rev. Hickson, the minister who conducted the ceremony, came from Shreveport and his train was late in arriving at Kingston. Also, when the marriage license was mailed from Mansfield, it was mistakenly addressed to Mitchell Judson Scott instead of Mitchell Judson Durham. Postmaster R. E. Scott refused to release this registered mail to the latter until the former returned from a hunting trip and confirmed that it did not belong to him.

32. Ibid., 141.

33. "Judson Burney Durham (1910-1993)—Find a Grave Memorial," http:www.findagrave.com/cgi-bin/fg.cgi?page=gr&GRid=88385879.

34. "Edith Eloise Whittington Durham (1910-2001)—Find a Grave Memorial," http:www.findagrave.com/cgi-bin/fg.cgi?page=gr&GRid=88385755.

35. James Michael Durham. Interview by author. 16 September 2001.

36. "Col. James Michael Durham," http://www.arlingtoncemetery.net/jmdurham.htm. Submitted by His Son, David B. Durham, Commander, United States Navy, January 2007.

37. "Obituary: Robert Scott Durham," *Fort Worth Star-Telegram,* 3 March 2013.

38. Thomas Whittington Durham. Interview by author. 11 March 2013.

39. Donald Smith Durham. Interview by author. 16 September 2001. When the writer first talked with Donald Durham in 1983, he was working at the Pentagon. After the terrorist attacks on the Pentagon on 11 September 2001, the writer contacted the retired colonel, saying "Thank God you are no longer at the Pentagon." Don told him that the scenes on television gave the impression that his former office was being hit.

40. "Obituary: Donald Smith Durham," *Kansas City Star,* 19 February 2006 http://www.legacy.com/obituaries/kansascity/obituary.aspx?pid=16759047#fbLoggedOut#storylink=cpy.

# Chapter 3

1. Lutie McNulty Durham, "Major William Strother Durham" http://freepages.genealogy.rootsweb.ancestry.com/--donnykrun/Durham.

2. "Corporal William Shedd Durham," http://freepages.genealogy.rootsweb.ancestry.com/--donnykrun/Durham.

3. *Fairfield County Cemeteries: Volume I: Church Cemeteries in the Western Section of the County* (Winnsboro, S. C., 2006), 8.

4. *Fairfield County Cemeteries, Vol. IV: Cemeteries in Adjacent Counties,* 17, 108.

5. John I. Sanders, "The Significance of Mr. Will Durham and His Country Store," 2-3.

6. U. S. Census (1870), per Heritage Quest Online.

7. U. S. Census (1880), per Heritage Quest Online.

8. U. S. Census (1900), per Heritage Quest Online. Due to a fire in Washington, D. C., much of the 1890 U. S. Census was destroyed and, thus, is not available.

9. U. S. Census (1910), per Heritage Quest Online.

10. U. S. Census (1920), per Heritage Quest Online.

11. "Durham," 1930 United States Federal Census—Ancestry.com. http://search.ancestry.com/cgi-bin/sse.dll?db=1930usfedcen&rank=1.

12. W. C. Durham. Letter to author. 14 April 1980.

13. Clara Durham. Interview by author. 6 May 1980. During my visit to Fairfield County on 23 August 2012, I learned that "Back Water" referred to the Lake Wateree area where many Durhams once lived.

14. Funeral program for Clara Durham.

15. Katherine Durham Pope. Interview by author. 23 August 2012.

16. Boykin Durham. Interview by author. 23 August 2012. Boykin, South Carolina is located in Kershaw County, which adjoins Fairfield County. It was named for the William Boykin family who settled the town in 1755. The Civil War officially ended with General Robert E. Lee's surrender to General Ulysses S. Grant at Appomatox Courthouse on 9 April 1865, but word traveled slowly. Union General Edward Potter was still raiding South Carolina for days thereafter. On 19 April, his troops engaged with Confederate regulars at Boykin's Mill. The outnumbered South Carolina troops were only able to slow the raiders by one day. Lieutenant Stevens of the 54th Massachusetts, killed in this battle, was the last known Federal officer to die in the Civil War. Fifteen-year-old Burwell Boykin, a volunteer with the South Carolina Home Guard and a descendent of Boykin's founder, was among those who defended his home that day; see "Boykin, South Carolina," http://www.sciway.net/city/boykin.html. Descendants of William Boykin included Mary Whitaker Boykin, the mother of Mary Boykin Miller, who married Confederate General James Chesnut, III and was the author of a journal entitled *Diary from Dixie*; see C. Vann Woodward, *Mary Chesnut's Civil War* (New Haven, Ct.: Yale University Press, 1993). Boykin Witherspoon was a planter who came overland from South Carolina and established Buena Vista Plantation in DeSoto Parish, Louisiana in 1854; see Means and Chrysler, *Images of America: DeSoto Parish*, 62.

17. *White Oak Baptist Cemetery Records.*

18. The writer is grateful to Johnny Harrison, Jr. and his uncle Tom Harrison (owner of a store in the Wateree area) for pointing out the Durham-Harrison connection and for helping him locate people and places relevant to this research; see Kevin Boozer, "Historian Connects with Locals," *Herald Independent*, 21 August 2012, http://heraldindependent.com/bookmark/19941692/article-Historian+-connects+with+locals.

19. Funeral program for William B. Durham.

20. Funeral program for Willie Mae Adams Durham.

21. Funeral program for Elie M. Durham.

22. : Funeral program for Herman "Slicks" Durham.

## Chapter 4

1. U. S. Census (1870), per Heritage Quest Online. http://persi.heritagequestonlin.com/hquoweb/library/do/census/results/hitlist?surname=Dur...References to Durhams born in Alabama more than likely indicates a connection with Capt. Osman L. Durham, who lived in Lowndes County, Alabama from 1839 until the late 1840s.

2. U. S. Census (1880), per Heritage Quest Online. http://persi.heritagequestonlin.com/hquoweb/library/do/census/results/hitlist?surname=Dur...

3. U. S. Census (1900), per Heritage Quest Online. http://persi.heritagequestonlin.com/hquoweb/library/do/census/results/hitlist?surname=Dur...

4. U. S. Census (1910), per Heritage Quest Online. http://persi.heritagequestonlin.com/hquoweb/library/do/census/results/hitlist?surname=Dur...

5. U. S. Census (1940)—Ancestry.com.http://search.ancestry.com/cgi-bin/sse.dll?indiv=1&db=1940usbedcen&rank=1&new=1&....

## Chapter 5

1. Mary Durham. Interview by author. 3 November 1978.

2. Mary Edwards. Interview by author. 3 November 1978.

3. Johnny Johnson, Jr. Interview by author. 20 August 1983.

4. Richard Durham, Jr. "The Durham Family Genealogy," 10 December 1999. This unpublished paper was written for a class in American History at Navarro College in Corsicana, Texas. The writer was the instructor of this class.

## Chapter 6

1. Mary O. Edwards. Interview by author. 3 November 1978.

2. "Texas Death Index, 1903-2000," Belton Durham, 1927. Certificate #62. https://familysearch.org/pal:/MM9.1.1/VZDK-L63

3. Mary O. Edwards. Interview by author. 3 November 1978.

4. Ibid.

5. Funeral program for General Beve Durham.

6. Mary Nelson Durham. Interview by author. 3 November 1978. Today, this congregation is called Rolling Hills Church of God in Christ and is located on Berry and Riverside in Fort Worth. Mary Durham died on 17 December 2008, in her 98th year. Her funeral was held at Greater Progressive Church of God in Christ in Fort Worth, followed by interment in Cedar Hill Memorial Park in Kennedale, Texas; see "Obituary: Mary Durham," *Fort Worth Star Telegram*, 21 December 2008.

7. Funeral program of Bealer Johnson.

8. "Obituary: Bib Durham." *Fairfield Recorder*, 29 April 1993, 4B.

9. Funeral program of Mary O. Edwards.

## Chapter 7

1. U. S. Census, 1880.

2. Eddie Marie Jones Durham, *Mama, 'Babe' and Me* (Bloomington, In.: Trafford Publishing, 2011 ), 65.

3. Eddie Marie Jones Durham. Letter to author. 6 November 1978.

4. Archie D. Durham, "Allen Durham," in *History of Freestone County, Texas, vol. 1* (Fairfield, Texas: Freestone County historical Commission, 1978), 349.

5. Eddie Marie Jones Durham, *Mama, 'Babe' and Me*, 65.

6. Eddie Marie Durham, "Rance Durham" in *History of Freestone County*. Pine Top Methodist Church was located next to Loan Star Cemetery. Union United Methodist Church is location on Interstate Highway 84 in Butler. Highway 84 goes directly from Fairfield, Texas to Mansfield, Louisiana.

7. *Marriage Records of Freestone County, Texas*. Freestone County Courthouse, Fairfield, Texas.

8. Eddie Marie Durham, "Rance Durham," in *History of Freestone County, Texas, vol. 1* (Fairfield, Texas: Freestone County historical Commission, 1978), 349.

9. Eddie Marie Durham, "Rance Durham." At that time, most African American voters were Republicans. After the Civil War, the Republican Party was identified with Abraham Lincoln and the Democratic Party was identified with the South and the defeated Confederacy. During the 1930s, many were helped by the programs of the New Deal and, as a result, abandoned the party of Lincoln for the party of Franklin D. Roosevelt.

10. Ibid.

11. Ibid.

12. Katie Mae Durham Tatum. Interview by author. 20 October 2001.

13. Eddie Marie Durham, "Rance Durham."

14. Ibid.

15. Ibid.

16. Aldessa Bass. Interview by author. 17 May 2001.

17. Standard Certificate of Death for Rance Durham.

18. Eddie Marie Durham, "Rance Durham."

19. Standard Certificate of Death for Alice Durham.

20. U. S. Census (1870). Another Taylor Durham, age 21 and born in South Carolina, is also listed in this census. Heritage Quest Online, http://persi.heritagequestonline.com/hqoweb/library/do/census/results/hitlist?surname=Dur..., 1.

21. U. S. Census, 1880.

22. Archie Durham, "Allen Durham," in *History of Freestone County, vol. I* (Fairfield, Tx.: Freestone County Historical Commission, 1978).

23. Mary O. Edwards. Interview by author. 1978.

24. Genealogy records at Palestine Public Library.

25. Eddie Marie Jones Durham, *Mama, 'Babe' and Me*, 65.

26. Ibid., 66. The writer worked for the Texas Department of Public Welfare (now Health and Human Services) in Teague from December 1974 to March 1977.

27. Funeral program for Luke Durham.

28. Standard Certificate of Death of Mollie Durham.

29. Eddie Marie Jones Durham, *Mama, 'Babe' and Me*, 66.

30. Ibid., 66-67.

31. Ibid.

32. Lonzo Durham. Interview by author. 21 July 2001.

33. Katie Mae Durham Tatum. Interview by author. 20 October 2001.

34. Freestone County Marriage Records.

35. Much information regarding the descendants of Willie Anderson and Ellen Titus Durham has been obtained from the investigations of Odis Rich, a researcher on the Titus family.

36. Standard Certificate of Death for Ellen Durham.

37. Laura Woodard. Interview by author. 19 November 2012. Following Papa Bud's death, Ruby married Will Goff, who operated a store and recreation center called the Dot Inn in Corsicana. Pinkie Morgan. Interview by author. 19 November 2012. Laura Woodard was born on 15 August 1910. She was the daughter of Jim and Pinkie Willis Allen. She married Paul Looney "Jack" Keeton, who died in 1991. She later married David Woodard, who died in 1996. She attended Owens Chapel School with the children of Anderson and Ellen Titus Durham. She remembers when Katie Mae Durham Tatum was born. Pinkie Morgan is the daughter of Laura Woodard.

38. Katie Mae Durham Tatum. Interview by author. 20 October 2001.

39. Ibid.

40. Ibid.

41. Standard Certificate of Death for Willie Anderson Durham.

42. Charles James Bate, *"It's Been a Long time" (And We've Come a Long Way): A History of Oklahoma Black Medical Providers (The Black Healers)* (Muskogee, Ok.: Hoffman Printing Co., Inc., 1986), 110. Knoxville College was founded in 1875. The Knoxville College Medical Department operated from 1895 to 1900 and became Knoxville Medical College in 1900 but closed in 1910; see "Black History Month: A Medical Perspective," http://www.mclibrary.duke.edu/hot/blkhist.html, 5. The closure of the school was the result of the Flexner Report. Abraham Flexner, a native of Louisville, Kentucky and graduate of Johns Hopkins University in Baltimore, Maryland, wrote a book entitled *The American College*, which was read by Henry Pritchett, the head of the Carnegie Foundation for the Advance-

ment of Teaching. Pritchett asked Flexner to make a detailed study of American medical schools. In December 1908, Flexner began his tour of 155 medical schools; see "1910 'Flexner Report' was Turning Point for School of Medicine," http://www.vanderbilt.edu/News/register/Dec03_01/story9. html, 1-2. This report led to the closing of a number of medical schools, including five of the seven black medical colleges then in existence. Only Howard University College of Medicine and Meharry Medical College were endorsed. Chapter XIV of the report was entitled "The Medical Education of the Negro." Reportedly: "The report fixed the pattern of admission of blacks into medical school well into the 1960s largely because the report put forward an outlook about black medical education that the American Medical Association readily accepted in formulating education policy. Gains in the higher standards for their medical training were diminished by the "separate but equal" education that the report perpetuated," see "Minorities in Medicine: The Flexner Report," http://otpt.ups.edu/ SCXT310/Approach/Allopathic/FlexnerRpiort.html, 1-2. At Knoxville, Flexner found entrance requirements nominal, a teaching staff of eleven, a budget of only $1,020, and no laboratory or clinical facilities. He depicted it and a white Tennessee medical college as "utterly wretched establishments . . . (which) would be wiped out if treated on their merits. After noting that the school occupied a floor of an undertaker's establishment, Flexner described the catalogue as "a tissue of misrepresentations from cover to cover."

43. Robin Hall, Director of Licensing, Oklahoma Board of Medical Licensure. Interview by author. 24 September 2002.

44. This town, whose population was originally all black, was founded in 1903. A local celebrity is blues legend D. C. Minner, who was born in Rentiesville on the spot where his Down Home Blues Club now sits and where his family has operated a business since 1911. After playing bass for a number of blues artists, he returned home in 1988 to reopen his grandmother's Crazy Corner as Down Home Blues Club, which is being transformed into a blues museum. In 1991, he and his wife founded the annual Dusk 'til Dawn Blues Festival; see "D. C. Minner's Down Home Blues Club," http://www. dcminnerblues.com, 1.

45. Leophia Carden. Interview by author. 22 October 2002. Mrs. Carden, the niece of Pinkie Strawther Durham, lived with Dr. and Mrs. Durham during the late 1920s.

46. Mildred Burkhalter. Interview by author. 8 October 2002.

47. "Texas Deaths, 1890-1976," Travis Durham, 1933, http://familysearch.org/pal:MM9.1.1/J61N-5ZV.

48. Archie D. Durham, "Durham, Archie D." *History of Freestone County, vol. II* (Fairfield, Tx.: Freestone County Historical Commission, 1989), 217.

49. Funeral program for Archie Dennis Durham.

50. Ibid

51. Ibid.

52. "Community Improvement Awards," *Fairfield Recorder*, 21 October 1982, 4A.

53. "NAACP Holds Freedom Fund Banquet," *Fairfield Recorder*, 27 April 1995, 3B.

54. "Willa Durham Obituary," *Fairfield Recorder*, 7 July 1994, 4B.

55. *Palestine Herald Press*, 3 November 1996.

56. Eddie Marie Jones Durham, *Mama, 'Babe' and Me*, 156-57.

57. Laura Woodard. Interview by author. 19 November 2012.

58. Clara Durham McIlvene. Interview by author. 24 November 2012.

59. Funeral program for Cuny Anderson Durham. Avant Prairie is off State Highway 179 four miles southeast of Teague. Early settlers included the Kilgores, the Comptons, the Highs, and the Blains. The community was originally called Durham and was probably named for Durham Avant, who obtained a land grant in the area. In 1903, eight students were enrolled in the white school and fifty-seven students were enrolled in the black school. Avant Prairie AME Church and the adjoining cemetery

remain open today; see Chris Cravens, "Avant Prairie, Texas," The Handbook of Texas Online, http://www.tshaonline.org/handbook/online/articles/hra87, 1.

60. "Roma Durham Obituary," *Fairfield Recorder*, 6 May 1999, 6B.

61. "Clara V. Peters Obituary," *Fairfield Recorder*, 6 May 1999, 6B-10B.

62. Funeral program for Lillie Elliott Durham Garietty.

63. Funeral program for Gladys Durham Henry.

64. Ibid.

65. Ibid. The street where this museum is located, was named for John Wesley Dobbs (26 March 1882 – 30 August 1961), an African American civic and political leader, who served as Grand Master of the Prince Hall Grand Lodge of Georgia, Free and Accepted Masons, from 1932 until his death. In 1994, Houston Street was renamed in Dobb's honor by his grandson Maynard Jackson, the first African American mayor of Atlanta; see "John Wesley Dobbs (1882-1961)", http://www.amistadresearchcenter.org/archon/?p=creators/creator&id=251

66. Funeral program for Gladys Durham Henry.

67. Aldessa Bass. Interview by author. 24 November 2012.

68. "Capoleon Y. Durham Obituary," *Fairfield Recorder*, 28 January 1988, 6B.

69. "Willie Delois Durham Obituary," *Fairfield Recorder*, 16 February 1999, 6B.

70. Funeral program for Walter Titus Durham.

71. Eddie Marie Durham, "Durham, Walter Titus," *History of Freestone County, Texas*, vol. II (Fairfield, Tx.: Freestone County Historical Commission, 1989), 218.

72. Ibid.

73. Ibid.

74. "To Restate Vows." *Fairfield Recorder*, 28 March 1985, 6A.

75. Eddie Marie Durham, *Mama, 'Babe' and Me*, 120-23.

76. Ibid.

77. Katie Mae Durham Tatum. Interview by author. 20 October 2001.

78. "Obituaries: Henry Tatum." *Fairfield Recorder*, 17 April 1986, 4B.

79. Katie Mae Durham Tatum. Interview by author. 20 October 2001.

80. Ibid; see Amanda Rogers, "Stitches in Time: Quilts Pieced together with Love and Patience Help Preserver Two Centuries of a Family's History," *Fort Worth Star-Telegram*, 13 April 2002.

81. Funeral program for Katie Mae Tatum.

82. Wilbur Thirkield Titus, ed. *Who Is Who In Hunter and Titus Families: A Profile of Courage and Achievement*, vol. 1 (Fairfield, Tx.: Hunter and Titus Family Reunion, 2003), 43.

83. Ibid.

84. Funeral program of Alonzo O'Neil (Lonzo) Durham.

85. "Annual Awards Presented: Senior Citizens Honored at Luncheon," The Fairfield Recorder, 24 May 1990, 4B.

86. Titus, *Who Is Who*, 57.

87. Funeral program for Alonzo O'Neil (Lonzo) Durham.

88. Harold Glenn Durham. Interview by author. 10 August 2002.

89. "Obituaries: Willie Durham," *Waco Tribune-Herald*, 29 September 1987.

90. Clara Durham McIlvene. Interview by author. 24 November 2012.

91. Funeral program for Clyde Henry.

92. Titus, *Who Is Who*, 126.

93. Ibid.

94. Funeral program for Coleman Henry.

95. Funeral program for Richmond Henry.

96. Aldessa Bass. Interview by author. 26 August 2012.

97. Robert L. Uzzel, "Mother-in-Law Celebrates 80th Birthday," *Ennis Daily News*, 13 September 2013.

98. The hospital in Fairfield, Freestone County, Texas was previously known as Fairfield Memorial Hospital--the name still used by the hospital in Winnsboro, Fairfield County, South Carolina. During the 1990s, the former facility was leased by East Texas Medical Center; see Robert L. Uzzel, "Mother-in-Law's Retirement is Sweet." *Ennis Daily News*, 28 February 2014, 5.

99. Aldessa Bass. Interview by author. 26 August 2012.

100. Ibid.

101. Ibid.

102. Bobby Jean Durham. Interview by author. 23 November 2001. While attending Shiloh Baptist Church as a child, Eddie Jones was mistakenly addressed as "Eddie Durham." She protested: "I'm not a Durham and I wouldn't be a Durham!" Little did she know that she would one day marry a Durham; see Eddie Marie Jones Durham, *Mama, 'Babe' and Me*, 68.

103. Titus, *Who Is Who*, 104. In a conversation with the writer, Archie Durham once compared James as an entrepreneur to the legendary Rance Durham.

104. James Artis Durham. Interview by author. 11 November 2001. His marriage to Delores Butler has been described as searching until he found a sweetheart named for his birthplace; see *Who Is Who*, 104.

105. Oneida Durham Steen. Interview by author. 25 November 2001.

106. Gene Durham. Interview by author. 25 November 2001.

107. Walter Titus Durham, Jr. Interview by author. 25 November 2001.

108. LaWanda Durham Mithcell. Interview by author. 25 November 2001.

109. Jo Lander Durham Mitchell. Interview by author. 25 November 2001.

110. Titus, ed. *Who Is Who*, 6.

111. Beauford Durham. Interview by author. 4 August 2001

112. Helen Durham Robinson. Interview by author. 25 November 2001.

113. Titus, *Who Is Who*, 6. Monson's roommate at Prairie View A&M was Hubert Reece, (1948-2014), Grand Secretary of the Prince Hall Grand Lodge of Texas, Free and Accepted Masons, and a long-time friend of the writer; see Robert L. Uzzel, "Remembering Grand Secretary Reece," *Ennis Daily News*, 13 June 2014, 8.

114. Ibid., 26.

115. Ibid. Humble Oil Company was founded in 1911. The name was changed to Exxon in 1972. Exxon and Mobil announced plans for merger in 1998; see Eric V. Thompson, "A Brief History of Major Oil Companies in the Gulf Region," http://www.virginia.edu/igpr/apagoilhistory.html, 8-9.

116. Earnestine Durham Williams. Interview by author. 21 August 2002.

117. Titus, Who Is Who, 26.

118. Ibid., 27.

119. Ibid., 26.

120. Ibid.

121. Harold Glenn Durham. Interview by author. 17 January 2014.

122. http://betterwayapostolic.org/pastors-bio.

123. Shirley Givens Durham. Interview by author. 4 June 2003.

124. http://betterwayapostolic.org/first-ladys-bio.

125. Titus, *Who Is Who*, 121.

126. Gale Lynn Durham. Interview by author. 25 July 2002.

127. Harold Glenn Durham. Interview by author. 25 July 2002.

128. Freddie Oneal Brackens, Sr. Interview by author. 25 November 2000.

129. Funeral program of McLenon Lee Brackens.

130. Titus, *Who Is Who*, 111-12.

131. Ibid., 111

132. Ibid., 112.

133. Ibid.

134. bid.

135. Rogers, *Stitches in Time*.

136. Titus, *Who Is Who*, 113.

137. Ibid.

138. Ibid.

139. Ibid.

140. Robert L. Uzzel, "Pastor's Wife Marks Six Decades of Life," *Ennis Daily News*, 26 July 2013, 5.

141. Debra Uzzel. Interview by author. 3 June 2014. Richard—the writer's oldest grandson—traveled with his grandfather and took a number of the pictures used in this book. On 5 July 2014, he won the domino tournament at the Isaac Durham Reunion in Butler.

142. JoAnna Parker. Interview by author. 3 June 2014.

143. Robert L. Uzzel, "Rob Uzzel and Audrey Wise Tie the Knot in Oklahoma." *Ennis Daily News*, 29 December 2013, 4. Audrey's family has roots in Freestone County. Her grandfather, Julian Wise, is the nephew of the late Uel Davis, Jr., long-time postmaster at Wortham, the Freestone County community that was the hometown of Blind Lemon Jefferson, the subject of the writer's first book. The writer is indebted to Davis for his help in research on Wortham's only celebrity; see Uzzel, *Blind Lemon Jefferson: His Life, His Death, and His Legacy.*

144. Kenneth LaClaire Bass. Interview by author. 4 June 2014.

145. Kevin Jabar Bass. E-mail to author. 3 June 2014.

146. Kimberly Bass Brown. E-mail to author. 3 June 2014.

147. Karen Sheanell Bass Dabney Jones. E-mail to author. 3 June 2014.

148. Celia Strickland. E-mail to author. 5 June 2014.

149. Cilkay Jessie. E-mail to author. 4 June 2014.

150. Teresa Haynes. Interview by author. 2 June 2013. The family of Clyde Anthony Haynes is from Bremond, Robertson County, Texas. The writer attended a DVD release party at the Texas Slavic and German Warehouse in Bremond on 5 November 2011; see Robert L. Uzzel, "The Waltz to Westphalia." *Ennis Daily News*, 10 November 2011, 3.

151. LaCharles Bass. E-mail to author. 3 June 2014.

# Chapter 8

1. Josephine Daniels. Interview by author. 24 August 2001.

2. U. S. Census (1920). Heritage Quest Online, http:persi.heritagequestonline.com/hqoweb/library/do/census/results/hitlist? Surname=Dur..., 1.

3. U. S. Census (1880).

4. Barnes, *Our African Heritage*, 6:8.

5. "Texas Deaths, 1890-1976," Saylor Bee Durham, 1937," https://familysearch.org/pal:/MM9:1,1/ J6MC-M31. Death certificate #14750.

6. Ibid.

7. "Texas Deaths, 1890-1976," Silliman Durham, 1920, https://familysearch.org/pal/MM9.1.1/JFZ6-HYM. Death certificate #16683.

8. Barnes, *Our African Heritage*, 6:8.

9. "Texas, Death Index, 1903-2000," Henry Durham, 1937. https://family search.org/pal:/MM9.1.1VZDH-DWY. Death certificate #20703.

10. Ibid.

11. Freestone County Marriage Records.

12. Mary Edwards. Personal interview. 23 June 2001.

13. U. S. Census (1920).

14. Josephine Daniels. Interview by author. 24 August 2001.

15. Standard Certificate of Death for Minor Durham, Jr.

16. U. S. Census (1920).

17. Ibid.

18. Ibid.

19. Barnes, *Our African Heritage*, 6;3.

20. Josephine Daniels. Interview by author. 24 August 2001.

21. Alice Jarmon. Interview by author. 30 May 2014.

22. Rosa Lee Quarles. Interview by author. 25 August 2001. Josephine Daniels stated that Blind Lemon, the blues singer from Wortham, was the first blind man she ever saw. see Robert L. Uzzel, *Blind Lemon Jefferson*, 93. Rosa Lee was a big help to this writer in his research on the latter volume. The name of the Wortham Black Cemetery was later changed to the Blind Lemon Jefferson Cemetery.

23. "Obituary: Rosa Lee Quarles." *Plainview Daily Herald*. 20 June 2003.

24. Funeral program for Frankie Lee Carter.

25. Alice Palmer Jarmon. Interview by author. 30 May 2014.

# Chapter 9

1. Chris told his son Mitcheola how rough slavery was. Mitcheola Durham. Interview by author. 20 August 1983. This interview was conducted at the McGee Nursing Home in Teague, Texas, where Mitcheola was a resident.

2. Freestone County Marriage Records.

3. U. S. Census (1920).

4. Mitcheola Durham. Interview by author. 20 August 1983. Chris' daughter Aretha was born in 1907. The year of his daughter Jessie's birth is unknown.

5. Ibid.

6. Julious Durham. Interview by author. 31 January 1980. This interview was conducted at Four Seasons Nursing Home in Dallas, where Julious was a resident.

7. "Freestone County Paupers," *Teague Chronicle*, 22 March 1918.

8. Mitcheola Durham. Interview by author. 20 August 1983. "Texas, Deaths 1890-1976," C. C. Durham, 1930. Certificate number 29029.

9. Funeral programs for Julious and Teaner Durham. Teaner Durham Johnson, the granddaughter

of Julious and Tener Durham, recalled that Julious rolled cigarettes from  Bull Durham tobacco and his wife used the tobacco bags to make a quilt lining.  Teaner Annie Durham Johnson.  Interview by author.  20 January 2014.

10. Ruby Jo Durham.  Interview by author.  25 December 2001.

11. "The Texas City Explosion." www.history.com/this...history/fertilizer-explosion-kills-581-in-texas, 1.

12. Mitcheola Durham.  Interview by author.  20 August 1983.

13. "Mitcheola Durham Obituary."  2 June 1994, 4B.

14. "Texas, Deaths 1890-1976," Booker T. Durham, 1931.  Certificate number 23462.

15. "Texas, Deaths 1890-1976," Major Durham, 1942.  Certificate number 12026.

16. Funeral programs for Isiah and Lillie Mae Durham.

17. "Obituary: John Durham." *Fairfield Recorder*, 6 June 2005.

18. Ike Durham.  Interview by author.  13 July 2013.

19. "Obituary: Isiah Durham, Jr." *Ennis Daily News*, 8 November 1985.

20. Isaac Durham.  Interview by author.  27 September 2014.

21. Teaner Annie Durham Johnson.  Interview by author.  20 January 2014.

22. Eddie Lee Durham.  Completed Questionnaire.

23. Teaner Annie Durham Johnson.  Interview by author.  20 January 2014.

24. Ibid.

25. "Obituary: Billy Rosee Durham, Sr." *Ennis Daily News*, 21 April 2000.

26. Teaner Annie Durham Johnson.  Interview by author.  20 January 2014

27. Lynda Kaye Durham Collins, completed questionnaire.

28. Jimmy R. Durham, completed questionnaire.

29. Teaner Annie Durham Johnson.  Interview by author.  20 January 2014.

# Chapter 10

1. U. S. Census (1880).

2. Freestone County Marriage Records.

3. U. S. Census (1880).

4. Freestone County Marriage Records.

5. U. S. Census (1880 and 1910).

6. Freestone County Records of Deeds, 9:279. John H. Reagan was a very prominent Texan. Born on 8 October 1818 in Sevier County, Tennessee, he came to Texas in 1839. He spent three years as a surveyor before being elected as a County and District Judge and a member of the Texas Legislature. On 27 December 1852, he was installed as Worshipful Master of Palestine Lodge #31 in Palestine, Texas. He held this position for two years. In1856 and again in 1858, he was elected to Congress. In 1861, he was elected to the Secession Convention and was sent to the Confederate Congress.  Confederate President Jefferson Davis appointed him as Postmaster-General and later as Secretary of the Treasury. After the Civil War, both Davis and Reagan were imprisoned at Boston, Massachusetts.  Upon his release in December 1865, Reagan returned to Palestine; see Charles Lee Steen, *The 150 Year History of Palestine Masonic Lodge #31, A.F.&A.M., Palestine, Texas: Sesquicentennial 1848-1998* (Palestine, Tx., 1998), 42. He purchased land at the former location of Fort Houston in Anderson County, where he farmed.  For awhile, he was unpopular with local citizens because he urged cooperation with the Reconstruction government; see ibid., 51.  However, he eventually regained their trust and, thus, was able to serve twelve years in Congress and win election to the U. S. Senate in 1887; see Pete Normand, *The Texas Masons: The Fraternity of Ancient Free & Accepted Masons in the History of Texas* (College

Station, Tx.: Brazos Valley Masonic Library and Museum Association, 1986), 25. In 1889, he voted for confirmation of President Benjamin Harrison's appointment of Norris Wright Cuney, a mulatto, as Collector of Customs in Galveston, Texas. Cuney was a member of Amity Lodge #4, F.&A.M., in Galveston and served as the first Grand Master of Prince Hall Masons in Texas; see Robert L. Uzzel, *Prince Hall Freemasonry in the Lone Star State: From Cuney to Curtis, 1875-2003* (Fort Worth, Tx.: Eakin Press, 2004), 1-15. In 1891, Reagan was appointed by Governor James S. Hogg as head of the newly created Texas Railroad Commission. He retired in 1903 and died on 6 March 1905. He was buried in East Hill Cemetery in Palestine, with the Texas Legislature attending his funeral as a body; see Normand, The Texas Masons, 25.

7. Andrews, *Our African Heritage*, 6:4.

8. Houston Slaughter. Interview by author. 27 December 1978. Slaughter, who is now deceased, lived for many years in Fort Worth.

9. U. S. Census (1920).

10. Freestone County Marriage Records.

11. Mary Durham Rabb. Interview by author. 25 May 2002.

12. "Texas, Deaths, 1890-1976," Jerome Durham, 1941, https://gfamilysearch.org/pal:/MM9.1.1/JF5G-H96.

13. Andrews, *Our African Heritage*, 6:11.

14. U. S. Census (1920).

15. Barnes, *Our African Heritage*, 6:11.

16. "Texas, Deaths, 1890-1976," Callie Durham, 1928, https://familysearch.org/pal:/MM9.1.1/J6BN-5XW.

17. "Texas, Deaths, 1890-1976," Sylvester Durham, 1935, https://familysearch.org/pal:/MM9.1.1/JNDZ-ID7.

18. Andrews, *Our African Heritage*, 6:11.

19. Standard Certificate of Death for Watson Durham, Freestone County Courthouse.

20. Mary Durham Rabb. Interview by author. 25 May 2002.

21. Standard Certificate of Death for Watson Durham, Freestone County Courthouse.

22. Andrews, *Our African Heritage*, 6:21.

23. Hellen Durham-Jones. Interview by author. 22 February 2003.

24. Clara Durham Page. Interview by author. 6 January 2002.

25. Ibid.

26. Hubert Durham. Interview by author. 20 July 2002.

27. "Obituaries: Hubert Durham," *Freestone County Times*, 25 May 2010. http:www.content.yudu.com/Library/A1nwvz/Freestone County Times/…, 1-2.

28. Standard Certificate of Death for Watson Durham, Jr., Freestone County Courthouse.

29. Gennelle Durham Moseley. Interview by author. 18 May 2003.

30. Hellen Durham-Jones. Interview by author. 22 February 2003.

31. Maurice Durham. Interview by author. 24 February 2003. Lameysha graduated from Lancaster High School and later attended Paul Quinn College. The writer has taught at both schools. She currently works for McGraw-Hill.

32. http://www.amazon.com/SECRETS-RESTAURANT-Lela-Bell/dp/B003D1AW5Q/ref=s-r_1_2?s=instant-video&ie=UTF8&qid=1390431978&sr=1-2&keywords=maurice+durham .

33. http://www.amazon.com/Race-Against-Time-SHARLA-BUTLER/dp/B008O62G2M/ref=s-r_1_1?s=instant-video&ie=UTF8&qid=1390431978&sr=1-1&keywords=maurice+durham.

## Chapter 11

1. Richard Durham, Jr., "The Durham Family Genealogy." Unpublished paper. 10 December 1999.

2 "Groundbreaking Ceremony Held Sunday at Lone Star Baptist Church." *Fairfield Recorder,* 12 October 2000, 2B. Lone Star Baptist Church was founded in 1879 under the leadership of Rev. G. W. Solomon. This church met under an arbor until Deacon Durham donated this land, on which the first building was built. The first deacons included Isaac and Belton Durham, Hanly Taylor, Lewis Wilson, John Welsey Jackson, Henry Howard, Andrew Love, Abe Simmons, Jeff Jackson, John Jackson, and Elec Smith. Another building was build during the pastoral administration of Rev. W. J. Manning but was later destroyed by fire. Palestine physician Dr. J. Don Jackson, the grandson of one of the founders and a lifelong member of Lone Star, recalled: "I remember when you could go by the church on Sunday morning and people would be everywhere. There would be a yard full of children. But most of us have moved away or died and the community is very sparsely populated now. It is just us stalwarts there."

3. Andrews, *Our African Heritage,* 6:4.

4. Ibid., 6:11-12.

5. Richard Durham, Jr., "The Durham Family Genealogy." Unpublished paper. 10 December 1999.

6. Andrews, *Our African Heritage,* 6:5.

7. Ibid., 6:12.

8. Ibid.

9. Ibid.

10. Ibid.

11. Hobart Durham, Jr. Interview by author. 24 November 2001.

12. Andrews, *Our African Heritage,* 6:21.

13. Richard Durham, Sr. Interview by author. 26 November 2001.

14. Andrews, *Our African Heritage,* 6:21.

15. Ibid.

16. Dorris "Jim Durham." Interview by author. 6 July 2003.

17. Funeral program for Dorris "Jim" Durham.

18. Thelma Lee Durham Roquemore. Interview by author. 5 July 2003.

19. Funeral program for Thelma Lee Durham Roquemore.

20. "Thomas A. Durham Obituary," *Fairfield Recorder,* 19 March 1998, 3B.

21. Therman Durham. Interview by author. 25 November 2001.

22. "Durham, Therman R." http://www.wacotrib.com/obituaries/durham-therman-r/article_10cfc853-fed0-54db-b634-44b4ba0290f3.html.

23. Hobart Durham, Jr. Interview by author. 24 November 2001.

24. Funeral program for Hobart Durham, Jr.

25. Homer G. Phillips Hospital, one of the country's most prestigious medical institutions, was designed by architect Albert Osburg. The hospital was opened in 1937, six years after the assassination of its benefactor and advocate Homer G. Phillips, a St. Louis-based African American lawyer. The hospital was built to serve the needs of more than 70,000 local African Americans, who became increasingly vocal about the lack of adequate health care and medical training. Along with Sumner High School, Antioch Baptist Church, and the Annie Malone Children's Home, Homer G. Phillips Hospital formed a closely related network of stability and pride in The Ville, St. Louis's premiere black community, during the years of restrictive covenants in housing and segregation in education. Homer G. Phillips Hospital became one of the few nationally-recognized, fully-equipped hospitals in the country where black doctors, nurses, and technicians could receive training. In less than a decade, Homer G. Phillips Hospital ranked in the upper third of the ten largest general hospitals in the country and gained a national reputation for treatment of the acutely injured. The staff was making valuable contributions to the development of techniques for intravenous protein feeding and for the treatment of gunshot

wounds, burns, and ulcers. In addition to providing a fully accredited training program for interns and residents of schools of nursing, the hospital established schools for x-ray technicians, laboratory technicians, and medical record library service. By the early 1950s, Homer G. Phillips Hospital offered advanced training to certified foreign doctors, which helped ease the staff of shortages and gave an opportunity to these physicians who were denied training in other hospitals due to race or creed. Yet by 1955, following an order from St. Louis Mayor Raymond Tucker that patients of any race, color, or creed living in the western part of the city must be admitted to the hospital, Homer G. Phillips was no longer an exclusively black institution. In August 1979, a wide range of complex issues surrounding Homer G. Phillips Hospital prompted its closure as a full-service facility. In the 1990s, the nurses' wing was renovated into low-income housing; and in 2004, the hospital was reopened as the Homer G. Phillips Dignity House, a residential care facility for the elderly; see Homer G. Phillips Hospital (1937-1979)www.blackpast.org/?q=aah/homer-g-phillips-hospital-1937-1979, 1.

26. Texanita Durham Bluitt. Interview by author. 6 July 2002. For more information on the Little Rock School desegregation crisis, see Daisy Bates, *The Long Shadow of Little Rock: A Memoir* (Fayetteville, Ark.: University of Arkansas Press, 1987). The writer had the pleasure of meeting Sis. Bates at the convention of the Phylaxis Society (a Prince Hall Masonic research organization) in Little Rock on 5 March 1994. Legendary civil rights activist Daisy Lee Gatson Bates (1914-1999) was a member of the Order of the Eastern Star. Her husband L. C. Bates (1904-1980) was a Prince Hall Mason.

27. Ibid. Texanita Durham Bluitt. Interview by author. 6 July 2002.

28. Ibid.

29. Ibid. This hospital was named for Rev. G. L. Prince, president of Mary Allen College, who had previously served as pastor of Galveston's Avenue L Baptist Church, one of the oldest black churches in Texas; and as president of the National Baptist Convention of America, see "Avenue L. Baptist Church," *Handbook of Texas* Online, http://www.tshaonline.org/handbook/online/articles/iva2.html , 1. G. L. Prince Hospital was built in 1950, with Dr. James Hilliard, Jr. serving as medical director. The Ford Foundation helped to underwrite the 24-bed facility with several grants. The hospital included an X-ray department, major and minor operating rooms, kitchen, nursery, laboratory, and personnel quarters. Both Dr. Hilliard and his wife Edna, a registered nurse, served as instructors in Mary Allen College's vocational nursing program; see Eliza Bishop, "Mary Allen College," *Houston Chronicle*, 21 January 1959.
The hospital operated about twenty years; see Eliza Bishop, "Mary Allen College Continues But Way Uncertain," *Houston Chronicle*, 9 December 1971.

30. Ibid. According to the 1982 Texas State Historical Marker placed at the site of this school: "In 1186 the Board of Missions for Freedmen of the Presbyterian Church in the United States, under the leadership of the group's secretary, the Rev. Richard Allen, began planning for the establishment of a black girls' school in Texas. After a statewide survey, they chose Crockett as the school site because of the area's large black population and because of a local black parochial school operated by the Rev. Samuel Fisher Tenney, pastor of the city's First Presbyterian Church. The Rev. Allen's wife Mary, for whom the school was named, was instrumental in raising the organizational funds for the new seminary. Dr. Byrd R. Smith became the school's first black president in 1924 and initiated a period of growth which included the adoption of new programs and the admission of male students. Transferred to the Missionary Baptist Convention of Texas in 1944, Mary Allen College became a 4-year liberal arts institution. In 1972, plagued by a series of legal and financial setbacks, the school closed. Once, the site of a 12-building campus and the home of a noted academic program of quality education and religion, this site serves as a reminder of the proud heritage of Texas' black population."

31. Ibid.

32. Ibid.

33. bid.

34. Ibid.

35. Ibid.

36. LaRue Durham Hooks. Interview by author, 12 January 2012.

37. "30 Years in Law Enforcement . . . Officer Retires from Force." *Fairfield Recorder*, 29 March 2001,

5A.

38. For more information on Routt, see Robert L. Uzzel, *Prince Hall Freemasonry in the Lone Star State: From Cuney to Curtis, 1875-2003* (Fort Worth, Tx.: Eakin Press, 2004), 152-164.

39. Isaac Newton Durham. Interview by author. 19 August 2001.

40. Ibid.

41. "Deputy of the Year Announced." *Fairfield Recorder*, 25 December 2003, 1A.

42. "Criminal Investigator Retiring." *Fairfield Recorder*, 1 March 2007, 1A.

43. "Veteran Lawman Takes Security Post," *Fairfield Recorder*, 30 December 2007.

44. "Durham Seeks Election to School Board," *Fairfield Recorder*, 12 April 2001, 2A.

45. "School Board Members Attend Seminar," *Fairfield Recorder*, 19 July 2001, 3B.

46. Isaac Newton Durham. Interview by author. 19 August 2001.

47. Richard Eugene Durham, Sr. Interview by author. 16 January 2013.

48. Richard Eugene Durham, Jr. "The Durham Family Genealogy." Unpublished paper. Navarro College. December 1999.

49. Richard Eugene Durham, Sr. Interview by author. 16 January 2013.

50. Allie Faye Durham Moore. Interview by author. 5 July 2003.

51. Bascom Gerald Durham, "Biographical Summary." Unpublished paper.

52. Ibid.

53. "Former Resident Earns Promotion." *Fairfield Recorder*, 28 June 2001.

54. Bascom Durham. Interview by author. 22 July 2003.

55. Bascom Gerald Durham, "Biographical Summary." Unpublished paper.

56. Ibid.

57. Bascom Durham. Interview by author. 6 July 2013.

58. Ibid.

59. James Ronnie Durham. Interview by author. 5 July 2014.

60. "30 Years in Law Enforcement . . . Officer Retires from Force." *Fairfield Recorder*, 29 March 2001, 5A.

61. Bryan Douglas Durham. Completed questionnaire.

62. Ramona Yvette Durham. Completed questionnaire.

63. Keith Isaac Durham. Interview by author. 30 June 2012.

64. Melissa Durham. Completed questionnaire.

65. Michael Cornell Durham. Completed questionnaire.

66. Cecilia Rena Durham Woods. Completed questionnaire.

67. Norah Burns Durham. Completed questionnaire.

68. Sophia Natasha Chrystal Durham. Completed questionnaire.

69. Daydrian Durham. Completed questionnaire.

70. Richard Eugene Durham, Jr. Completed questionnaire.

71. Amy Durham. Completed questionnaire.

72. Bascom Durham. Interview by author. 6 July 2013.

73. Raquila Durham. Completed questionnaire.

# Chapter 12

1. The writer wonders if "Strawther" is a variation of "Strother" in view of previous references to William Strother Durham and General Richard Strother Taylor.

2. Dorsey Strawther. Interview by author. 17 August 1983.

3. U. S. Census (1880).

# Chapter 13

1. George Brown Tindall, *South Carolina Negroes, 1877-1900* (University of South Carolina Press, 1952), 204. The 1850 South Carolina Slave Schedules list a farmer named James Durham among the slaveholders. He was probably the owner of J. J. Durham. In 1850, Fairfield and Spartanburg are the only South Carolina counties where any Durhams are listed among slaveholders.

2. Ibid.

3. Ibid., 204-05.

4. Ibid.

5. According Robert F. Durden, retired chair of the History Department at Duke University: "Seeking a name for his manufactured smoking tobacco shortly after the Civil War, John R. Green of Durham drew inspiration from a popular brand of mustard made in Durham, England, that featured the head of a Durham bull on its label. Green chose to use the image of a whole bull, and his trademark-soon the subject of extensive litigation to protect it-became one of the most recognizable product advertisements in the country. Green made William T. Blackwell his partner in 1867, and when Green died two years later, Blackwell bought the entire business from the Green estate. Subsequently, with James R. Day and Julian S. Carr as his partners, Blackwell led the William T. Blackwell Company to a dominant position in Durham's burgeoning tobacco industry. Bull Durham smoking tobacco was widely advertised and was one of the world's best-known American products of the late nineteenth and early twentieth centuries. The 1988 blockbuster film *Bull Durham*, starring Kevin Costner, Susan Sarandon, and Tim Robbins, brought national attention to both the famous tobacco moniker and the Durham Bulls, Durham's popular minor league baseball team"; see Robert F. Durden, "Bull Durham Tobacco," http://ncpedia.org/bull-durham-tobacco. In 1898, Blackwell's Durham Tobacco Company was bought out by Union Tobacco Company. In 1899, the Duke-owned American Tobacco company bought out Union and, thus, acquired the Bull Durham brand; see Robert F. Durden, *The Dukes of Durham*, 1865-1929 (Durham, N. C.; Duke University Press, 1975), 68-69. Dr. Durden wrote: "I know of no one named Durham who was involved with the Dukes in the tobacco business."; see Robert F. Durden. Letter to author. 24 January 1979. Many African Americans were employed in Durham's tobacco factories but not often in managerial roles; see Leslie Brown, *Uplifting Black Durham: Gender, Class, and Black Community Development in the Jim Crow South* (Chapel Hill, N. C.: University of North Carolina Press, 2008).

6. William L. Durham Jr. and Mary Snipes." Ancestry.com. http://freepages.genealogy.rootsweb.ancestry.com/~clearcreek/durham_william-lindsey-jr.html.

7. "Durhamville to Durham," *Durham Sun*, 23 June 1964, 6D.

8. Jim Wise, "Moving Dr. Durham: City Namesake Mobile in Life and After," http://www.henry-nicholson.com/dr_durham.htm, 3-4.

9. George Lougee, "Dr. Durham Gambled on Future and Won Enduring Fame in City," *Durham Morning Herald*, 6 February 1966, 1A. In 1806, Haw River Mountain Church was established. In 1830, it was relocated to Orange County as Antioch Baptist Church; see "CCG William L. Durham and Mary Snipes," http://freepages.genealogy.rootweb.ancestry.com/-clearcreek/durham_william-lindsey-Jr.h..., 2.

10. Lougee, "Dr. Durham Gambled on Future and Won Enduring Fame in City," 1A. Maplewood Cemetery was established in 1872 by the purchase of an empty field of land at what is now Kent Street and Morehead Avenue. Prior to the establishment of the cemetery, people had been buried in the churchyards of their particular churches. Apparently Dr. Durham was not the only person exhumed from church yards and reburied at Maplewood but his re-burial received the most publicity; see "Endangered Durham: Maplewood Cemetery," http://endangereddurham.blogspot.com/2008/05/maplewood-cemetery.html, 1.

11. The latter quotation is of Egyptian origin. Indeed, the successors to Dr. Durham have done even

better. The growth and progress of Durham owed much to a remarkable family named Duke who made millions of dollars in tobacco, textiles, and electric power. Duke university is a product of the Duke philanthropy; see Robert F. Durden, *The Dukes of Durham, 1865-1929.*

12. "CCG William L. Durham and Mary Snipes," 2.

13. "Wise, "Moving Dr. Durham,"4.

14. The writer has sought without success to locate a will and/or estate papers for Dr. Durham. The absence of such might be partially explained by his death at such an early age.

15. *The American Slave: A Composite Bibliography, North Carolina Narratives, Part I Vol. 14:* 285-90.

16. According to his nephew, the late Dallas attorney William E. Walton, Lawyer Durham's father was a white man who came to Texas from North Carolina on a cattle drive. William E. Walton. Interview by author. 5 June 2001.

17. Richard Allen Burns. "Durham, William J." *Handbook of Texas Online,* http://www.tshaonline. org/handbook/online/articles/fdu46. When the two major parties began to seek the black vote, Lawyer Durham became the leading black Democrat in Texas while Dr. L. G. Pinkston, a Dallas physician, became the leading black Republican.

18. Ibid.

19. Ibid.

20. "Durham's Rites Set Saturday," *The Dallas Morning News,* 25 December 1970, 8B.

21. Dave Oliphant, "Durham, Eddie." *Handbook of Texas Online,* http://www.tshaonline.org/hand-book/online/articles/fduqk.

22. Ibid.

23. Ibid.

24. Ibid.

25. Archer L. Durham. Letter to author, 20 March 1987. In response to the author's letter regarding the Durhams of Fairfield, General Durham wrote: "None of the names nor locations that you listed relate to my family history to the best of my knowledge."

26. Major General Archer L. Durham, U. S. Air Force Website, http://www.af.mil/information/bios/bio.asp?bioID=5304.

# *Bibliography*

## Documents

DeSoto Parish Conveyance Records, J:232.
_____. M:4.
Freestone County Records of Deeds, 9:279.
Military Records. Bureau of Pensions—V.L.M.—9418.
Standard Certificate of Death for Alice Durham.
Standard Certificate of Death for Ellen Durham.
Standard Certificate of Death for Minor Durham, Jr.
Standard Certificate of Death for Mollie Durham.
Standard Certificate of Death for Rance Durham.
Standard Certificate of Death for Watson Durham.
Standard Certificate of Death for Willie Anderson Durham.
U. S. Census (1870).
U. S. Census (1880)
U. S. Census (1900).
U. S. Census (1910).
U. S. Census (1920).
U. S. Census (1930).
U. S. Census (1940).

## Books

The American Slave: *A Composite Bibliography, North Carolina Narratives,*
Part I Vol. 14: 285-90.

Andrews, Paula D. Woodard, *Our African Heritage: We Are Family!!!* Dallas, Tx., 2002.

Bate, Charles James. *"It's Been a long Time' (And We've Come a Long Way):*
*A History of Oklahoma Black Medical Providers (The Black Healers).*
Muskogee, Ok.: Hoffman Printing Co., Inc., 1986.

Bates, Daisy. *The Long Shadow of Little Rock: A Memoir.* Fayetteville, Ark.:
University of Arkansas Press, 1987.

*Biographical and Historical Memoirs of Northwest Louisiana.* Nashville, Tenn.:
Southern Publishing Co. 1890.

Brown, Leslie. *Uplifting Black Durham: Gender, Class, and Black Communithy*
*Development in the Jim Crow South.* Chapel Hill, N. C.: University
of North Carolina Press, 2008.

Carter, James David. *Education and Masonry in Texas, 1846 to 1861.*
Waco, Tx.; Committee on Masonic Education and Service
for the Grand Lodge of Texas, A.F&A.M., 1963.

Durden, Robert F. *The Dukes of Durham, 1865-1929.* Durham, N. C.:
Duke University Press, 1975.

Durham, Eddie Marie Jones. *Mama, 'Babe' and Me* (Bloomington, In.: Trafford Publishing, 2011), 65.

*Fairfield County Cemeteries: Volume I: Church Cemeteries in the Western Section* of the County (Winnsboro, S. C., 2006), 8.

*Fairfield County Cemeteries: Volume IV: Church Cemeteries in the Adjacent Counties* (Winnsboro, S. C., 2006), 8.

Hill, Samuel S., ed. *Varieties of Southern Religious Experience.* Baton Rouge, La.: Louisiana State University Press, 1988.

*History of Freestone County, vol. I.* Fairfield, Tx.; Freestone County Historical Commission, 1978.

*History of Freestone County, vol. II.* Fairfield, Tx.; Freestone County Historical Commission, 1989.

Jeffries, Hasan Kwame. *Bloody Lowndes: Civil Rights and Black Power in Alabama's Black Belt.* New York: New York University Press, 2010.

Kennedy, James Ronald and Kennedy, Walter Donald. *The South was Right!* Gretna, La.: Pelican Publishing Co., 2006.

McMaster, Fitz Hugh. *History of Fairfield County, South Carolina: From "Before the White Man Came" to 1942.* Spartanburg, S. C.: The Reprint Company, 2003.

Means, Emilia Gay Griffith and Chrysler, Liz. *DeSoto Parish (Images of America).* Charleston, S. C.: Arcadia Publishing, 2011.

Nelson, Ouida Warner, and Nelson, Edward Kenneth. *The Nelsons and Scotts of DeSoto Parish, Louisiana and Related Families.* Shreveport, La., 1969.

Normand, Pete. *The Texas Masons: The Fraternity of Ancient Free & Accepted Masons in the History of Texas.* College Station, Tx.: Brazos Valley Masonic Library and Museum Association, 1986.

*Records of Louisiana Confederate Soldiers and Commands.* Baton Rouge, La.: Louisiana Commission on Military Records.

Roberts, Allen E. *House Undivided: The Story of Freemasonry and the Civil War* Richmond, Va.: Macoy Publishing & Masonic Supply Co., Inc., 1990.

Steen, Charles Lee. *The 150 Year History of Palestine Masonic Lodge No. 31, A.F.&A.M. Palestine, Texas: Sesquicentennial 1848-1998.* Palestine, Tx., 1998.

Tindall, George Brown. *South Carolina Negroes, 1877-1900.* Columbia, S. C.: University of South Carolina Press, 1952.

Titus, Wilbur Thirkield, ed. *Who Is Who in Hunter and Titus Families: A Profile of Courage and Achievement, vol. 1.* Fairfield, Tx.: Hunter and Titus Family Reunion, 2003.

Uzzel, Robert L. *Blind Lemon Jefferson: His Life, His Death, and His Legacy.* Fort Worth, Tx.: Eakin Press, 2002.

_____. *Prince Hall Freemasonry in the Lone Star State; From Cuney to Curtis, 1875-2003.* Fort Worth, Tx.: Eakin Press, 2004.

Walkes, Jr., Joseph A. *Jno. G. Lewis, Jr.—End of an Era: The History of the Prince Hall Grand Lodge of Louisiana, 1842-1979.* Kansas City, Mo.: Midtown Printing and Publishing Co., 1986.

Woodward, C. Vann. *Mary Chesnut's Civil War.* New Haven, Ct.: Yale University Press, 1993.

**Articles**

"Annual Awards Presented: Senior Citizens Honored at Luncheon." *Fairfield Recorder,* 24 May 1990, 4B.

Bannerman, Sally Moss. "Reminiscing About the First Commencement of the Mansfield Female College." http://www.countygenweb.com/DeSotoParishLA/commencement.htmn.

Baugh, Judy. "Mansfield Female College." http://www.countygenwb.com/DeSotoParishLA/mansfield_female_college.htm.

Bishop, Eliza. "Mary Allen College." *Houston Chronicle,* 21 January 1959.

_____. "Mary Allen College Continues But Way Uncertain." *Houston Chronicle,* 6 December 1971.

Boozer, Kevin. "Historian Connects with Locals." *The Herald Independent* 31 August 2012, 5.

_____. "Professor Seeks Locals to Help with Book." *The Herald Independent* 21 August 2012, 5.

"Community Improvement Awards." *Fairfield Recorder,* 21 October 1982, 4A.

"Criminal Investigator Retiring." *Fairfield Recorder,* 1 March 2007, 1A.

"Deputy of the Year Announced." *Fairfield Recorder,* 25 December 2003, 1A.

"Durham Seeks Election to School Board." *Fairfield Recorder,* 12 April 2001, 2A.

"Durhamville to Durham." *Durham Sun,* 23 June 1964, 6D.

"Durham's Last Rites Set Saturday." *Dallas Morning News,* 25 December 1970, 8B.

"Fairfield, Alabama." http://www.citytowninfo.com/places/alabama/fairfield.

"Family Tree." Jet, 18 March 1991.

"Former Resident Earns Promotion." *Fairfield Recorder,* 28 June 2001, 5A.

"Freestone County Historian Dies." *Fairfield Recorder,* 11 April 1991.

"Freestone County Paupers." *Teague Chronicle,* 22 March 1918.

"Groundbreaking Ceremony Held Sunday at Lone Star Baptist Church." *Fairfield Recorder,* 12 October 2000, 2F.

Lougee, George. "Dr. Durham Gambled on Future and Won Enduring Fame in City." *Durham Morning Herald,* 6 February 1966, 1A.

"NAACP Holds Freedom Fund Banquet. *Fairfield Recorder,* 27 April 1995, 3B.

"Obituary: Bib Durham." *Fairfield Recorder,* 29 April 1993, 4B.

"Obituary: Billy Ross Durham, Sr." *Ennis Daily News,* 21 April 2000.

"Obituary: Capoleon Yale Durham." *Fairfield Recorder,* 28 January 1988, 6B.

"Obituary: Clara Durham Peters." *Fairfield Recorder,* 6 May 1999, 6B-10B.

"Obituary: Donald Smith Durham." *Kansas City Star*, 19 February 2006.

"Obituary: Ella Durham McClure." *Palestine Herald Press*, 3 November 1996.

"Obituary: Henry Tatum." *Fairfield Recorder,* 17 April 1986, 4B.

"Obituary: Hubert Durham." *Freestone County Times*, 25 May 2010.

"Obituary: Isiah Durham, Jr." *Ennis Daily News*, 8 November 1985.

"Obituary: John Durham." *Fairfield Recorder*, 10 January 2005, 4B.

"Obituary: Mary Durham." *Fort Worth Star-Telegram.* 21 December 2008.

"Obituary: Mitcheola Durham." *Fairfield Recorder*, 2 June 1994, 4B.

"Obituary: Robert Scott Durham." *Fort Worth Star-Telegram*, 3 March 2013.

"Obituary: Roma Durham." *Fairfield Recorder,* 6 May 1999, 6B.

"Obituary: Thomas A. Durham." *Fairfield Recorder*, 19 March 1998, 3B.

"Obituary: Willa Durham." *Fairfield Recorder*, 7 July 1994, 4B.

"Obituary: Willie Durham." *Waco Tribune-Herald*, 29 September 1987.

Rogers, Amanda. "Stitches in Time: Quilts Pieced Together with Love and Patience Help Preserve Two Centuries of a Family's History." *Fort Worth Star-Telegram*, 13 April 2002.

"School Board Members Attend Seminar." *Fairfield Recorder*, 19 July 2001, 3B.

Sessions, J. R. R. "Alderman's Store Cotton Gin," *Freestone County Times*, 2 September 2003, 7-B.

Stotts, "History of Mansfield Female College: the Oldest Female College West of the Mississippi River, 1855-1930.

"30 years in Law Enforcement . . . Officer Retires from Force." *Fairfield Recorder*, 29 March 2001, 5A.

"To Restate Vows." *Fairfield Recorder*, 28 March 1985, 6A.

Uzzel, Robert L. "Battle of Mansfield Remembered." Ennis Daily News, 11 May 2014, 8.

_____. "Mother-in-Law Celebrates 80th Birthday." Ennis Daily News, 13 September 2013, 5.

_____. "Mother-in-Law's Retirement is Sweet." Ennis Daily News, 28 February 2014, 5.

_____. "Pastor's Wife Marks Six Decades of Life.' Ennis Daily News, 26 July 2013, 5.

_____."Remembering Grand Secretary Reece." Ennis Daily News. 13 June 2014, 8.

_____. "The Waltz to Westphalia." Ennis Daily News, 10 November 2011, 3.

"Val Verde Cannon, FHS Band to Mansfield." *Fairfield Recorder*, 2 April 1864, 1.

"Veteran Lawman Takes Security Post." *Fairfield Recorder*, 30 December 2003, 1A.

## Internet Sources
"About D. L. Dykes, Jr." D. L. Dykes, Jr. Foundation for Faith and Reason. http://faithandreason.org/index.php/about.

"Avenue L. Baptist Church." *Handbook of Texas Online.*

http://www.tshaonline.org/handbook/online/articles/iva2.html.

"Better Way Apostolic Church." http://www.betterwayapostolic.com.

"Black History Month: A Medical Perspective."
http://www.mclibrary.duke.edu/hot/blkhist.html, 5.

Blake, Tom "Fairfield County, South Carolina: Largest Slaveholders from 1860
Census Schedules and Surname Matches for African Americans on
on 1870 Census," 2.

"Boykin, South Carolina," http://www.sciway.net/city/boykin.html.

Brock, Eric J. "Honoring a Black Man Who Offered His Services to the Confederate
Army: Levy S. Carnine is Remembered Today as a Civil War 'Hero.'"
*Shreveport Journal*, www.countygenweb.com/.../canine.htm.

Burns, Richard Allen. "Durham, William J." *Handbook of Texas Online*,
http:www.tsha.utexas.edu/handbook/online/articles/fdu46, 1.

"Captain Charnel Durham (1753-1836).
http:freepages.genealogy.rootsweb.ancestry.com/-donnykrun/Durham.

"CCG William L. Durham and Mary Snipes,"
http://freepages.genealogy.tootweb.ancesgtry.com/-clearcreek/durham_
william-lindsey-Jr.h..., 2.

"Corporal William Shedd Durham."
http://freepages.genealogy.rootsweb.ancestry.com/--donnykrun/Durham.

Cravens, Chris. "Avant Prairie, Texas." *The Handbook of Texas Online*.
http://www.tshaonline.org/handbook/online/articles/hra87, 1.

"D. C. Minner's Down Home Blues Club," http://www.dcminnerblues.com, 1.

"DeSoto Parish History."
http://www.centrallouisiana.net/almanac/parishes/desoto.html.

"Dobbs, John Wesley." En.wikipedia.org/wiki/John_Wesley_Dobbs, 1.

Durden, Robert F. "Bull Durham Tobacco,"
http://ncpedia.org/bull-durham-tobacco.

"Edith Eloise Whittington Durham (1910-2001)—Find a Grave Memorial."
http:www.finda grav e.com/cgi-bin/fg.cg?page=gr&GRid=88385755.

Durham, Lutie McNulty. "Major William Strother Durham."
http://freepages.genealogy.rootsweb.ancestry.com/--donnykrun/
Durham.

"Endangered Durham: Maplewood Cemetery," http://endangereddurham.blogspot.
com/2008/05/maplewood-cemetery.html, 1.

"Fairfield County, SC—History," http.www.fairfieldsc.com/secondary.aspx?pageID=176.

"Filmmaker-Nurse to Present Documentary about Homer Phillips Hospital
at School of Nursing Event." http://slu.edu/readstory/newslink/976, 1.

"Freestone County Historian Dies." Fairfield Recorder, 11 April 1991, 1A.

"The Homer G. Phillips Hospital (1937-1979)."

www.blackpast.org/?=aah/homer-g-phillips-hospital-1937-1979, 1.

"Judson Burney Durham (1910-1993)—Find a Grave Memorial." http://endangereddurham.blogspot.com/2008/05/maplewood-cemetery.html, 1.

Latimer, Truett. "Avenue L Baptist Church." *Handbook of Texas Online,* http:www.tsha.utexas.edu/handbook/online/articles/view/AA/iva2.html, 1.

Leffler, John. "Freestone County." *Handbook of Texas Online,* http:www.tsha.utexas.edu/handbook/online/articles/view/FF/bcf9.html, 1.

"Major General Archer L. Durham." *U. S. Air Force Website.* http://www.af.mil/information/bios/bio.asp?bioID=5304.

"Mansfield Female College Museum." http://cityofmansfield.net/photo_gallery/ Mansfield_female_college_museum.html.

McArthur, Judith N. "Johnson, Rebekah Baines." *Handbook of Texas Online,* http:www.tsha.utexas.edu/handbook/online/articles/tj022, 1.

"Nathaniel P. Banks." www.civilwar.org/.../biographies/nathaniel.banks.html.

"1910 'Flexner Report' was Turning Point for School of Medicine." http://www.vanderbilt.edu/News/register/Dec03_01/story9html.

"The Old Val Verde Cannon." http://www.fairfieldtx.com/cannon.htm, 1.

Oliphant, Dave. "Durham, Eddie." *Handbook of Texas Online,* http:www.tsha.utexas.edu/handbook/online/articles/view/DD/fduqk.html,  1.

Patenaude, Lionel V. "Jones, Jesse Holman," *Handbook of Texas Online,* http:www.tsha.utexas.edu/handbook/online/articles/fjo53,  1.

"Richard Taylor: Confederate General." http://www.civilwarreference.com/people/index.php?peopleID=1199.

"Robert Winfield Durham." http://stith.packent.com/ged2/d0000/g0000039.html.

Rogers, Amanda. "Stitches in Time: Quilts Pieced Together with Love and Patience Help Preserve Two Centuries of a Family's History." *Fort Worth Star-Telegram,* 13.

"South Carolina Reference Room: Counties: Fairfield." http://www.state.sc.us/seal.fair.html, 1.

Summerlin, Travis L. "Baines, Sr., George Washington," *Handbook of Texas Online,* http:www.tsha.utexas.edu/handbook/online/articles/fba14,  1.

"The Texas City Disaster, April 16 and 17, 1947." http://www.texas-city-tx.org/docs/exp.html, 1-2.

"The Texas City Disaster." www.history.com/this . . .history/fertilizer-explosion--kills-581-in-texas, 1.

Thompson, Eric V. "A Brief History of Major Oil Companies in the Gulf Region.' http://www.virginia.edu.igpr/apagolhistory.html, 8-9.

"William L. Durham, Jr. and Mary Snipes." Ancestry.com. http//freepages.genealogy.rootsweb.ancestry.com/~clearcreek/ durham_william-lindsey-jr.html.

"Winnsboro." Ioguide.congress.gov/scripts/biodisplay.pl?index=W000637.

"Winnsboro Cotton Mill Blues." http://labornotes.org/2011/01/winnsboro-cotton-mill-blues, 1-2.

Wise, Jim. "Moving Dr. Durham: City Namesake Mobile in Life and After," http://www.henry-nicholson.com/dr_durham.htm.

**Films**

Durham, Maurice. *Secrets and the Restaurants.* http://www.amazon.com/SECRETS-RESTUIARANT-Lela-Bell/dp/B003D1AW5Q/ref+sr_1_2?s=instant-viedo&ie=UTF8&qid=1390431978&sr=1-2&keywords=maurice+durham.

_____. *A Race Against Time: The Sharla Butler Story.* http://www.amazon.com/Race-Against-Time-SHARLA-BUTLER/dp/B008062G2M/ref=sr_1_1?s=instant-video&ie=UTF8&qid=1390431978&sr=1-1&keywords= maurice+durham.

**Correspondence**

Bass, Kevin Jabar. E-mail to author. 3 June 2014.

Bass, LaCharles Michael. E-mail to author. 3 June 2014.

Brown, Kimberly Bass. E-mail to author. 3 June 2014.

Durham, Archer L. Letter to author. 20 March 1987.

Durham, Donald Smith. Letter to author. 24 February 1983.

Durham, Eddie Marie Jones. Letter to author. 6 November 1978.

Durham, W. C. Letter to author. 14 April 1980.

Jessie, Cilkay. E-mail to author. 4 June 2014.

Jones, Karen Sheanell Bass Dabney. E-mail to author. 3 June 2014

Stevenson, Ruth M. Letter to author, 3 January 1984.

Strickland, Celia. E-mail to author. 5 June 2014.

**Marriage Records**

Durham, Anderson and Calhoun, Ellen. 13 July 1870.

Durham, Anderson and Rhodes, Laura. 10 September 1874.

Durham, Jerome and Simmons, Matilda. 18 December 1901.

Durham, Jr., Minor and Turner, Delia. 27 December 1894.

Durham, Rance and McDonald, Alice. 2 January 1879.

Durham, Willie Anderson and Titus, Ellen Anna. 21 October 1899.

**Death Certificates**

Durham, Alice. 18 October 1957.

Durham, Belton. June 1927.

Durham, Booker T. 7 May 1931.

Durham, Callie. 16 August 1928.

Durham, Christopher Columbus. 24 June 1930.

Durham, Ellen Titus. 15 June 1929.

Durham, Henry. 6 April 1937.

Durham, Jerome. 12 May 1941.

Durham, Major. 26 March 1942.

Durham, Jr., Minor. 13 March 1963.

Durham, Mollie. 17 August 1947.

Durham, Rance.  6 March 1950.
Durham, Saylor Bee.  23 May 1937.
Durham, Sillimon.  7 May 1920.
Durham, Sylvester.  16 July 1935.
Durham, Travis.  24 June 1933.
Durham, Watson.  1 October 1973.

## Funeral Programs

Brackens, McLenon Lee.
Durham, Alonzo O'Neil (Lonzo).
Durham, Archie Dennis.
Durham, Clara.
Durham, Dorris Jim.
Durham, Elie M.
Durham, Henry.
Durham, Herman.
Durham, Jr., Hobart.
Durham, Isiah.
Durham, John.
Durham, Julious Durham.
Durham, Lillie Mae.
Durham, Luke.
Durham, Teaner.
Durham, Therman Rogene.
Durham, W. M.
Durham, Walter Titus.
Durham, William B.
Durham, Willie Mae Adams
Garietty, Lillie Elliott Durham.
Henry, Clyde.
Henry, Coleman.
Henry, Gladys Durham.
Henry, Richmond.
Johnson, Bealer.
Roquemore, Thelma Lee Durham.

## Unpublished Materials

Collins, Lynda Kaye Durham.  Completed Questionnaire.
Durham, Amy.  Completed Questionnaire.
Durham, Bascom Gerald.  "Biographical Summary."
Durham, Bryan Douglas.  Completed Questionnaire.
Durham, Nora Burns.  Completed Questionnaire.
Durham, Eddie Lee.  Completed Questionnaire.
Durham, Jimmy R.  Completed Questionnaire.
Durham, Michael Cornell.  Completed Questionnaire.
Durham Jr., Richard Eugene.  Completed Questionnaire.

_____. "The Durham Family Genealogy." 10 December 1999.

Sanders, John I. "The Significance of Mr. Will Durham and His Country Store." Winnsboro, S. C., 2007.

White Oak Baptist Cemetery Records.

Woods, Cecilia Rena Durham. Completed Questionnaire.

### Interviews

Bass, Aldessa. Interview by author. 17 May 2001 and 24 November 2012.

Bass, Kenneth LaClaire. Interview by author. 4 June 2014.

Bass, LaCharles Michael. Interview by author. 16 October 2011.

Bluitt, Texanita Durham. Interview by author. 6 July 2002.

Brackens, Sr., Freddie Oneal. Interview by author. 25 November 2000.

Burkhalter, Mildred. Interview by author. 8 October 2002.

Carden, Leophia. Interview by author. 22 October 2002.

Daniels, Josephine. Interview by author. 24 August 2001.

Durham, Clara. Interview by author. 6 May 1980.

Durham Bascom. Interview by author. 22 July 2003 and 5 July 2014.

Durham, Beauford. Interview by author. 4 August 2002.

Durham, Bobby Jean. Interview by author. 23 November 2001.

Durham, Boykin. Interview by author. 3 August 2012.

Durham, Daydrian. Interview by author. 5 July 2014.

Durham, Donald Smith. Interview by author. 15 September 2001.

Durham, Dorris Jim. Interview by author. 6 July 2003.

Durham, Gale Lynn. Interview by author. 25 July 2002.

Durham, Gene. Interview by author. 25 November 2001.

Durham, Harold Glenn. Interview by author. 10 August 2002.

Durham, Jr., Hobart. Interview by author. 24 November 2001.

Durham, Hubert. Interview by author. 20 July 2002.

Durham, Ike. Interview by author. 13 July 2013.

Durham, Isaac Newton. Interview by author. 19 August 2001.

Durham, James Artis. Interview by author. 16 October 2001.

Durham, James Michael. Interview by author. 16 September 2001.

Durham, James Ronnie. Interview by author. 5 July 2014.

Durham, Julious. Interview by author. 31 January 1980.

Durham, Keith Isaac. Interview by author. 30 June 2012 and 5 July 2014.

Durham, Lonzo. Interview by author. 21 July 2001.

Durham, Luke. Interview by author. 3 November 1978.

Durham, Maurice. Interview by author. 24 Feburary 2003.

Durham, Mary Nelson. Interview by author. 3 November 1978.

Durham, Maurice. Interview by author. 23 January 2013.

Durham, Mitcheola. Interview by author. 20 August 1983.

Durham, Sr., Richard Eugene. Interview by author. 27 November 2001 and 16 January 2013.

Durham, Robert Lemont Christopher. Interview by author. 5 July 2014.

Durham, Ruby Jo. Interview by author. 25 December 2001.

Durham, Shirley Givens. Interview by author. 4 June 2003.

Durham, Therman. Interview by author. 25 November 2001.

Durham, J., Walter Titus. Interview by author. 25 November 2001.

Edwards, Mary O. Interview by author. 3 November 1978 and 23 June 2001.

Hall, Robin. Interview by author. 24 September 2002.

Haynes, Teresa Bass. Interview by author. 16 October 2011.

Hooks, LaRue Durham. Inteview by author. 12 January 2012.

Jarmon, Alice. Interview by author. 25 August 2001.

Jessie, Cilkaye Bass. Interview by author. 7 June 2003.

Johnson, Jr., Johnny. Interview by author. 20 August 1983.

Johnson, Teaner Annie Durham. Interview by author. 20 January 2014.

Jones, Hellen Durham. Interview by author. 22 February 2003.

McIlvene, Clara Durham. Interview by author. 24 November 2012.

Mitchell, JoLander Durham. Interview by author. 25 November 2001.

Mitchell, LaWanda Durham. Interview by author. 25 November 2001.

Moore, Allie Faye Durham. Interview by author. 5 July 2003.

Moseley, Gennelle Durham. Interview by author. 20 July 2002.

Page, Clara Durham. Interview by author. 6 January 2002.

Parker, JoAnna. Interview by author. 3 June 2014.

Pope, Katherine Durham. Interview by author. 23 August 2012.

Quarles, Rosa Lee. Interview by author. 25 August 2001.

Rabb, Mary Durham. Interview by author. 25 May 2002.

Robinson, Helen Durham. Interview by author. 25 November 2001.

Roquemore, Thelma Lee Durham. Interview by author. 5 July 2003.

Simmons, Charles. Interview by author. 23 June 2001.

Slaughter, Houston. Interview by author. 27 December 1978.

Strawther, Birdiola. Interview by author. 20 August 1983.

Strawther, Dimple. Interview by author. 20 August 1983.

Strawther, Dorsey. Interview by author. 20 August 1983.

Strickland, Celia Bass. Interview by author. 7 July 2003.

Tatum, Katie Mae Durham. Interview by author. 20 October 2001.

Walton, William E. Interview by author. 5 June 2001.

Williams, Ernestine Durham. Interview by author. 21 August 2002.

Woodard, Laura. 19 November 2012.

# About the Author

Robert L. Uzzel was born on 22 May 1951 in Waco, Texas. He graduated from Waco High School in 1969 and received an Associate of Arts degree from McLennan Community College in 1971. He received a Bachelor of Arts in Religion and Sociology in 1973, a Master of Arts in Church-State Studies in 1976, and a Ph.D. in World Religions in 1995 from Baylor University. He received a Master of Arts in Political Science from the University of Texas at Arlington in 2008.

He was ordained an itinerant deacon in 1975 and an itinerant elder in 1977 by Rt. Rev. John Hurst Adams, the 87th Bishop of the African Methodist Episcopal Church. He has served as pastor of Texas AME congregations in Dallas, Fort Worth, Kaufman, Blooming Grove, and Maypearl. He has served as pastor of Wayman Chapel AME Church in Ennis since November 2002.

He has taught a wide variety of courses in Religion, History, and Political Science at Paul Quinn College, Cedar Valley College, Mountain View College, Tarrant County College, Temple College, Navarro College, and Hill College.

An active Prince Hall Freemason since 1981, he holds Certificates of Literature from both the Philalethes Society and the Phylaxis Society. He is a Fellow of the Phylaxis Society, a member of this society's Harry A. Williamson Hall of Fame, a recipient of the society's Dr. Charles H. Wesley Medal of History, a Founding Fellow of the Masonic Society, and member of the Society of Blue Friars (an invitation-only organization for Masonic authors and editors).

His previous books include *Blind Lemon Jefferson: His Life, His Death, and His Legacy* (2002); *Prince Hall Freemasonry in the Lone Star State: From Cuney to Curtis, 1875-2003* (2004); and *Éliphas Lévi and the Kabbalah: The Masonic and French Connection of the American Mystery Tradition* (2006). His articles on theological and historical subjects have appeared in a number of newspapers, magazines, and journals.

He is married to the former Debra Bass, a native of Fairfield, Texas. They have four children, seven grandchildren, and one great-grandchild.

CPSIA information can be obtained at www.ICGtesting.com
Printed in the USA
LVOW04s0242020615

440816LV00029B/771/P